Newness of Life

A Study in the Thought of Paul

NEWNESS OF LIFE

Even so we also should walk in newness of life
—Rom. 6:4

by
Richard E. Howard

Beacon Hill Press of Kansas City
Kansas City, Missouri

Quotations·from the following copyrighted versions of the Bible have been used and permission to do so is acknowledged with thanks:

New American Standard Bible (NASB), copyright © The Lockman Foundation, 1960, 1962, 1963, 1968, 1971.

Revised Standard Version of the Bible (RSV), copyrighted 1946 and 1952.

The New English Bible (NEB), © The Delegates of the Oxford University Press and the Syndics of the Cambridge University Press, 1961, 1970.

The New Testament in Modern English (Phillips), copyright © by J. B. Phillips, 1958. Used by permission of the Macmillan Co.

The *Amplified New Testament* (Amp.), copyright 1958 by the Lockman Foundation, La Habra, Calif.

Contents

Foreword

In 1725, after reading Bishop Taylor's *Rule and Exercises of Holy Living and Dying,* John Wesley resolved to make the whole of his life "a sacrifice to God." For the next dozen years he applied himself to a single-minded quest for holiness. His service to God and his fellows through the Holy Club and his ministry in Georgia were expressions of this quest.

Upon returning from his abortive ministry in America Wesley met Moravian Peter Bohler, who patiently explained to him why his quest for holiness had failed: he was seeking to make *his* life a sacrifice to God before he had received by simple faith the benefits of *Christ's* atoning sacrifice. He was seeking to be sanctified before he had been justified. Late in his ministry Wesley makes reference to this revolution Bohler initiated in his life. Speaking of his brother Charles and himself, he wrote: "In 1729, two young men reading the Bible, saw that they could not be saved without holiness [an allusion to the Holy Club]. In 1737 they saw holiness comes by faith. They saw likewise, that men are justified before they are sanctified."

"Men are justified before they are sanctified." *The indicative of grace precedes the imperative to holiness.* Not until we have been absolved from the guilt and released from the power of sin through simple trust in Christ's atonement can we present our bodies as "a sacrifice to God" and experience the power of sanctification.

In this scholarly but eminently practical study of Pauline theology, Professor Howard shows how this basic distinction between the indicative of grace and the imperative to holiness constitute the warp and woof of the Pauline gospel and ethic. Drawing upon his doctoral research at Harvard University, tested and refined by years in both the pulpit and the classroom, the author brings to us a wealth of exegetical insights from the Pauline Epistles. His Pauline theology is set within the broader frame of biblical theology, as he shows how the apostle's doctrines of man and sin have their roots in Old Testament thought.

John Wesley himself was a biblical theologian, who constantly tested his interpretation of scripture by Christian experience, as well as by reason and tradition. Unfortunately, his followers have not always been so careful. Wesleyan theology has tended to be more systematic than biblical, and Wesleyan preaching has drawn heavily on Christian experience, often being more topical than expositional. These tendencies have been the source of concern to many of us who believe that doctrine must always bow to scripture, in its detailed expression as well as in its general outlines. While the basic biblical relationship of justification and sanctification has been maintained and the message of full salvation faithfully proclaimed, Wesleyan teachers and preachers have not always been good exegetes. The time has come to launch a vigorous, new exegetical study of scripture in evangelical circles.

Professor Howard calls us to this kind of investigation. His conviction is that the Scriptures must be the final Arbiter of doctrine. The Bible must be permitted to reshape cherished notions and rephrase time-honored clichés. If the message of holiness is true, we have nothing to fear but everything to gain from submitting our theology to the crucible of honest, rigorous, biblical study such as we have in this volume.

I have known the author for many years, as both a scholar and as a brother in Christ. We have conversed and debated countless hours about some of the issues raised in these pages. While we have not been able to agree on all points, through these discussions I have been driven back again and again to scripture and a deeper immersion in the gospel. This is all to the good. "We can do nothing against the truth, but for the truth." The truth of the gospel must be our consuming passion. No one can give serious attention to this volume without being enveloped afresh in that truth.

I predict that this work will prove helpful not only to preachers and teachers but also to thoughtful laymen who are seeking stronger biblical foundations for their faith and witness. I am happy to commend it to you for your prayerful study.

WILLIAM M. GREATHOUSE, *President*
Nazarene Theological Seminary
Kansas City, Missouri

Preface

A century ago Wesleyan theology stood at the forefront of evangelicalism. Great leaders, like Finney and Moody, were deeply influenced by the call to a life of inward and outward holiness. However, today, in most evangelical circles the Wesleyan message is considered extreme and even fanatical. At the same time there has been a greatly increased interest in biblical theology among Evangelicals, primarily in the Calvinistic and Reformed traditions. In my opinion there is a vital correlation between these two developments. Wesleyanism has not shown sufficient interest in biblical theology. It is to this need that the present study is addressed.

Much of this material was first prepared under the discipline of doctoral research. I have attempted to "detechnicalize" it, so that it would be intelligible to those not trained in theology.

Publication of this material is the fulfillment of a dream, which I am afraid at times has seemed more like a nightmare. I had often heard and read that writing was difficult. Thomas Wolfe reportedly said: "Writing is easy. Just put a sheet of paper in the typewriter and start bleeding." The ideas were clear and the outline came easy, *but* when it came to putting them on paper it was another matter. Minutes, hours, days were squeezed into an overloaded schedule. It was writing, writing, and then rewriting and rewriting—for more than six and a half years.

After the first draft, friends read and kindly criticized—constructively. What came hardest was "style"—I almost hated that word! After preaching for more than 30 years, writing style came hard. I remembered what a kindly Harvard professor remarked: "Dick, you use exclamation marks like clubs." My closest colleague friend repeatedly told me that *thus* was fine in a sermon ("Thus saith the Lord"!) but was monotonous in writing—over and over again. A librarian friend read every word of the first draft —sometimes by midnight oil—and made many constructive criticisms.

In more than twoscore churches I have tested the exegesis and terminology. Hundreds of my students have listened to the *fact* of the indicative and the *appeal* of the imperative. A dozen honest and searching graduate students critiqued the first draft in a seminar.

Then there was the complete revision that took over three years' free time (so-called) in a professor's life. My patient English-professor-wife, Winifred, read every word at least twice, correcting the spelling and improving sentence structure. Through the years my children, Judith and Roy, have had to share their dad with "the book" for many, many hours.

Can anyone adequately understand, let alone acknowledge, his debt to his teachers? Several made the New Testament come alive to me, from my first instructor (Ralph Earle at Eastern Nazarene College) to my last (Krister Stendhal at Harvard Divinity School). Albert Harper and Edgar S. Brightman disciplined my mind through philosophy. Samuel Young and Nels Ferré opened up for me the depths of theology.

Rob Staples, a close friend and colleague, prodded and encouraged me and read thoroughly both drafts of the manuscript. William M. Greathouse, the president of Nazarene Theological Seminary, who kindly consented to write the Foreword for this volume, also read both drafts and made many valuable suggestions, both practical and theological.

Two of my secretaries typed much of the early draft, and the final copy was expertly typed by Rita Lewis. Much of the tedious proofreading (checking every scripture reference) was cheerfully done by Ronoyce Grate.

But my deepest gratitude is to God! For more than 10 years I have known that I must write this material in book form. Although I seriously doubted if it would ever be worthy of publication—write I must! Times without number—late at night and early in the morning—I sensed His insistent encouragement. Without this I would have deserted the project a hundred times. Any credit of accomplishment is His.

Finally, I am dedicating this volume to my mother, Catherine Howard, who, although past 70 years of age, found "Newness of Life" as this volume was being prepared.

—RICHARD E. HOWARD
Bethany, Oklahoma

Introduction

Is the Bible relevant? Can the Scriptures communicate to men today in their predicament? Much is heard about the modern generation that is caught up in self-assertion and social rebellion. Does the gospel of Jesus Christ relate to the burning issues of war, poverty, human rights, and discrimination?

Tragically, some think not. The Church speaks but they are not listening. They have turned God off. Sometimes He is dismissed from His universe, but more often He is ignored as indifferent and unnecessary. The Bible is considered outmoded, the irrelevant residue of a past culture. It seems to speak another language that fails to communicate. It is out of touch with the explosive issues of today.

Why? What is wrong? Could it be that the voice of God has been confused with the dogma of men? Have they been hearing what men think and not what God says? When men have listened for the Divine Word have they instead heard human theology—not being able to tell the difference?

Make no mistake—theology *is* crucially necessary. It is the manner in which man understands God. Everyone has a theology, regardless of what it is called. But theology must not be confused with revelation. God has spoken in the Scriptures which contain the *facts* of revelation. In a truly biblical theology this data is structured into dogma. Our "theology" is the systematic organization of thought that best relates for us *all the truths* of the Bible.[1]

The choice is not between theology and revelation. Instead the question is one of authority. Does theological dogma or scriptural revelation take precedence? Does our theology determine what the

---

1. It is necessary to be candid. Much of biblical theology is by implication—based on what is implied and not *explicitly stated* in scripture. Any given theological doctrine is the thought pattern in which the factual knowledge available is best understood. Divergent doctrine is basically a matter of *difference in understanding* and not the result of ignorance or prejudice.

Bible means, or does the Bible determine what our theology shall be? This is the crucial issue of authority.

When we accept the Scriptures as our Authority, the implications are staggering. Are we willing—have we the courage and faith —to allow the Bible to speak to us? Such an authority must be definitive. No other criterion, such as reason or experience or even theological dogma, can be given precedence over it.

When our theology provides the framework in which we can best understand the facts of biblical revelation, it will of necessity be dynamic. The Word of God is an exhaustless Source of spiritual truth, and the continuing flow of these revealed facts breathes new life into our theology. On the other hand, if Christian dogma is theologically or even experientially oriented, the result can only be increased sterility. The pages of church history eloquently testify to this fact.

Only the living Word of God can keep doctrine alive. Without such life, Christian experience becomes an empty formalism. Could this be why many believers are unconcerned and unchallenged, and the multitudes are unconvinced and untouched?

But what is meant by authority? Few would deny their allegiance to the Bible, so it is necessary to have a clear understanding of the authority of scripture. The Bible is God's *Message* to man. Admittedly it has been received through finite channels. Yet it can be a Message only when it is used contextually and not as a "book of magic." We cannot extract fragments from it as proof texts and claim for them supernatural power and authority.

The New Testament must *first* be understood in the context of its message to the specific historical situation that called forth its appearance. What was God saying to them *back there*? Such questions as "why," "when," and "to whom" any specific portion of it was written are of great importance. Concepts and customs change with civilizations, and we can miss God's revelation if we attempt to understand an ancient message on the basis of modern concepts. We misuse the Bible when we modernize it.

Yet the miracle of scripture is that, as we listen and understand *what God says back there,* we can *hear Him speak here.* Through the illumination and guidance of the Holy Spirit there is an application of the message of scripture to us—today. It has an application and fulfillment to men today that makes it unique.

This message has the power of divine authority. It is God's Message for us and cannot be rejected, ignored, or modified without eternal loss to those who so treat it.

A truly biblical message is far more than the use of scripture for an illustration or a topic. Instead, it is the anointed proclamation of God's eternal message to man, as revealed in His Word. Only then does it possess the authority of divine revelation.

If our faith is to be built upon the authority of the Bible, we must acquaint ourselves with scriptural terminology, which is much more than words. It is the use of scriptural terms to describe biblical concepts and ideas. Only in this way can the great majority of believers relate doctrine to scripture.

This study seeks to examine the thought of Paul[2] on the vital subject of salvation by treating his concepts in his terminology. It is exciting to discover how relevant Paul's thought is today. When we understand his terminology we find that he has much to say to us.

How did Paul view man? The terminology he used to depict man is often quite foreign to us today, and any attempt to understand it on the basis of modern presuppositions produces endless confusion. Yet it is striking how much we can learn about ourselves when we grasp Paul's thought.

Paul, however, did not think of man in theoretical terms. Instead he viewed man *as he was*—either in sin or in Christ. His understanding of sin and its power over man poses an answer to many of today's haunting questions. Why does man rebel? What is man searching for? Why is man often his own worst enemy? Can man ever do his "own thing"?

Yet Paul is not writing to men in sin. All of that is in the past, viewed now only in reminiscence. Instead, he is rejoicing with the new men of faith, who are in Christ. With his converts he stands—and bows—in wonder before the Cross. He is amazed that

---

2. When reference is made to the "thought of Paul," it is important to keep clearly in mind the nature of his writings. They are letters and not carefully worked out theology. In these letters are found many varied moods determined by the needs the specific letter is addressed to (cf. Galatians, Corinthians, Colossians, etc.). Paul's thought on any given subject can be determined only by an examination of the various references he makes to it, keeping in mind the context in which it is found.

God should love him so. As man responds in faith to that Cross of love, he stands before God righteous and reconciled. By grace he becomes a new creature as he lives a new life in the Christian family.

Here is found more than the answer to man's questions. This is the remedy for man's need. It strikes a responsive chord in the heart of the modern "pilgrim," whether he be Pharisee or prodigal. In Christ there is life—newness of life!

Surprisingly, Paul is not satisfied. Man does not become a whole person when he *finds* life in Christ. The wise apostle realized that man must *give* as well as *receive* in order to become a "total" man. So Paul exhorts his converts—with repeated imperatives— to *give back to God* the new life they have found in Christ. Only then can they find true freedom. As they lose their lives in God, they will then fully find them. The key is sovereignty. Under the rule of the Spirit the new man discovers the rich treasure of total living. His life is increasingly filled with the fruit of the Spirit until at last he meets his Lord face-to-face.

One of the greatest spiritual phenomena of the twentieth century has been the revival of biblical theology. Unfortunately this, all too often, has not left the classroom or reached beyond the scholar's pen. It is not enough for the theological professor to be convinced that the only Authority for faith is the Bible. This message must sound forth from the pulpits of the Church today. Even more, a truly biblical faith must be the possession of the man in the pew. Perhaps this study of Pauline thought will make a modest contribution to the fulfillment of this vital need.

SPECIAL NOTE

This might not be the place for *you* to start reading. Part I attempts to examine briefly the way that Paul understood man. This might be a little technical for the reader who is untrained in theology. *Yet it is important.* If we are to grasp *Paul's ideas,* and not simply follow our own, we must understand *his distinction* between the inner and outer man, and *his meaning* of the terms *heart, spirit, soul, flesh,* and *body.* As the study continues, it will become clear how this understanding will prove to be a vital key that unlocks the door to many questions, such as: how sin works, the present and future aspects of salvation, the distinction between human weakness and sinful failure, etc. Confusion about such questions results primarily from the failure to understand Paul's view of man.

So if these first pages prove to be too technical for you, jump to Part II. Then at a later time this introductory section can be read with greater profit.

—R. E. H.

PART I

MAN: AS VIEWED BY PAUL

Paul's Ideas or Ours?
What Is Man?
What Is the Flesh?

Chapter 1

Paul's Ideas or Ours?

Do we read Paul's letters in the light of *his* ideas or *ours*? Unfortunately the two are not always the same. The great apostle lived a long time ago, when men did not think in the carefully defined scientific categories that have become a natural part of modern thought. Instead, life was viewed from a much simpler perspective that can be described as "practical" or even "functional."

To further complicate our problem, a decisive transition took place very early in the Church. The New Testament was written by men of Hebrew heritage and training, with the single exception of Luke, who was overwhelmingly influenced by such men. Consequently, the scriptural record was channeled through their ideas and concepts, which today are termed "Semitic." Then there was a marked shift of leadership, which started before the close of the first century. Bishops, teachers, evangelists, and pastors were increasingly selected from among Greek converts until the leadership from the diminishing Jewish segment of the Church entirely disappeared. Within two or three generations after the New Testament was written, it was being interpreted by men with different, and sometimes conflicting, concepts and ideas.

Serious problems resulted. More and more of the basic theological doctrines were expressed in Greek concepts rather than with the Semitic ideas with which the New Testament was written. One graphic example is the development of the doctrine of the immortality of the soul, which is basically a Greek concept that differs quite significantly from the New Testament truth of the resurrection of the body.[1]

This confusion between Greek and Semitic concepts is reflected in the manner in which Paul's view of man has been understood. His concept of man is basically Semitic[2]—seeing man in a *functional* manner. He can use one part of man to represent the whole and vice versa. A physical organ can depict much more extensive functions (cf. *heart, bowels*). It is a mistake to attempt to force Paul's use of terms, relating to man, into carefully defined and systematized categories, which characterize Greek thought and are the basis for much of the modern methods of analytical physiology and psychology. Instead, Paul simply understood man as he appeared to be and act.

Actually, Paul was not concerned about what man *is*—theoretically. He did not philosophize about the nature of man, for this would be acting as "wise [men] according to the flesh"[3] (1 Cor. 1:26), and be the "philosophy and empty deception" (Col. 2:8) that he repeatedly warned against. There is no formulation of a doctrine of man, *per se*, in his writings because he had no interest in such.

---

1. This will be specifically examined and explained in a later chapter.

2. For centuries Pauline scholars were convinced that the apostle's anthropology was basically Hellenistic, reflecting the influence of the Greek culture in which he was reared and educated. Early in the twentieth century British and German New Testament scholars challenged this assumption. Through detailed analysis they demonstrated that Paul's terminology of man was not Hellenistic. Some scholars drew the opposite conclusion, that it was exclusively Jewish. Two significant developments served to modify both of these extreme positions. The discovery of the Dead Sea Scrolls (1947) confirmed a growing persuasion that there was a remarkable degree of syncretism between Jewish and Hellenistic cultures in the thought pattern of the first century. A second development was that further studies reveal that, although Paul was what he claimed to be (a Hebrew of the Hebrews), and was also not left uninfluenced by the Hellenistic culture in which he so extensively lived, yet no language or background can adequately sum up the life and experience Paul knew as Christian. He attached to all terms, Greek and Hebrew, a meaning all his own. "Paul was neither a Jew nor Greek. He may have been debtor to both, and especially to the Jew; but, in the crucial matter of God and His ways with men, he was a Christian, born beside the Damascus Road" (W. D. Stacey, *The Pauline View of Man* [New York: St. Martin's Press, 1956], p. 241).

3. All Bible quotations are from the *New American Standard Bible*, unless otherwise noted.

Instead, Paul was supremely interested in man's relationship with God, and with other men. His concern was religious, with the result that his terminology is directly related to whether he is thinking of man under wrath or under grace, before or after faith, in sin or in Christ, as the old or new man, etc.

There is some complexity in Paul's terminology because he attached to some key words a meaning all his own, regardless of whether they came from Hebrew or Hellenistic backgrounds.[4] On occasions he uses a more general term with a limited or technical significance, generally within a limited context.[5] Only a study of the context and the use of the term elsewhere in Paul's writings can reveal the shade of meaning in the Apostle's thought. Unless this qualified meaning is discovered the import of what he is saying appears confusing and can be entirely lost.

As we approach the study of Paul's thought we shall attempt to discover first his ideas about man. He must have a concept of the constituent nature of man that forms the background for the transforming change that was always in the foreground of his thinking. It is still a *man* who is changed. Without such a basic understanding his religious concern would be most difficult, if not impossible, to grasp. Although he has no explicit formulation of anthropology (doctrine of man), we shall attempt to project his basic views.

There is understandably a danger in such a projection, namely, the peril of modernizing Paul. The natural tendency is to allow our own ideas to influence our understanding of the terms and concepts of someone else. This is serious enough when those involved are from the same age and culture, but to attempt to understand Paul on the basis of our ideas—reflecting the theological presuppositions of almost two millennia of disputation—is futile. We must seek to grasp *Paul's* ideas in their original context.

---

4. Cf. footnote 2 above.

5. Rudolph Bultmann recognized this distinction and called the technical usage of terms "ontic" terminology as distinct from "ontological" (*Theology of the New Testament*, tr. Kendrik Grobel [New York: Charles Scribner's Sons, 1955], 1: 212, 227). The outstanding example of this is Paul's use of "flesh" (*sarx*) in Romans 8 and Galatians 5.

Chapter 2

What Is Man?

The Psalmist asked: "What is man, that thou art mindful of him?" (Ps. 8:4, KJV). He was looking at man in his wretched, sinful condition and rightly wondered how God could love him. In the study that follows, an answer to the total question will be attempted, but at this point we are interested only in the part, "What is man?"

Paul, as does the rest of the New Testament, uses two terms to refer to man. Although *anthrōpos* and *anēr* have some minor differences,[1] for all practical purposes they are synonyms, with the former being used more extensively by Paul. These terms refer to man as a human being but do not tell us anything about what man, as a human being, is.

Paul does, however, use terms that relate to what man is, but modern thought has been extensively influenced by Greek ideas. The result is that these terms are understood today with connotations that reflect Greek ideas rather than specifically those of Paul.

In Greek thought, all of reality was divided into two parts,

---

1. Technically *anthrōpos* relates to man as a human being, in distinction from other forms of life—plant, animal, angelic, etc. *Anēr* contrasts the male with the female (husband and wife, man and woman) or a single man from a crowd of men. (Cf. W. F. Arndt and F. W. Gingrich, *A Greek-English Lexicon of the New Testament* [Chicago: University of Chicago Press, 1957]. All references to this lexicon will be identified as "A and G.")

such as spirit and matter, good and evil, immortal and mortal.[2] Consequently, the Greeks thought of man in "two parts." The human body was entirely physical and, as a part of the material world, was evil and mortal. On the other hand, man's soul was seen as spiritual and immortal, and intrinsically good. While living in this world, the soul was helplessly imprisoned in the body. Salvation was impossible in this world and came only when man escaped from the body to a pure life of spirit.

In actuality the Greek idea of man ended up with *two men.* Most significantly, the spiritual man (the soul or mind) can, and one day will, exist separate from the body as a disembodied soul. The Greek view of man is called *analytical,* because it divides man up into separate *parts.* In contrast, Paul's concept of man is typically Semitic and specifically Jewish. He sees man as a *unity,* living in various *functional relationships.*

One of the clearest examples of the basic difference in the Jewish and Greek ideas of man is seen in the use of the term *soul* (*psyche*). Paul used *soul* as it is used throughout the Old Testament[3] and the New Testament[4] to designate man as a *whole. Soul* is the closest biblical synonym for *self* or *person.* Paul exhorts: "Let every person [*psyche*] be in subjection to the governing authorities" (Rom. 13:1). At other times the term means man's physical life, the loss of which is death. Paul used *soul* when referring to Elijah's complaint that his enemies were seeking his life (cf. Rom. 11:3).

At times it is not clear whether Paul means person or physical life, with either fitting the context well (cf. 1 Thess. 2:8; 2 Cor. 12:15). It is important, however, to recognize that when Paul uses *soul* to mean life, it is clearly *physical* life. As in the rest of the New Testament, Paul uses another term, *zōē,* for life in the larger meaning of eternal or spiritual life.

Due to the influence of Greek thought, the term *soul* is instinctively contrasted with *body,* and we speak of saving or losing it in a

---

2. This is termed "metaphysical dualism." This is obviously an oversimplification, but it can be safely concluded that to some degree this metaphysical dualism is characteristic of Greek thought in general and was highly developed in what came to be known as gnosticism.

3. In the Hebrew OT *nephesh* and the LXX *psyche*.

4. Cf. footnote 6 below.

spiritual sense.[5] Paul never speaks of "saving the soul."[6] He does not think of the soul as the inner, immortal part of man. This idea is basically Greek and not Semitic.

It might be asked: Don't Paul and the New Testament speak of two parts of man? How does this differ from the Greek ideas? It is true that Paul, and the New Testament, view man in a twofold sense; however, it is not *two men*, but rather two *sides* or aspects of *one man*. Thus Paul can speak of the inner and outer man. "Therefore we do not lose heart, but though our outer man is decaying, yet our inner man is being renewed day by day" (2 Cor. 4:16).[7] These two aspects of man are vitally related, with the inner expressing itself in the outer and the activity of the outer manifesting the inner. The inner man is known only to God and man himself, while the outer man is seen and known to other men. Of greatest significance is the fact that *no existence is possible without both.* Man is not man without both the inner and outer aspects of his being. That is why the present outer man will one day be replaced with a *new outer* man through the resurrection. Man cannot exist without a body.[8]

Due to the hiddenness of the inner man, the contrast between inner and outer is also described in terms of hidden and manifest (cf. Rom. 2:28-29; 1 Cor. 4:5; 14:25). This distinction is fundamental to the Semitic concept of man, as seen in Samuel's classic statement when seeking a replacement for King Saul: "Man looks at the outward appearance, but the Lord looks at the heart" (1 Sam. 16:7).

What terms does Paul use to refer to these two aspects or sides

---

5. There are a few instances when Paul uses *soul* to mean inward purpose or will, which is similar in meaning to *heart* (*kardia*), and is even translated "heart" (Eph. 6:6; cf. Col. 3:23) and "mind" (Phil. 1:27). However, *soul* is *never* contrasted with *body* (*soma*) or *flesh* (*sarx*) by Paul.

6. There has been needless confusion about Matt. 16:25-26: "For whoever would save his life will lose it, and whoever loses his life for my sake will find it. For what will it profit a man, if he gains the whole world and forfeits his life? Or what shall a man give in return for his life?" (RSV). The RSV properly translates *psyche* as "life" in both v. 25 and v. 26, whereas the KJV (and the NASB) unfortunately translate *psyche* as "life" in v. 25 and as "soul" in v. 26.

7. Cf. also Rom. 7:22; Eph. 4:16; Rom. 2:28-29.

8. This is termed "somatic existence" and in philosophical terms is metaphysical monism.

of man? We have already suggested some. Unquestionably the most extensively used term to denote the inner man is *heart* (*kardia*).[9] However, the Semitic meaning of *heart* is quite distinct from the Hellenistic concept that has so extensively influenced modern ideas. The Greeks used *heart* with reference to the emotions or feelings as distinguished from the intellect (mind) and will (volition). The New Testament uses *heart* to mean the *total* inner man.

Often *heart* is a synonym for *within* and by implication is in contrast to that which is without. "And hope does not disappoint; because the love of God has been poured out within our hearts through the Holy Spirit who was given to us" (Rom. 5:5).[10] Yet *heart* indicates more—it is the *center* of man, and as such is identified with understanding (cf. 2 Cor. 3:15; Eph. 1:18; 4:18) as well as man's deepest emotions (cf. 2 Cor. 8:16; Rom. 9:2; 10:1).

The heart can depict both what a man *is* and the motivation for what he *does*—his character and his conduct. Actually, what a man *is* (in his heart) determines what he *does*.[11] The New Testament knows nothing of modern psychological concepts,[12] but it does recognize that certain activities come from the heart and others do not. It is the heart activity, with thought and intent, that has a moral quality. Here is where both good and evil are to be found (cf. Rom. 6:17; 2 Cor. 8:16; 2 Thess. 3:5).[13]

What about "mind" (*nous*)? Very interestingly, Paul is the only one in the New Testament who significantly uses this term.[14] Although Paul borrowed the word from Greek thought, he gave it a new meaning. In Hellenistic usage the mind was thought to be intrinsically good and immortal. In later chapters it will be seen

---

9. *Kardia* is used over 150 times in the NT and is consistent in meaning with its antecedents in the OT.

10. Cf. also 2 Cor. 1:22; Gal. 4:6; Eph. 3:17.

11. "The good man out of the good treasure of his heart brings forth what is good; and the evil man out of the evil treasure brings forth what is evil; for his mouth speaks from that which fills his heart" (Luke 6:45).

12. Cf. environmental stimuli, involuntary or unconscious response, volitional activity, conscious will, etc.

13. Cf. Jesus' identification of a lustful look as an attitude of adultery in the heart (cf. Matt. 5:28). This is true of a whole catalogue of sins (cf. Mark 7:21-23).

14. The only place *nous* is found outside of the writings of Paul in the NT is in Luke 24:25; Rev. 13:18; 17:9.

that the mind can be either good or evil, as understood by Paul. His use of the term is practically synonymous in meaning with *heart,* with any distinctiveness being an emphasis on the rational process of the inner man (cf. Rom. 14:5).[15] We should, however, not confuse the mind with the brain. In actuality the brain is part of the outer man, through which the mind expresses itself.

One final term that relates to the inner man is *spirit* (*pneuma*). The Greeks viewed man's spirit as immortal and good, even as his soul and mind. If Paul's use of the term is understood in this manner, one of the most important aspects of his thought is lost.

The Old Testament[16] and the Synoptic Gospels use the term *spirit* to depict the inner man, comparable to *heart* and *mind.* In a few instances Paul appears to use the term in this way (cf. 1 Cor. 5:5; 7:34; 2 Cor. 7:1), but his primary meaning of the term is distinctive, depicting in all practicality an original idea. Whereas the Synoptics and Acts clearly distinguish between the human and the divine spirit, Paul blends the two concepts into one. When he is speaking of the Holy Spirit working through man it is difficult to distinguish between the human and the divine unless they are clearly identified.[17] In references to the human spirit there are always overtones of the Divine Spirit and vice versa. For example, "The grace of the Lord Jesus Christ be with your spirit" (Phil. 4:23).[18]

Yet this must not be misunderstood! It will be clearly examined in a later chapter, but at this point it should be emphasized that this "Divine invasion" is not an absorption or unchristian spiritual pantheism that destroys man's identity. Instead, unless clearly identified as either divine or human (cf. Rom. 8:14-16),

---

15. A verse in Philippians demonstrates this similarity of usage. "And the peace of God, which surpasses all comprehension [*nous*] shall guard your hearts [*kardia*] and your minds [*noēma*—lit. 'thoughts'] in Christ Jesus" (Phil. 4:7).

16. The Hebrew word that is generally used is *ruach.*

17. This is readily seen in most English translations, by the variations of "spirit" and "Spirit." In the earliest MSS (uncials) all letters were capitals.

18. Cf. 1 Cor. 5:3-5: "For I, on my part, though absent in body but present in spirit, have already judged him who has so committed this, as though I were present. In the name of our Lord Jesus . . . I have decided to deliver such a one to Satan for the destruction of his flesh, that his spirit may be saved in the day of the Lord Jesus." Paul would seem to be speaking of being present in the Holy Spirit and not in some nebulous sense of "thought," etc.

spirit represents the new inner man as indwelt by the Divine Presence. As William Barclay explains it:

> For Paul the spirit of a man is the indwelling power of God in that man, or, to put it another way, it is the risen Christ resident within him. The spirit of a man is that part of man which has kinship with God.[19]

We have examined several terms that relate to the *inner* man, but what about the *outer* man? Quite naturally we think of the word *body* (*soma*), and it is right that we should because it is one of the most important words referring to the outer man. But what does Paul mean by *body*? Again, a great part of our difficulty in understanding Paul is due to the fact that the modern concept of *body* is greatly influenced by Greek thought. For instance, we distinguish between the *physical* body (and its organs) and the *non-physical* or psychological functions of the mind or psyche.

Paul's concept of man is basically Semitic and not Greek, yet his use of *body* is a marked development over the use of the term in the Old Testament and throughout the rest of the New Testament. In the Old Testament the word *body* was used to refer to the various parts of the body, but there is no concept of the body as a whole.[20] Later, in the Synoptics, *body* begins to take on a collective significance, as seen by Jesus' reference to "clothing the body,"[21] but it often means a dead carcass.[22] The only time *body* is used in Acts (9:40) it has this latter meaning.

How did Paul use the term *body*? He speaks of the members (*melē*) of the body, which in some contexts appear to be *physical* organs (cf. 1 Cor. 12:14f.; Rom. 12:4f.), but elsewhere they refer to much broader functions (cf. Rom. 6:13, 19; Col. 3:5). Paul also speaks of man's desires (*epithumia*), passions or propensities (*pathēmata*), wishes (*thelēmata*), and longings (*orexis*), but these are primarily associated with the flesh (*sarx*). In the next chapter

---

19. William Barclay, *Flesh and Spirit* (Nashville: Abingdon Press, 1962), p. 62.

20. In the OT, "body" is a translation (KJV) of the following: *belly, bones, back, thigh, sheath, carcass, flesh,* and even *soul* (*nephesh*). In the LXX, *soma* (*body*) translates more than 10 Hebrew words.

21. Cf. Matt. 6:25f. Note the interesting contrast in this verse where food and drink are for the life (*psyche*) and clothing is for the body (*soma*). Cf. also Matt. 5:29-30; 6:22-23; Mark 5:29.

22. Cf. Matt. 27:52, 58-59; Mark 15:43; Luke 17:37. In some late MSS *soma* (*body*) is changed to *ptōma* (*corpse*); cf. Matt. 14:12; Mark 15:43.

the relationship of the body (*soma*) and flesh (*sarx*) will be examined, particularly with reference to the outer man.

Paul expresses the urgent desire that "Christ shall even now, as always, be exalted *in my body* [italics added], whether by life or by death" (Phil. 1:20; cf. 2 Cor. 4:10). He also warns that "we must all appear before the judgment seat of Christ, that each one may be recompensed for his *deeds in the body* [italics added], according to what he has done, whether good or bad" (2 Cor. 5:10; cf. Rom. 8:13). The deeds of the body which exalt Christ and for which man must face judgment would certainly be more than physical functions or activities.

It seems clear that by *body* Paul means the *total outer man*, and not simply a physical organism. Through this body the inner man of the heart lives, and it is with it and through it that the inner man acts, expressing itself in thoughts, feelings, desires, speech, etc. The body is thus directly contrasted with the heart, as the outer and inner man (cf. Rom. 1:24). In simple terms, Paul views man's body, or outer man, as *all that is at present* decaying or wasting away (cf. 2 Cor. 4:16).

Although we can distinguish in our thinking between the *physical* desires of the body and the *psychological* instincts or drives of the mind or psyche, it is becoming increasingly clear to medical science that the fine line of separation is difficult, if not impossible, to determine. They discover that many physical symptoms have nonphysical causes, and probably vice versa. For Paul the body is this closely interwoven psychosomatic person, made up of physical organs, the brain and its intricate nervous system, and all the basic human instincts. It can only result in confusion if we equate *body* only with the physical part of man.

It is of special importance to realize that Paul and the rest of the New Testament writers *never* use the term *body* (*soma*) in any other way than what has just been examined.[23] This usage is termed anthropological. Even Paul's familiar allegory of the

---

23. In Jas. 3:3 there is reference to a horse's body, and in Heb. 13:11 a beast's body is mentioned. In the context of Paul's major teaching on the resurrection of man's body he speaks of the body of a seed (1 Cor. 15:38) and possibly of the sun, moon, and stars as heavenly bodies (1 Cor. 15:40-41—some commentators have a different interpretation; cf. G. C. Findley, "1 Corinthians," *Expositor's Greek*

Church as the body of Christ is based on the physical and human body with its members, etc. (cf. 1 Cor. 12:15 f.). Arndt and Gingrich, in their authoritative New Testament lexicon, substantiate the exclusive anthropological use of *soma* by Paul and the rest of the New Testament writers. It will be seen later that this has a significant theological importance.

There is one more important term that Paul extensively uses to refer to man[24] and that is flesh (*sarx*). But due to its involved meaning, we will devote the entire next chapter to an examination of it.

Testament, pp. 935-36). Yet in every case the body represents the *outward* form, and in this sense can be classified as anthropological. At no time is *soma* used to depict a mass of matter such as a body of water, etc.

24. It would be unnecessary and far too involved to consider all of Paul's terminology relating to man. There is little question about the practical meaning of such terms as *conscience, life, will,* etc.

Chapter 3

What Is the Flesh?

The last term we shall examine, that Paul uses in relation to man, is *flesh* (*sarx*). Immediately we are faced with confusion. Quite obviously this vital term has many, and even widely varying, meanings.[1] How do we know which way the term is being used? Is it possible to escape being arbitrary? Is there one basic idea that ties all of these meanings together?

As already suggested, one fact must be always kept clear. Paul does not use terminology in a theoretical manner—as if he looked at man in a showcase. Instead, he views man in his *actual situation*. This is of particular significance in regard to *flesh*, for we shall see in later chapters that there is a vital relationship between *flesh* and *sin*. However, as we examine Paul's use of the term we should be able to discover his basic concept or idea. Nevertheless, we must remember that this is a projection for the purpose of *our* understanding.

One reason why we have difficulty in grasping the meaning of flesh is our tendency to understand it as simply a *part* of man. We shall see that such is indeed true, but there is also a much larger meaning that is unlike the other anthropological terms we have been examining. For instance, we can quite properly describe man *as* flesh, but not *as* heart or mind or body. Also man has a relation-

---

1. Cf. any standard dictionary of Bible terms or a Greek lexicon like A and G.,

ship to flesh—often described as living "according to [*kata*] the flesh"—which is not true of these other terms.

It will help us to better understand the term *flesh* if we realize that it has a strong *descriptive* significance, which we normally associate with an adjective. For all practical purposes it is used as an adjective—in an absolute sense. The object which it modifies is not stated but is provided by the context. Thus you need to ask first—flesh *what*?[2]

Our problem is that we don't use the term *flesh* in ordinary conversation, *as Paul did*. To us *flesh* means the soft parts of the body of a man or animal, as distinct from the skeleton or bone structure. But what did Paul mean by this descriptive term? In his first letter to the Corinthians we find an indication of his meaning.

> And I, brethren, could not speak to you as to spiritual men, but as to men of flesh, as to babes in Christ. I gave you milk to drink, not solid food; for you were not yet able to receive it. Indeed even now you are not yet able, for you are still fleshly. For since there is jealousy and strife among you, are you not fleshly, and *are you not walking like mere men*? For when one says, "I am of Paul," and another, "I am of Apollos," *are you not mere men*? (1 Cor. 3:1-4, italics added).[3]

Quite plainly *flesh* is here tied to *man living like a man*. A term we use quite commonly fits this description closely. It is the word *human*. This term means "that which is related to or characteristic of man." It can quite easily represent what man possesses or produces.[4] Strikingly—*there is no Greek word that is translated "human"*! Furthermore, the English term *human* has had an interesting development. Until relatively recent years *human* was strictly an adjective and it was considered improper English to use it without an accompanying noun that it modified. But it was so extensively used in an absolute sense—without an accompanying

---

2. Greek is a definitive language and often distinctions are expressed by different words rather than modifying adjectives. It is common for an adjective to be used nominally—as a noun. The adjective form of *flesh* (*sarkinos*) is used in this manner (cf. 1 Cor. 3:1).

3. It is significant that the KJV translates the end of v. 4: "Are ye not yet carnal [fleshly]?"

4. The NEB translates 1 Cor. 3:4 very significantly: "When one says, 'I am Paul's man', and another, 'I am for Apollos', *are you not all too human*?" (italics added).

noun—it is now listed in the dictionary as both an adjective and a noun. It still has a strong descriptive meaning and you need to ask —human *what?*

There is one further shade of meaning in *flesh* that needs to be seen. It always has the overtones of earthly.[5] There is no thought of the flesh being redeemed or transformed for existence in a future life beyond this world, as is true of the body. The flesh always is related to man's present life on earth.

The term *flesh*, with its basic meaning of "human," can be seen in three significant relationships to man. *The flesh is something man is.* It is descriptive of man as a human being. Man *is* flesh—that is his *basis of existence.* Paul writes to the Romans that "by the works of the Law no flesh will be justified in His sight."[6] Every man *exists* as flesh, even as Jesus told Nicodemus: "That which is born of the flesh is flesh" (John 3:6). When John described the truth of the Incarnation he said: "And the Word became flesh, and dwelt among us" (John 1:14; cf. Rom. 8:3). When Christ became a man—a human being—He became flesh.

The flesh is also *something that man has.* There are repeated references to man possessing the flesh, and the possessive pronoun (*my, your, our*) is sometimes used with it.[7] This is man's *sphere of existence* or *where man* (inner) *lives.* As such *the flesh* often is a synonym for the human body, or the outer man.[8] Paul refers to his "thorn in the flesh" (2 Cor. 12:7) and speaks of the life that he lived in the flesh (Gal. 2:20). Like *body* (*soma*), the term *flesh* is used by Paul to depict the outer man as it is contrasted with the inner man of the heart (cf. Rom. 2:28-29; Col. 2:5). Actually the total concept is the fleshly (human) body.[9] As such, it is the *sphere* in which man

---

5. The few times that the word *earthly* (*epigeios*) is used, the term *flesh* or *human* can be equally meaningful. Compare 1 Cor. 15:40; 2 Cor. 5:1; Phil. 2:10; 3:19. Compare 1 Cor. 1:26, where *sarx* is used, with Jas. 3:15, where *epigeios* is used—both to refer to "earthly wisdom."

6. Rom. 3:20; cf. 1 Cor. 1:29; Gal. 2:16. This is in keeping with the use of the term elsewhere in the NT; cf. Matt. 24:22; Luke 3:6.

7. Cf. Eph. 2:3; Rom. 6:19. In Greek often this possessive meaning is not explicitly stated; cf. Gal. 5:16, 19.

8. Cf. the parallels in 2 Cor. 4:10-11 and compare 1 Cor. 5:3 with Col. 2:5.

9. Cf. Col. 2:11, where Paul uses this exact expression (*sōmatos tēs sarkos*). It is interesting that he can also speak of the "flesh mind" (*tou noos tēs sarkos*), meaning the human *inner* man (cf. Col. 2:18).

lives out his earthly life. As long as man lives in this world he must live *in the flesh.*[10]

The fleshly (human) body possesses desires (*epithumia*), propensities (*pathēmata*), and wishes (*thelēmata*),[11] which can be filled or satisfied (cf. Gal. 5:16; Col. 2:23).

It is of special interest that at least once Paul speaks of *flesh* as the sphere of man's existence in the larger sense of the world in which he lives. "But if you should marry, you have not sinned; and if a virgin should marry, she has not sinned. Yet such will have trouble in this life [flesh, *sarx*], and I am trying to spare you" (1 Cor. 7:28). This underscores the fact that *the flesh* signifies the *earthly sphere* in which man lives, with its primary meaning being the human body.

What makes *flesh* such a difficult concept for the modern mind to grasp is that it also represents *something man uses.* The flesh *can be* the means or basis for living, revealing *how man lives.* Often this unique relationship is expressed by the phrase "according to the flesh" (*kata sarka*),[12] depicting a variety of meanings.[13] However, as with the other uses of *flesh* treated above, the basic concept of "human" can be seen throughout.

"According to the flesh" can represent a relationship with others such as human lineage (Rom. 4:1; 9:3) and human masters (Eph. 6:5; Col. 3:22). This phrase also can indicate similarity or conformity to a norm, thus meaning "in accordance with the flesh" or even "for the purpose of the flesh." Thus Paul speaks of human

---

10. This relationship to the flesh is often expressed by the dative case, which can have a strong locative (sphere) meaning (cf. 2 Cor. 12:7; 1 Cor. 7:28), or by the preposition "in" (*en*) with the dative case (*en sarki*) to emphasize the locative (sphere) meaning (cf. Gal. 2:20; Rom. 2:28; Phil. 3:3-4; 2 Cor. 10:3).

11. Cf. Rom. 13:14; Eph. 2:3; Gal. 5:24. Paul uses the expression "lusts of the *heart*" (*epithumiais ton kardiōn*) in Rom. 1:24. Strictly speaking, he appears to mean the desires of the fleshly (human) body that have the *consent* of the heart (cf. the discussion in the previous chapter on heart activity). Compare also Eph. 2:3, "desires [*thelēmata*] . . . of the mind [*dianoiōn*]."

12. This relationship to the flesh is also depicted by the instrumental force of the dative case (cf. Gal. 3:3), and particularly so when this dative of means is strengthened by the preposition *en* (cf. Rom. 7:5; 8:8-9; note the context, especially 8:4-5). It is best translated "by" or "by means of."

13. Cf. *kata* with the accusative case in A and G.

wisdom (1 Cor. 1:26) and human intent (2 Cor. 1:17). This is the key to understanding the following passage:

> Therefore from now on we recognize no man according to the flesh [*kata sarka*]; even though we have known Christ according to the flesh [*kata sarka*], yet now we know *Him thus* no longer. Therefore if any man is in Christ, *he is* a new creature; the old things passed away; behold, new things have come (2 Cor. 5:16-17).

Much has been written as to whether Paul is referring here to knowing Christ before His death. This is very unlikely. Instead he is describing one of the results of being a new creature in Christ as having *a new basis of knowledge*. We do not view Christ or men simply on the basis of human knowledge. Instead, we know Christ and men in a new way.

To use the flesh as the basis for living is to live by means of human strength, power and resources—by human dynamic. In actuality to so live can only result in weakness as can be vividly seen in these words of Paul:

> I ask that when I am present I may not be bold with the confidence with which I propose to be courageous against some, who regard us as if we walked according to the flesh [*kata sarka*]. For though we walk in the flesh [*en sarki*], we do not war according to the flesh [*kata sarka*], for the weapons of our warfare are not of the flesh, but divinely powerful for the destruction of fortresses (2 Cor. 10:2-4).

Although Paul admitted he walked *in the flesh* (*en sarki*), as his sphere of existence, he adamantly denied warring *according to the flesh* (*kata sarka*), which would be using the flesh as his means of living. He wanted it plainly understood that his weapons of warfare were not fleshly (*sarkika*).

Paul considered the results or products of living according to the flesh (*kata sarka*) as merely human works and values, which he strongly depreciated. If he were to trust in his Jewish heritage and zealous activity it would be to trust in the flesh as human works and values (cf. Phil. 3:3-7). Even more significantly, he considered any reference to his Christian sufferings and sacrifices as boasting according to the flesh, because all such were human works (cf. 2 Cor. 11:18).

In actuality when a man lives according to the flesh (*kata sarka*), he is living *according to himself.*[14] Because of the basic nature of man, this means that the person living *by* the flesh also lives *for* the flesh. Not only does he live by means of his own strength and resources (human means), but he lives for himself. The consequence is that to live *kata sarka* results in the improper satisfaction of the demands of the fleshly (human) body—its desires, propensities, and wishes. We shall see in later chapters that this is the arena of the struggle against sin (cf. Gal. 5:13-25; Eph. 2:1-3; Rom. 7:5; 8:1-13). This is why the flesh is termed man's lower nature in some modern translations.

To some, Paul's Semitic concept of man, which views him as a basic unity with diversified functions, has been considered so primitively naive that it has little meaning for contemporary thought. However, it is quite significant that, as the mysteries of psychosomatic behavior are explored, the interrelation of the inner and outer man takes on increased importance. Even more striking are the modern theories of personality, in which the inner style of life is in direct interplay with the outer creative self. The main trend of present-day psychological thought is holistic.[15] This is not too foreign to Paul's thought.

Of most importance, these unfamiliar ideas about man must be "translated" into concepts that have theological and practical meaning to men today. It is to this task that we now turn.

---

14. It is interesting that Augustine recognized this: "The 'living according to the flesh' is equivalent in meaning to the 'living according to one's self,' 'according to man'" (De Civ Dei, xiv, 2-4).

15. Cf. Calvin S. Hall and Gardner Lindsey, *Theories of Personality* (New York: John Wiley and Sons, Inc., 1957).

PART II

THE OLD MAN: IN SIN

Sin is Universal
Sin Rules Man
Sin and the Law
Sin and Death

We have seen that Paul basically viewed man from a religious perspective. He is either "in Christ" or "in sin"—there is no middle ground. However, Paul was writing to the new men of faith who had joyfully received the gospel he proclaimed. Therefore his consideration of the man "in sin" is always by way of reminiscence. He is looking back at what once had been—even occasionally of himself. This former life in sin is picturesquely described as "the old man" or "the man we once were" (Rom. 6:6, NEB), and is even directly contrasted with the "new man," who is in Christ (cf. Eph. 4:22-24; Col. 3:9-10).

Chapter 4

Sin Is Universal

Paul's conclusion that "all have sinned and fall short of the glory of God" is well known (Rom. 3:23). He graphically describes the sin of the Gentile world, not only as a historical background for his presentation of the good news of the gospel (cf. Rom. 1:18-32), but with a very intimate reminiscence of the life from which his beloved converts had been delivered (cf. Col. 3:5-7). Even the Jew, with all of his benefits through the holy law, was no less a transgressor (cf. Rom. 2:21-24). Thus Paul "charged that both Jews and Greeks are all under sin" (Rom. 3:9).

Is this not true today? An elaborate argument is not needed to bring any perceptive observer to the same disheartening conclusion. Forms of expression may have altered through the centuries—although surprisingly many have not—but the basic fact of sin is all too apparent. Often it is seen in gross vulgarity and dissipation, while among many others it wears a sophisticated cloak that is more compatible with social mores, which themselves are in a constant state of moral degeneracy. All have sinned—today.

Paul has a perfectly plausible explanation of what *caused* the universality of sin. Even as his Jewish contemporaries, he directly traced man's sinful condition to Adam.[1] Yet Paul gives the matter surprisingly little attention. His one clear reference[2] to the relationship between Adam's fall and man's sin is secondary in nature —almost an afterthought. In Rom. 5:12-21, Paul's primary concern is not to trace the *origin* of sin. If this were his intent, then such a discussion belongs *before* he considered sin and its consequences (1:18—3:19). Further, if such were his objective, he failed to treat two of the most vital questions—how and what. Paul's interpreters have made the repeated and unfortunate mistake of trying to discover and explain *what Paul never attempted to say*.

Having considered sin and its consequences (1:18—3:19), and the new way of righteousness by faith (3:20—5:11), Paul concludes the *comparison* of sin and righteousness with a vivid *contrast*. This is clearly seen in his grand conclusion: "As sin reigned in death, even so grace might reign through righteousness to eternal life through Jesus Christ our Lord" (Rom. 5:21). All of the consequences extending from the one trespass[3] of Adam to all men were abundantly remedied through the one redeeming act of Christ with its consequences to all men. "For as through the one man's disobedience the many were made sinners, even so through the obedience of the One the many will be made righteous" (Rom. 5:19).

Almost incidental to this is Paul's hesitation—right in the midst of a sentence[4]—to *explain*[5] that through Adam sin entered

---

1. Cf. the brief, but thorough, study of this question by William Sanday and A. C. Headlam in *The Epistle to the Romans, International Critical Commentary* (New York: Charles Scribner's Sons, 1899), pp. 136-38, with their conclusion that "there is no fundamental inconsistency between his [Paul's] views and those of his contemporaries."

2. Cf. 1 Cor. 15:21-22, where Paul relates man's universal death to Adam, but he does not mention sin. The emphasis of the chapter is that life (resurrection) comes through Christ.

3. The Greek term (*paraptōma*) means "to fall" or "to slip"; cf. A and G.

4. The Greek construction shows a broken sentence which Paul never completes. It is a protasis with no apodosis.

5. It is the *explanation* that appears to be an afterthought. The *fact* of the contrast between Adam and Christ, as described in Rom. 5:12-21, is central to Paul's thought.

into the world (Rom. 5:12). "Through the one man's disobedience the many were made sinners" (Rom. 5:19).

This would not be too difficult to understand, simply in terms of Adam setting in motion a chain of sinful acts, except for some important additional facts that begin to emerge. Perhaps most significant is the *basic illustration—in antithetical parallelism.*[6] The sinful condition of *all* men was somehow to be traced to a *single* disobedience in Adam, even as the remedy of grace for *all* men can be traced to a *single* obedience in Jesus Christ. Man's sinful plight is *not* due simply to his own actions. This is what Paul pauses to explain: "All sinned—for until the Law sin was in the world; but sin is not imputed[7] when there is no law. Nevertheless death reigned from Adam until Moses, even over those who had not sinned in the likeness of Adam's offense" (Rom. 5:12-14).

To be sure, man sinned; but before the law was given on Mount Sinai, it was unlike Adam's *transgression* because Adam had disobeyed God's express commandment. Most significantly, the universal consequence of death—which extended to all men— was not *caused* by man's *own* sin, *but Adam's.* Paul makes this abundantly clear in the graphic contrast that follows (cf. vv. 15-19).

Of further crucial significance is the portrayal of sin in the succeeding context. In Rom. 5:12—8:10, Paul extensively uses only *one* word for sin[8] and always in the singular number[9] and usually with the definite article.[10] Through a succession of Greek cases he increasingly personifies sin; first as the sphere and even the *personal object* of man's action,[11] then as a *possessing agent,*[12] and finally as a *ruling power* that reigns over man (6:12) as his mas-

---

6. Although the single acts with their multiple consequences—of Adam and Christ—are *directly parallel,* the nature of both the acts and consequences are in *vivid antithesis.*

7. The Greek word (*ellogeō*) is a commercial term, which literally means to "charge to someone's account"; cf. A and G.

8. The word is *hamartia* and is used 40 times, which is twice as much as in all the rest of Paul's writings.

9. The one exception is 7:5.

10. The definite article (*ho,* "the") is used over 30 times.

11. The *dative* case is used; cf. 6:1-2, 6c.

12. The *genitive* case is used; cf. 6:6b; see also 6:17, 20, 22-23.

ter.[13] In the light of this usage of the word *hamartia*, it is quite significant that in chapter 5, although Paul uses four terms, to describe Adam's "fall,"[14] *he never uses "hamartia."* Instead, *hamartia* came into the world as the result or consequence of Adam's act. "There is an undercurrent all through this passage, showing how something else is at work besides the guilt of individuals."[15] We shall see that in this most extensive passage on sin in the Bible (Rom. 5:12—8:10), it (sin) is described as *much more than an act.* Instead, it is portrayed as an irresistible power that captures and controls man, making him its helpless slave.

Paul traces sin and its consequences directly to Adam. "Through one man sin entered into the world, and death through sin, and so death spread to all men, because all sinned" (Rom. 5:12); and "Through the one man's disobedience the many were made sinners" (Rom. 5:19). Adam, holy by creation, committed an *act* of disobedience, a trespass or fall. As the result of this he was depraved. In this sense *sin,* as a ruling power (*hamartia*), came into the world. Consequently all men (his posterity) sinned because of the sin that came into the world through Adam. Adam's depravity was at the same time the depravity of his posterity. This alone gives a proper significance to the nature of *hamartia.*

There is, however, a *further* sense in which "the many were made sinners." Paul makes it clear that the death of Adam's posterity was not the result of *their* sin, because their sin was not in the likeness of Adam's offense. Adam had transgressed or crossed a line. Man could not transgress because he was without the commandment (from Adam to Moses). Man's death, as well as his sin, was the result of Adam's fall. Death cannot be the result of depravity (*hamartia*)—it must be the result of action that brings guilt. Man's *own* action, before the coming of the law, could not produce such guilt. The exegesis indicates Adam's posterity *sinned* in Adam. Such a conclusion alone points to the guilt and resulting death from Adam to Moses. So men were made sinners in Adam in

---

13. The *nominative* case is used; cf. 6:12, 14; 7:8-9, 13 (three times), 17, 20.

14. He uses *paraptōma* (trespass, fall, slip) six times, *parabasis* (transgression, crossing of a line), *parakoē* (disobedience), and *hamartanō* (to sin). The last term is the verb form of the root from which the noun *hamartia* is derived, but it is the latter that has technical significance.

15. Sanday and Headlam, *Epistle to the Romans,* p. 134.

a *twofold sense.* They were depraved in Adam and they were guilty in Adam—resulting in death. Anything short of this twofold explanation does not do justice to *all* of the facets of Paul's thought. Is this not why Paul could so confidently charge that all men are under sin?

This still leaves a most intriguing question—How? In what way were all men depraved *and* guilty in Adam? Legion have been the attempts to explain this theologically. The simple fact is, however, that Paul never attempted to answer this question. This was not his concern. In recent years, biblical and theological students have found at least a partial answer in the ancient concept of the total solidarity of mankind.[16] This simply means that what happens to one happens to all. When Adam transgressed, all of mankind became as guilty as he—and thus die. Further, as Adam was depraved as the result of his transgression, so are all men.

An immediate modern reaction is that this is no answer. Perhaps it is best to admit that we do not know how. Yet the *fact* remains too apparent to deny. We, his interpreters, can do no better than Paul, who was content to leave this question in a shroud of mystery. Lest we impatiently demand an answer, let us be reminded that there is much in the good news of the gospel that we know to be true—yet we cannot explain. *How* is a man righteous by faith, or *how* does one die with Christ? Can we explain it? Such we can understand no more than Nicodemus did the new birth.

Furthermore, it is obvious that Paul made no attempt to explain *what the sin is* that entered into the world through Adam. It has been identified above as depravity and guilt. This depravity, as *hamartia,* is graphically *described* in Romans 6—8 as a ruling and reigning power. This is precisely the difficulty. Although Paul *describes what sin does,* he never did work out a *generic definition of what sin is.* This has produced a problem from his day to ours. All too often a description has been mistaken for a definition.

It is necessary for us to "translate" Paul's dramatic personification of sin into concepts that are meaningful to men today. In

---

16. As representative, cf. William Barclay's comments on Rom. 5:12-21, *The Daily Study Bible* (Philadelphia: The Westminster Press, 1959).

this task we must be guided by *two facts* that are recognized as basic to a biblical theology: (1) This sin is *original,* meaning that *man is born with it.* (2) This sin *remains* in the life of the regenerated believer. However we understand sin, it must be consistent with these two facts.

When original sin is identified as an attitude of rebellion toward God and/or enmity toward man, it is a matter of confusing *results* with *causes.* Man is not born with these attitudes and it is difficult to reconcile them with an experience of regeneration. Rebellion and enmity are the *consequences* of original sin and not that sin itself.

Sometimes original sin is equated with man's so-called "lower nature," meaning his depraved outer man—his desires, passions, appetites, propensities, etc. This reflects a failure to understand Paul's basic anthropology. *Original sin is a corruption of the inner man—man's heart.* We are not born with a depraved outer man. Instead this, too, is the *consequence* of original sin.

Sin has been *described* as a destructive principle, a wrongness, a corruption of human nature, an evil attitude or inclination, an hereditary disease, hostility, etc. All such descriptions reflect a groping after the meaning of sin in terms of a mysterious intruder, who has invaded human personality.

When an attempt *is* made to *define* this mysterious intruder, a striking similarity appears. Sin has been defined as self-delusion, self-reliance, listening to oneself instead of listening to God, man's self-assertion in rebellion against God, turning toward oneself and making oneself the center of his self. No clearer definition can be found than that offered by H. Orton Wiley in his treatment of sin as unrighteousness (*adikia*): "Sin, then, is self-separation from God in the sense of decentralization, the place which should be occupied by God being assumed by the self."[17]

It can be seen that, thus understood, sin is a relationship—*a perverted relationship* between God and man. How can sin be anything else if it is related to persons? Can this understanding of

---

17. H. Orton Wiley, *Christian Theology* (Kansas City: Beacon Hill Press, 1952), 2:84.

the nature of sin be meaningfully related to the Scriptures—specifically to Adam's fall? What does the Genesis record reveal in regard to the beginning of sin? It is well known that Satan's appeal was to eat of the forbidden tree—to disobey the explicit command of God. The tempter's enticing promise was that, as a result, "you surely shall not die! For God knows that in the day you eat from it your eyes will be opened, and *you will be like God, knowing good and evil*" (Gen. 3:4-5, italics added). As Eve pondered the promise, she saw that "the tree was desirable to *make one wise*" (Gen. 3:6, italics added).[18] What is not generally associated with this is the remark of God, when He sent Adam and Eve from the garden after they had transgressed—"*Behold, the man has become like one of Us, knowing good and evil*" (Gen. 3:22, italics added). This is one time the devil told the truth. Man did become like God through the Fall.

The question immediately arises—how did man become like God through his trespass? The answer, of course, is his coming to know good and evil. This *cannot* mean to know the *difference between* good and evil *per se*, because such knowledge is indispensable to moral behavior. Rather, does it not mean to know (or presume to know) what is good or evil *for myself*? Until this time God had been sovereign and man had been subject, but in that act of rebellion man *usurped his sovereignty* and became the *god or lord of his own life*. "The place which should be occupied by God, is assumed by the self," as Wiley points out.

This is the depravity that possesses all men—they are born into this world in the grip of self-sovereignty. We shall see how this sin rules man, which alone explains the inescapable fact of the universality of sin.

Sometimes objection has been made to this understanding of the nature of sin, suggesting that it makes sin practically synonymous with free will. Such a conclusion arises from a failure to see a basic—even the dictionary—distinction. Sovereignty is the *power of control,* while free will is the *power of choice.* Man cannot be man without the power of choice. At no time in his relationship

---

18. Cf. Rom. 1:19-22, where Paul describes the working of this "wisdom."

with God is such freedom lost or even transgressed.[19] It was precisely such a power of choice that *enabled* Adam to transgress—he
used his freedom to rebel and thus *chose* to rule or control his own
life. Man, in the highest state of grace, still possesses the power of
choice, but he has *chosen* to surrender to his Lord the power to *control* his life. He has made Him the Lord of his life.

---

19. Freedom of choice does not mean the *power* to produce righteous action.
Fallen man is a slave to sin. Cf. Augustine's "bondage of the will."

Chapter 5

Sin Rules Man

We don't read very far in the New Testament before coming to a startling discovery about sin. Not only is it universal—but it has a stranglehold on men. Instead of the common idea that sin is a series of unrelated evil acts, or even thoughts, sin is seen to be an evil power that holds man in its grip. Jesus repeatedly taught that a man was not defiled by a superficial and external contamination, but that the true source of evil was the power that ruled deep within a man's heart (cf. Mark 7:1-23). A careful examination of the Sermon on the Mount (Matthew 5—7) reveals that the Master Teacher was urgently seeking to explain this basic truth.

In the New Testament passage most intensively dealing with sin (Romans 5—8), the word for *sin* (*hamartia*) is increasingly personified. Sin rules man, making him its helpless pawn. Using two vivid metaphors, Paul *describes* sin in Rom. 6:12 as a "reigning king" (*basileuō*) and in 6:14 as a "ruling lord" (*kurieuō*). In the culture of that day that meant total subservience. Not only does sin possess man, making him a bondslave (cf. Rom. 6:17), but it takes advantage of him for its own objectives (cf. Rom. 7:8). This power is so overwhelming that the victim exclaims: "So now, no longer am I the one doing it, but sin which indwells me" (Rom. 7: 17); and, "Wretched man that I am! Who will set me free from the body of this death?" (Rom. 7:24). Here is the full Pauline concept of sin—a power that holds man helplessly in its enslaving grip.

This graphic portrayal of sin has caused many to wonder if Paul, in keeping with the current ideas of his day, saw sin primarily as evil powers or demons.[1] However, New Testament scholars generally conclude that this vivid, metaphorical language should not be literalized—certainly not mythologized. The strongest support for this conclusion is the manner in which Paul relates sin to his basic twofold concept of man.

The inner man of the heart is vitally related to character and conduct. A man is—spiritually, morally, and ethically—what he is in his heart, because what he is inwardly determines what he does outwardly. It is, therefore, important to understand what sin does to the heart of man. In the dismal picture of sin wreaking havoc on man in Rom. 1:18-32, the following verses are of special significance.

> For even though they knew God, they did not honor Him as God, or give thanks; but they became futile in their speculations, and their foolish heart was darkened. . . . And just as they did not see fit to acknowledge God any longer, God gave them over to a depraved mind, to do those things which are not proper (Rom. 1:21, 28).[2]

The *heart was darkened* and the *mind was depraved.* But this was not only true of the pagan victim of sin. Paul charges *all men* to be under sin, which includes the Jewish moralists with their holy law. What caused the hypocrisy of the Jews, resulting in their despising of God's kindness, forbearance, and long-suffering (cf. Rom. 2:4)? "But because of your stubbornness and unrepentant heart you are storing up wrath for yourself in the day of wrath and revelation of the righteous judgment of God" (Rom. 2:5). The problem was a *hard and impenitent heart.*

How does man's heart become darkened and hardened? This is clearly seen when original sin or depravity is understood as self-sovereignty. Every man is born with a bias—he is turned in on himself and away from God. His relationship with God is perverted because he is lord of his own life. He presumes to know what is good

---

1. Cf. Sanday and Headlam, *Epistle to the Romans,* pp. 143-46; also Col. 2:15.
2. There is a graphic play on words in v. 28. As they thought God not good enough for them, so God gave them up to a "reprobate mind," which literally means a mind that is not fit.

and evil for himself. Devoid of the light of God's sovereign presence, his heart is hardened in darkness. The only possible result is impenitence and rebellion toward God and enmity toward men.

But a word of caution is necessary here. *Man is not born a rebel; he becomes such by exercising his sovereignty.* This is a vital distinction that must be clearly understood. Rebellion and enmity toward God and men are not original sin, but the *results* of original sin at work in the human heart. In theological terms, these evil attitudes of the inner man are examples of *acquired* depravity and not original depravity.

This inner man, now doubly depraved, finds expression in the outer man where the enslaving power of sin is most graphically seen. Sin reigns as a king in man's mortal body (cf. Rom. 6:12) and his members, obviously of the body, serve uncleanness and iniquity (cf. Rom. 6:19). Paul speaks in Rom. 6:6 of the "body of sin" (*to sōma tēs hamartias*), meaning that man's body (the outer man) is under the total domination and control of sin. It is a "sinful body" or even "sin's body."[3] It is a mistake to interpret the word "body" (*soma*) with a nonanthropological meaning, such as making it mean a "mystical body of evil," a "mass," "totality" or the "nature" of sin. Such an interpretation has no precedence in the biblical uses of the term, and there is serious doubt if there is any to be found in nonbiblical usage.[4] Sin so contaminates and controls the outer man—expressing itself through it and using it—that man's body is pictured *as sin's own body.*

Sin's rule of the outer man is most graphically seen in Paul's portrayal of the flesh as sin's instrument. "For while we were in the flesh, the sinful passions, which were *aroused* by the Law, were at work in the members of our body to bear fruit for death" (Rom. 7:5). What does Paul mean when he speaks of a time when we *were* in the flesh? The clear implication is that they *were not* at the present time. Obviously he is not speaking of the flesh as the basis

---

3. The genitive case can be either descriptive or possessive in meaning. The personification of sin in the context—where it is clearly shown to have a possessive character (cf. Rom. 6:16-17, 20)—would argue strongly for the possessive meaning of the genitive. Cf. Marvin R. Vincent, *Word Studies in the New Testament* (Grand Rapids, Mich.: William B. Eerdmans Publishing Co., 1957), 3:69.

4. Cf. chapter 2 and the treatment of *soma* (body).

or sphere of man's existence, because such a relationship to the flesh cannot cease as long as a man is living. Instead, he is referring to the time when the flesh was used as the *basis or dynamic for living*.[5]

When a man uses his flesh as the dynamic for living, the result is that "the sinful passions . . . were [are] at work in the members of our body" (Rom. 7:5). What does Paul mean by *sinful passions*? Are a sinner's propensities[6] intrinsically evil? How and when do these human propensities become sinful? What happens?

Our propensities and desires are morally neutral *per se*, but they quickly take on the character of their direction of fulfillment and *become biased in that direction*.[7] The sinful heart of man finds expression in the desires of the flesh and thus these desires become evil and sinful. Man's desires are not evil because they are of the flesh, but because sin is at work in the flesh (cf. Rom. 8:3). *Theoretically* our fleshly desires are morally neutral, but *actually*—because of sin's rule—our fleshly desires are evil. And we must always remember that Paul viewed man *as he actually is*.

The propensities and desires of the flesh bear the corrupting mark of years (individually) and centuries (racially) of sinful and evil indulgence.

> Flesh is man (outer) as man has made himself in contrast with what God has made him. . . . The flesh stands for the total effect upon man of his own sin and of the sin of his fathers and of the sin of all men who have gone before him. The flesh is human nature as it has become through sin.[8]

---

5. Cf. chapter 3 and the distinctions in Paul's use of *sarx* (flesh). This relationship is generally described as living *kata sarka* (according to the flesh), as in Rom. 8:4-5, but here the same result is accomplished by the instrumental dative case with *en* (in), *en sarki*. Cf. Rom. 8:8-9 for the same construction.

6. The word is *pathēmata*, which is used to mean a passive disposition or propensity rather than an outburst of emotion. The translation "propensity" is preferable to "passion" because of the modern connotations of the latter, cf. Rom. 7:5; Gal. 5:24. Cf. "*pathos*" in Rom. 1:26. Paul used several other terms to describe man's drives and desires: *epithumia* ("desire," Gal. 5:24; Eph. 2:3), *thelēmata* ("wish," Eph. 2:3), *orexis* ("longing," Rom. 1:27).

7. It is startling to discover that every evil work of the flesh (Gal. 5:19-21) is a corruption of a *potentially good* propensity, which could have had a proper and good expression or fulfillment.

8. Barclay, *Flesh and Spirit*, p. 22.

Thus, for the sinner to live *for* the flesh—to satisfy its desires and propensities—is to live in sin, because sin is ruling him through his own flesh.

Such a picture is hard for us to understand because we naturally think of our desires as being *within us.* Of course this is true, but in New Testament terms our desires (propensities, instincts, drives, etc.) are part of the flesh, which is our outer man (see chap. 3). We do speak of desiring or wishing in the sense of preference, purpose, or intent, *which is an attitude of the inner man,*[9] but this must be clearly distinguished from the basic appetites, instincts, and desires of the outer man.

As seen in Rom. 7:5, our sinful passions work—are outwardly expressed—*in our members* or in outward actions. Here is the tragic climax of the rule of sin. *First,* sin depraves our hearts, producing evil attitudes and motives. *Second,* these evil attitudes corrupt and misdirect the desires of our flesh. *Finally,* these desires, now sinful, find expression in outward deeds and actions. Thus sin rules man through his flesh, making him a slave of his own desires and propensities until he cries: "Wretched man that I am! Who will set me free from the body of this death?" (Rom. 7: 24).

Nowhere is the sinful bias of the flesh, with its desires and propensities, more clearly portrayed than in Romans 8:5-7:

> For those who are according to the flesh [*kata sarka*] set their minds on the things of the flesh, but those who are according to the Spirit [*kata Pneuma*], the things of the Spirit. For the mind set on the flesh is death, but the mind set on the Spirit is life and peace; because the mind set on the flesh is hostile toward God; for it does not subject itself to the Law of God, for it is not even able *to do so.*

Paul uses here a very graphic word, as both a noun and a verb,[10] which means to "set one's mind,"[11] or more accurately translated to "aim," to "aspire," or to "strive."[12] When a man uses his flesh

---

9. Cf. Rom. 7:15-25, where Paul describes wishing or liking (*thelō*) as an attitude of the *nous* (mind).

10. Cf. *phronēma* (noun) in vv. 6-7 and *phroneō* (verb) in v. 5.

11. The word "mind" in this translation must not be understood to mean the human mind—it is not the Greek word *nous*.

12. Cf. A and G.

for the dynamic of living—living by means of the flesh—his aim or aspiration is death, is enmity against God, and is not and cannot be subject to God's law. This is what sin, which is direct antipathy to God, has done to man's flesh.

The only possible result of such living is to produce the things of the flesh which Paul graphically describes as the works of the flesh.[13] It is significant that this graphic catalogue is *primarily* concerned with interhuman relations, which underscores the fact that sin, in its enslaving rule over man, is horizontal as well as vertical in its dimensions. Not only does Paul see man as a helpless sinner in relationship to God, but also in relationship to his fellow-men and to himself. Although he does not associate the two dimensions as dogmatically as is found in James and First John, there is no question as to his viewing them in direct interrelationship. In practically every letter Paul's concern about sin on the horizontal plane is painfully obvious.[14]

To live by the flesh is to be in sin's bondage, with the passions of sin working havoc in our members. The flesh, with its insistent desires and propensities, is an irresistible, compulsive force for evil. Man can only exclaim: "For I know that nothing good dwells in me, that is, in my flesh" (Rom. 7:18). Sin is ruling man through his flesh.

It is at this point that serious confusion develops. Does all this mean that the flesh is intrinsically evil, or *forever* the helpless pawn of sin? How are we to understand the relationship between sin and the flesh? Is the flesh sin? Sometimes the flesh is equated with the total depravity of man. One view properly considers flesh to be the outer man, but improperly concludes that because man lives *in* the flesh he cannot help living *by* and *for* the flesh. In other words, as long as a man is a man he is the helpless victim of sin. Another view equates the flesh with the *inner principle* of sin that depraves the heart of man, and suggests that this flesh can be cleansed out of a man.

---

13. Cf. Gal. 5:19-21 and the author's commentary on it in Vol. 9 of *Beacon Bible Commentary* (Kansas City: Beacon Hill Press, 1965).
14. Cf. the following examples where the emphasis is interpersonal: Rom. 1:18-32; 1 Cor. 6:8-10, 16-20; 2 Cor. 12:20—13:2; Gal. 5:14-15, 19-21; Eph. 2:1-5; Col. 3:5-9; 1 Thess. 4:1-7.

Both of these erroneous views are based on a misunderstanding of Paul's basic anthropology. Either view, whether it is completely pessimistic or unrealistically optimistic—with regard to deliverance from the flesh—would make Paul's exhortations relative to the flesh totally meaningless.[15] Also, it must be remembered that *Jesus came in the flesh.* "For what the Law could not do, weak as it was through the flesh, God *did:* sending His own Son in the likeness of sinful flesh and *as an offering* for sin, He condemned sin in the flesh" (Rom. 8:3).

Jesus came in the *likeness* of sinful flesh—He came in the flesh and yet without sin. This makes it plain that the flesh does not have to be sinful. His purpose was to condemn sin in the flesh.

No—the flesh is not sin. Instead, sin uses the flesh. This is its instrument to enslave man. Man is totally helpless to save himself —he is a wretched victim.

Nowhere is this total servitude to sin more vividly portrayed than in Paul's description of his own past experience.

> For the good that I wish, I do not do; but I practice the very evil that I do not wish. But if I am doing the very thing I do not wish, I am no longer the one doing it, but sin which dwells in me. Wretched man that I am! Who will set me free from the body of this death? (Rom. 7:19-20, 24).

It is true that this portion of Romans 7 (14-25) has been a theological battleground since the days of the Reformation and even back to the Greek and Latin fathers. The crucial question is the *status* of the person identified as "I." Is Paul talking about himself—is it autobiographical? Most New Testament scholars agree that this deeply personal language could be nothing else. If Paul is indeed speaking of himself, then what period of his life does he refer to? Is this his experience as an unregenerated Jew under the law, or as a newborn Christian struggling against sin? Sometimes it has been suggested that this describes Paul as a "partial" Christian, who is saved but not yet living in the fullness of God's grace. How can such *total* spiritual wretchedness be reconciled

---

15. This will be treated in a later chapter. Paul does not counsel either despair or deliverance, but discipline.

with the saving grace of God?[16] Instead, this graphic picture is most likely how Paul views the life he once lived under the law—but *now* seen through the eyes of his new life in Christ. A man's perspective makes a great difference. Undoubtedly that is not how his life appeared to him while he was actually living it.

Regardless of how this crucial passage is understood, there can be no doubt that it portrays total enslavement to sin. The inability to do the good desired and the compulsion to do the evil hated—is slavery indeed. Such is the condition of the man living under sin's ruling control. Total wretchedness is the only possible result while living in the body of death.

Paul not only portrays the rule of sin in terms of bondage, but also in the vivid figure of alienation or estrangement. "The mind [that is] set on the flesh is hostile [lit., "at enmity"] toward God . . . for it is not even able *to do so*" (Rom. 8:7). The sinner has actually made himself the *enemy* of God. The result is tragic estrangement. Paul reminded the Colossians that they "were formerly alienated and hostile in mind" toward God (Col. 1:21). Included in his description of the evil Gentile walk was the fact that such alienated them from the life of God (cf. Eph. 4:18, KJV).

The most extensive and revealing passage in the writings of Paul on alienation from God as the result of sin is Eph. 2:12-19:

> *Remember* that you were at that time separate from Christ, excluded from the commonwealth of Israel, and strangers to the covenants of promise, having no hope and without God in the world. But now in Christ Jesus you who formerly were far off have been brought near by the blood of Christ. For He Himself is our peace, who made both *groups into* one, and broke down the barrier of the dividing wall, by abolishing in His flesh the enmity, *which is* the Law of commandments *contained* in ordinances, that in Himself He might make the two into one new man, *thus* establishing peace, and might reconcile them both in one body to God through the cross, by it having put to death the enmity. AND HE CAME AND PREACHED PEACE TO YOU WHO WERE FAR AWAY, AND PEACE TO THOSE WHO WERE NEAR; for through Him we both have our access in one Spirit to the Father. So then you are no longer

---

16. If this is a picture of a Christian, then he is a defeated Christian, and this defeat is the result of trying to live *kata sarka*. This will be considered in a later chapter.

> strangers and aliens, but you are fellow-citizens with the saints, and are of God's household.

How graphic is the picture—strangers and aliens living far off from God in enmity and alienation!

However, there is a *double* alienation here! Not only is the Gentile separated from God, but there is a barrier between Gentile and Jew. This points to a crucial fact that is often overlooked when sin's alienating power is considered. Such alienation is on both the vertical and horizontal planes. It will be seen shortly that one of Paul's primary concerns is the result of sin on interhuman relationships.

It is often heard in modern ears that this biblical picture of sin is hopelessly irrelevant and meaningless to man today—that it is nothing but myth. But stop and consider! Is it any wonder that sin is thus described in the Bible? Without the benefits of modern psychology, how better could such a concept be grasped by or explained to primitive minds? When a man's body is attacked by the insidious blight of malignancy it is often—by modern sophisticated man—objectified as an external power that is fastening its tentacles upon him and bringing him into subjection and helplessness. When Dr. Tom Dooley, the famed missionary doctor, was stricken with cancer at the height of his brilliant career, he described his reaction to this horrible blight. The graphic description of his final days is a veritable objectifying of the malignancy as a power against which he desperately fought because it was compelling him to leave the work to which he was so deeply dedicated. Such is certainly not unlike the compulsive power that an alcoholic or narcotic addict objectifies. Is the power of sin really much different?

However, it is supremely important to "translate" this strange terminology of Paul—with its dramatic personification of sin—into concepts that are meaningful to man today. Can this enslaving rule of sin be related to the conclusion in the previous chapter as to the nature of original sin? It was suggested that every man is born into this world as the sovereign or lord of his own life—with the will to rule. Sometimes it is thought that such is far too anemic an understanding of the nature of sin. How woeful an error this is! This perverted relationship places man at odds with God—his true Lord. Antipathy, enmity, and hostility are inevitable. As he

asserts his sovereignty, man's heart becomes darkened in blind-
ness, hardened in rebellion, impenitent, and worthless.[17] Tragically, this condition has intensified as depravity has built up through
the centuries.

At the same time, the outer man is controlled by this sinful
heart—as its helpless slave. As man is driven by his own appetites
—his "instincts" for self-esteem and self-indulgence—he is con-
sumed by the supreme passion to *satisfy himself.* This is what
motivates every prodigal—be he in the far country or sitting
hypocritically on the church pew. The specific nature of the self-
expression is determined by the factors of heredity, environment,
culture, and education—or its lack. This is so often forgotten—
all sinners are not alike!

The *fact* of slavery to sin is well known by experience. Within
man there is a self-sovereignty that causes him to disobey God, to
break His laws, transgress His commandments, and spurn or even
despise His overtures and entreaties. Men—driven by such evil
hearts—find ingenious ways to sin against their fellowmen. Again,
this is not always with profanity, but at times is with sophisticated malice. Often men are found in the grip of miserable habits
of body, tongue, and mind, but slavery is not necessarily vile and
vulgar. Many times greed, jealousy, hatred, ill will, unforgiveness,
meanness, etc., are cloaked with respectability and accepted
socially. Any attempt to save oneself meets with total failure and
frustration. Even the knowledge of the right (law or conscience) is
not sufficient to counteract or overcome the power of sin, because
man, using the flesh as his dynamic for living, is weak and powerless. Most horrible of all is the tragic fact that this grip and power
of sin *intensifies,* not unlike a creeping malignancy that is almost
demonic. Such a life is actually a living death of utter wretchedness, as man faces the prospect of eternity without God.

Such a man is in reality a slave! He is truly in the grip of sin
—although he would well desire to be free. Thus, a man is the helpless victim of *his own* propensities and desires—a supreme passion
for self-indulgence and self-satisfaction. Without help he can only
destroy himself!

---

17. Cf. the meaning of *edokimasan* in Rom. 1:28.

Chapter 6

Sin and the Law

There is an important dimension of sin's tyranny over man that we have not yet considered. Paul writes that "while we were in the flesh, the sinful passions, which were *aroused* by the Law, were at work" (Rom. 7:5). He goes on to say: "For apart from the Law sin *is* dead" (Rom. 7:8). Even more pointedly he wrote: "The power of sin is the law" (1 Cor. 15:56). How strange this sounds to us today! Even if this were true in Paul's day—against the background of Judaism—what meaning does it have for us? Is the law the power of sin today in our lives?

To understand this strange tie between sin and the law we must see what Paul meant by *the law (nomos)*. As a Jew, he identified the law with the Mosaic covenant, given at Mount Sinai as a divine revelation.[1] Yet Paul makes a crucial distinction in the meaning of *law!* In the Mosaic covenant there was a legalistic sys-

---

1. This is the *primary*, if not exclusive, meaning of *nomos* for Paul; cf. Rom. 4:13-15; 7:9; Gal. 3:10-24. Note especially Rom. 5:13-14; Gal. 3:17, 19. In Rom. 2:14-15, Paul speaks *hypothetically* of "when Gentiles who do not have the Law do instinctively the *things* of the Law, these, not having the Law, are a law to themselves, in that they show the *work* of the Law written in their hearts, their conscience bearing witness, and their thoughts alternately accusing or else defending themselves." Paul does *not* say the Gentiles have the *nomos*, but they "do the things" of the *nomos* and "show the works" of the *nomos*. Thus the *nomos*, as the Mosaic covenant, is basic to this passage. Although Paul recognizes that in some way God's will for man is written on the hearts of men, presumably from creation, *he is very careful not to call this "nomos."* However he does say that the Gentiles are a *nomos* to themselves, but quite distinct from the Mosaic covenant.

tem of works that contained commandments, statutes, regulations, rites, sacrifices, etc.; but this legalistic system was intended
to be a *means* and not an *end.* Like his Lord before him, Paul saw
the fundamental ethical principles of the true law of God. This is
the divine will—God's standard or ethic for man—*lying behind the
legalistic system as its goal or end.*[2]

This distinction—between the law as the divine standard and
the legalistic system—explains Paul's apparent paradoxical attitude toward the law. On the one hand he describes the law as
something noble, spiritual, and holy, and stoutly defends it; while
on the other hand *in the very same passage* (Rom. 7:6-14) he warns
that the law reveals and promotes sin, and says he died to it (cf.
Gal. 2:19). The key issue is whether the law is viewed as God's
ethic (the goal) or a system of human works (the means). In these
two senses, Paul can even place the law in direct antithesis to itself. "Where then is boasting? It is excluded. By what kind of law?
Of works? No, but by a law of faith" (Rom. 3:27; cf. 3:21; 7:23).

Tragically, Judaism was captivated by the means and lost
sight of the end. The typical Jew, in practicality, viewed the law—
both the written law and the endless collection of oral traditions
added to it—only in terms of a rigid and external legalism that
was pursued through a slavish obedience to commandments, rites,
etc. As a result, for the Jews, the law was virtually synonymous
with human works.

So Paul attacked this common Jewish concept of law as human works. This is seen primarily in his letters that contain his
polemic against Jewish legalism, which sought salvation by the
works of the law rather than through faith and grace.[3] Significantly, in these letters Paul primarily used the word "law" *(nomos) as*

---

2. It is possible to distinguish between civil, ceremonial, and moral regulations, but they are so intertwined a complete separation is virtually impossible.
Such classifications as "ethical and cultic," "moral and ceremonial," and even
"statutes and principles," are most difficult to substantiate. It is better to understand the distinction as that between a total legalistic system of human works and
the divine standard that lies behind this system.

3. Paul uses *nomos* over 100 times in Romans and Galatians, but less than 15
times in the rest of the letters.

his opponents did for purposes of argumentation.[4] He argued that mere possession of the law was not enough, because only the doers of the law are justified with God (cf. Rom. 2:13). Those living by means of the law are obligated to do all the law. "For as many as are of the works of the Law are under a curse; for it is written, 'CURSED IS EVERY ONE WHO DOES NOT ABIDE BY ALL THINGS WRITTEN IN THE BOOK OF THE LAW, TO PERFORM THEM'" (Gal. 3:10).

Man finds this impossible, so that the law is a total failure *as a means of salvation.*

Then what was the purpose of the law, understood as the Mosaic legalistic system? Why had God given it to the Jewish nation if it brought only a curse and condemnation? Paul argues that God never intended it to be *permanent!* No man can be justified by the works of the law.[5] If such were possible, then there would be no need of Christ. "If righteousness *comes* through the Law, then Christ died needlessly" (Gal. 2:21; cf. 3:18, 21).

Instead Paul says the function of the law is *temporary*—for a very specific purpose. He asks: "Why the Law then?" and answers: "It was added because of transgressions" (cf. Gal. 3:19). Here again is the strange tie between sin and the law. What does it mean? It is only through the law that the knowledge of sin comes to man (cf. Rom. 3:20). In fact, "Where there is no law there is no transgression" (Rom. 4:15, RSV; cf. 5:20). Paul graphically describes this from personal experience:

> What shall we say then? Is the Law sin? May it never be! On the contrary, I would not have come to know sin except through the Law; for I would not have known about coveting if the Law had not said, "YOU SHALL NOT COVET." But sin, taking opportunity through the commandment, produced in me coveting of every kind; for apart from the Law sin *is* dead. And I was once alive apart from the Law; but when the commandment came, sin became alive, and I died; and this commandment, which was to result in life, proved to result in death for me; for sin, taking opportunity through the commandment deceived me, and through it killed me. So then, the Law is holy, and the com-

---

4. Cf. Rom. 3:27 and the use of the term "works" *(erga)* in place of "law" *(nomos)* in Rom. 4:2, 6; 9:12, 32; 11:6; Eph. 2:9. Cf. also the expression "works of the law" in Rom. 3:20, 28; Gal. 2:16; 3:2, 5, 10.

5. Cf. Rom. 1:17; 3:20; Gal. 2:16; 3:11.

mandment is holy and righteous and good. Therefore did that which is good become *a cause of* death for me? May it never be! Rather it was sin, in order that it might be shown to be sin by effecting my death through that which is good, that through the commandment sin might become utterly sinful (Rom. 7:7-13).

As seen in this testimonial, or confession, the law not only brings the knowledge of sin, *but it becomes the unwitting accomplice of sin!* "And the Law came in that the transgression might increase" (Rom. 5:20). Because of the weakness of the flesh, sin "takes opportunity"[6] through the law, deceiving and slaying man. Paul adamantly denies that this makes the law sinful. Instead, the law reveals the true nature of sin, as it (sin) uses what is good (law) to accomplish its evil ends.[7]

Even more startling is Paul's contention that this relationship between sin and law is for a grand purpose—*to prepare men for Christ!* Through the law men were *shut up . . . under sin* (Gal. 3:22) and were *shut up to the faith* (Gal. 3:23). To illustrate this, Paul pictures the law as a slave custodian,[8] a guardian or manager,[9] which keeps man under surveillance as a virtual slave.

So we can conclude that Paul saw this strange tie between sin and law because the men of his day failed to recognize the crucial relationship between their legalistic standards and the divine ethic that lies behind them. When viewed as only human works, the law can only result in sin. Tragically, this has been misunderstood to mean that Paul rejected all law. Nothing could be further from

---

6. The Greek metaphor is very vivid, using the term *aphormē,* which is a military term, meaning "the starting point or base of operations for an expedition, then generally the resources needed to carry through an undertaking" (A and G).

7. Paul also refers to "elemental things" *(stoicheia)* that had previously enslaved his Gentile converts, and warns that to take up the law *(nomos)* would bring them back into this bondage (cf. Gal. 4:3-9; Col. 2:8, 21). New Testament scholars have two basic views as to what the *stoicheia* were, namely, either rudimentary principles or elementary spirits (even demons). The association of the *stoicheia* with the *nomos* (with similar functions) strongly suggests that the preferable conclusion is that they referred to the rites, regulations, fasts, festivals, holy days, etc., through which the pious pagans sought to find peace with their gods.

8. Cf. Gal. 3:24-25. The Greek word is *paidagōgos,* which indicates a slave whose duty is to conduct a boy or youth to and from school and to superintend his conduct generally. He was not a teacher! The KJV translation ("schoolmaster") is unfortunate.

9. Cf. Gal. 4:2 and the discussion in BBC, Vol. IX, *en loc.*

the truth! In the study to follow it will be seen that the law—as the divine standard—can and must be fulfilled. But such a fulfillment is not by human works. It is by faith in Christ and through the life of the Spirit, which brings fulfillment in love.

How does Paul's understanding of sin and law relate to men today, particularly in our nonlegalistic culture? Is the law the power of sin in every man's life? Did Paul observe a crucially important relationship between sin and the law that even spans cultures? Can this thought—that the power of sin is the law—be psychologically meaningful today?

The apostle recognized that among the Gentiles many of the things required by the law of God were written in their hearts and brought to light by their consciences (cf. Rom. 2:15). Intrinsic to the constitution of man is the awareness of God's law—*in every man!*

When the essential nature of sin is understood as self-sovereignty, as previously discussed, then the relationship of sin to the law becomes glaringly apparent. As a man holds the reins of rule in his own hands—what is his greatest threat? Is it not the command of God, against which he defiantly rebels? There can be no issue, no conflict, without the law. In the truest sense, without the law there is no knowledge of sin. It is the sovereignty of God that puts man's own sovereignty into "comic relief," as he shakes his puny little finger in the face of Omnipotence. Yet—mystery of mysteries—divine sovereignty respects human sovereignty!

It is the very presence of the law that causes sinful man to intensify his rebellion. His own inner conscience, coupled with the outward moral pressures of social standards and mores, as well as the law of the state, challenge his will to rule. His only defense is self-assertion against any and every demand. How tragically this is being seen in the mid-twentieth-century social revolution! Far beneath any racial or other sociological or economic cause is the more basic problem of sin, confronted by law. As a result, man's self-sovereignty runs rampant. The theme of this revolution is the violent demand for, and the exertion of, man's *rights,* the most basic of which is interpreted as the right of anarchy and *lawlessness.* As will be seen in later chapters, the only solution to this problem is to be found in surrendered sovereignty—to God.

Yet the relationship between sin and law, as viewed by Paul, must also be seen in an entirely different sphere. Not only is the law the power of sin in the rebelling sinner, but also in the man seeking salvation by human works. Clearly, this was Paul's primary concern. Today men have their modern laws or "elemental things" through which they hope to make peace with God. Often it is found in the institutional church, with its rites and regulations; but it is not uncommon for man to thus seek God on a lonely pilgrimage. Many times men reject all external compulsion and claim allegiance only to their own consciences. But the results are all the same. The way of the law can only lead to sinful bondage.

Paul's explanation is still valid today! The problem is not in the church, in the external compulsion of society, or in the inner conscience. The problem is within man himself! He cannot save himself, however earnestly and anxiously he might try. The sinful nature of man—his own self-sovereignty—uses the law under which he chooses to live as an accomplice. Instead of peace he finds only frustration, despair, condemnation, and guilt. The law proves indeed to be the power of sin!

Chapter 7

Sin and Death

What is the consequence or result[1] of sin's rule over man? Paul saw only one possibility—that was death! "For the wages of sin is death" (Rom. 6:23). "For the outcome of those things [servitude to sin] is death" (Rom. 6:21). "Do you not know . . . you are [the] slaves of the one whom you obey, either of *sin resulting in death,* or of obedience resulting in righteousness?" (Rom. 6:16, italics added). This appears simple enough to understand, until some questions are asked. *What* kind of death is the result of sin? *When* does this death occur?

Paul traced death, even as sin, to Adam. "But now Christ has been raised from the dead, the first fruits of those who are asleep. For since by a man *came* death, by a man also *came* the resurrection of the dead. For as in Adam all die, so also in Christ all shall be made alive" (1 Cor. 15:20-22).[2] There seems to be little question that here, in his most extensive treatment of bodily resurrection (which includes the entire chapter), Paul was referring to death as the cessation of earthly life.

---

1. The term *penalty* is never used in the New Testament (or Old Testament) in relation to sin. Such a concept is extra-scriptural. Cf. any standard Bible concordance.

2. In these few verses are found most of the New Testament words for *death:* "dead" *(nekros),* "asleep" *(koimaō),* "death" *(thanatos),* and "die" *(apothnēsko).* The Greek preposition *dia,* translated "by" (*"by* a man came death, *by* a man also came") literally means "through."

In another passage, that relates death to Adam, Paul states that death, as well as sin, came into the world *through Adam's transgression.*

> Therefore, just as through one man sin entered into the world, and death through sin, and so death spread to all men, because all sinned . . . Nevertheless death reigned from Adam until Moses. . . . For if by the transgression of the one the many died . . . For if by the transgression of the one, death reigned through the one . . . As sin reigned in death (Rom. 5:12-21).

In order for Paul to use death as an illustration it must be *physical* death that reigned from Adam to Moses, upon those who did not have their own sins charged to their accounts (see chapter 4). It seems quite clear that Paul traced human mortality to man's sin (in Adam).[3]

However, as the general context is examined (Rom. 5:13—8:39), it becomes apparent that Paul viewed death as *far more than physical in nature.*

> The sinful passions . . . were at work in the members of our body to bear fruit for death. . . . When the commandment came, sin became alive, and I died; and this commandment . . . proved to result in death for me; for sin . . . deceived me, and through it [the commandment] killed me. . . . It was sin, in order that it might be shown to be sin by effecting my death through that which is good (Rom. 7:5-13).

Paul called man's body, under the rule of sin, a "wretched body of death."[4] From these scriptures it can be readily seen that death is here portrayed as the experience of man *while he is still alive physically.* Death is not simply what is experienced at the *end* of this earthly life, but is experienced *in this life.* Other references in Paul's writings graphically picture death as just such a present experience. "And you were dead in your trespasses and sins. . . . even when we were dead in our transgressions" (Eph. 2:1, 5). "And when you were dead in your transgressions and the uncircumcision of your flesh" (Col. 2:13).

---

3. The general Jewish belief of Paul's day was that Adam was created immortal and became mortal through his transgression.

4. Cf. Rom. 7:24. There is no support in the Greek for the translation in the NEB ("this body doomed to death"). There is good reason to interpret the genitive *(thanatou)* as possessive—"death's body."

A closer examination of these scriptures reveals that death is the result of sin in yet a further dimension. Not only is there physical death at the *end* of this life and a present spiritual death *in* this life, but there is also an eternal death *after* this life. *Physical* death makes *eternal* the *spiritual* death that exists in this life as the consequence of sin.

There is certainly a cause-and-effect relationship between sin and death, but it is a serious mistake to understand Paul's thought here in *impersonal terms.*[5] *The death of the sinner is to be directly related to the wrath of God.*

> Let no one deceive you with empty words, for because of these things [catalogue of evil] the wrath of God comes upon the sons of disobedience (Eph. 5:6). But because of your stubbornness and unrepentant heart you are storing up wrath for yourself in the day of wrath and revelation of the righteous judgment of God (Rom. 2:5).

Sometimes the wrath of God against man's sin can be seen *in this life.* "For the wrath of God is revealed from heaven against all ungodliness and unrighteousness of men, who suppress the truth in unrighteousness" (Rom. 1:18). Following this verse is a picture of human degradation and depravity that defies description. The key to the passage is that *God gave them up.*[6] *He abandoned them!* The worst punishment sinful man can receive is to be abandoned by God to his sins. This is death and hell!

But that is not the end of the matter. The passage ends with the following words: "And, although they know the ordinance of God, that those who practice such things are *worthy of death* [italics added], they not only do the same, but also give hearty approval to those who practice them" (Rom. 1:32).

There is a day of judgment for every man—*free moral agency demands it!* "For we must all appear before the judgment-seat of Christ, that each one may be recompensed for his deeds in the body, according to what he has done, whether good or bad" (2 Cor. 5:10). The judgment upon the sinner is death or eternal separation

---

5. Paul's Jewish training would make it impossible for him to think in terms of an impersonal cause-and-effect chain of events.

6. Cf. Rom. 1:24, 26, 28. The Greek word is *paradidōmi,* which in this context means "to abandon." Cf. A and G.

from God. God *must*—because of His divine nature—abandon the sinner, forever. Nothing reveals the seriousness of sin quite so much as God's wrath against sin. The hope of the Christian is to be saved from this wrath. "Much more then, having now been justified by His blood, we shall be saved from the wrath *of God* through Him" (Rom. 5:9).

But it is extremely important that we understand what the wrath of God is. It is not, as Leon Morris puts it,

> some irrational passion bursting forth uncontrollably, but a burning zeal for the right coupled with a perfect hatred of everything that is evil. It may be that wrath is not a perfect word to describe such an attitude, but no better has been suggested, and we must refuse to accept alternatives which do not give expression to the truth in question.[7]

Certainly God's wrath is not capricious, giving vent to personal vindictiveness. The sinner is not punished—let alone tortured—because God desires to "get even" or "make him pay" for his sin. Such ideas are a shameful sacrilege and reflect a tragic misunderstanding of the nature of God. Perhaps that is how we would treat a sinner—but not God! We find it difficult to reconcile compassion and wrath, mainly because we seldom see it existing among men. But that is precisely the nature of God's wrath—*compassionate wrath*. When God abandons a sinner it is not with satisfaction, but with a broken heart!

Again the question is faced. Does Paul's clear teaching on sin and death have significant meaning today? The question of the relationship between sin and physical death is purely academic. There is no question that all men today are mortal, regardless of what Adam originally was. Such mortality can very well be the result of the sinfulness of the human race—starting from man's beginning.

However, the matter of death in a deeper, nonphysical sense is another matter! Exactly what does this mean for man today? As in so much of Pauline thought, the key to understanding is found in his antithetical concepts. The full meaning of death can be grasped only when it is seen to be the direct opposite of life.

---

7. *The Apostolic Preaching of the Cross* (Grand Rapids, Mich.: Wm. B. Eerdmans Publishing Co., 1965), p. 209.

There is one clear concept that *is* readily understandable and meaningful to man today. *Sin alienates!* When sin is understood as self-sovereignty, this truth is vividly seen. Self-rule can only result in "solitariness"—alienation from God and man! No man *can be* an island, but the very essence of sin is seen in the eternal attempt to be such! The only result possible is self-destruction. This is why the sinner is his own worst enemy, as his sin builds an impassable barrier between him and God. There is no more tragic sight than to see a man destroy himself, as he persistently *cuts himself off* from all that brings reality and fulfillment. What he mistakes for *self-realization* proves to be *self-destruction.*[8] Yet, such is the essential nature of sin.

This is what Paul means by death—a living death and hell. If spiritual life is *union* with God, then spiritual death is *separation* from God! The horrible thing is that this cavern dug by sin becomes deeper and deeper. As each day passes, God is farther and farther away. It is no wonder that multitudes find such a living death and hell unbearable and seek escape by suicide.

Yet—here is sin's most tragic irony! There is no escape because there is death after this life. Such is only the eternal fixation of the state of spiritual death experienced here. Eternal death is eternal separation from God. As Jesus described it: "Between us and you there is a great chasm fixed, in order that those who wish to come over from here to you may not be able, and *that* none may cross over from there to us" (Luke 16:26).

Such is indeed a bleak, black picture! But it must be remembered that only against such a background—a realistic picture of sin—can the full brightness of the message of the gospel be seen. It is cause for constant praise and hope that those to whom Paul was writing had been delivered from the reigning power of sin. The "old man in sin" was a *fact of the past!* Instead they were "new men in Christ"—a study of which we will now pursue.

---

8. Olin A. Curtis vividly describes the reality of death: "Death says to the sinner, 'You would not obey God, you would not love your fellow men, you lived for self, you wanted self—THEN TAKE IT!!'" (*The Christian Faith* [New York: Eaton and Mains, 1905], p. 297.) Cf. his discussion of the significance of death, pp. 295-99.

PART III

THE NEW MAN: IN CHRIST

The Divine Initiative
The Human Response
The New Relationship (Union)
The New Status (Standing)
The New Creation (Person)
The New Life
The New Fellowship (Church)

The gospel of Jesus Christ *is* good news! Through Christ—specifically His crucifixion and resurrection—God Almighty has provided a remedy for the tragic condition that sin has caused among men. Through the centuries men have come to understand more clearly this "great salvation." But there is a basic distinction between *provision* and *possession*. The Protestant Reformation clarified, for all time, the truth that faith alone can unite the two. Man's works can never merit God's gracious gift. However, there is also the further distinction, equally crucial, between man's objective *status* with God and his subjective spiritual *state*. The believer is not only a forgiven sinner, but also a new creation.

Much of the theological controversy of the intervening centuries has centered around these basic ideas. The concern that motivates this study of the thought of Paul is a feeling of necessity to relate these theological ideas to scripture—in concepts and terms. Having done this, we must face the question: Is this message of good news relevant to the present age? History shows unmistakably that, in repeated instances, it has revolutionized the world—of another day. Can it do a repeat performance in this present world that totters on the brink of self-destruction? If the Scriptures are indeed God's eternal Message to man, the answer can only be "Yes." Is it possible that a great segment of modern society—even to a large extent the Church that names the name of Christ—has turned scornfully from its only means of redemption? This would not be the first time! However, this *is* the first atomic generation!

Chapter 8

The Divine Initiative

One fact makes Christianity absolutely unique among all the religions known to man. God Almighty *acted first* to save sinful men! In every other religion the action of God is in response to the approach of man, but in Christianity all that man does is in response to what God has done first. God has taken the initiative to save man! Paul understood this divine initiative in terms of love *(agapē)*. "But God, being rich in mercy, because of His great love with which He loved us . . ." (Eph. 2:4). One thing alone moved the heart of God toward a race of sinful men—love!

This love was manifested in a concrete expression. "But God demonstrates His own love toward us, in that while we were yet sinners, Christ died for us" (Rom. 5:8). This is the Pauline counterpart to the "golden text" of the Bible—"For God so loved the world, that He gave His only begotten Son, that whoever believes in Him should not perish, but have eternal life" (John 3:16). What John graphically portrays, Paul specifically states: "Christ also loved you, and gave Himself up for us, an offering and a sacrifice to God as a fragrant aroma" (Eph. 5:2). "For while we were still helpless, at the right time Christ died for the ungodly" (Rom. 5:6). God Almighty expressed His love for sinful men by the love gift of His Son, who in turn "loved me, and delivered Himself up for me" (Gal. 2:20).

It is significant and surprising that, in contrast to the Gospels, Paul's message is not about the birth, life, teachings, and miracles of Christ. Instead, he sees God's love in the death and resurrection of Christ. The Cross, and the Resurrection which vindicated it, was absolutely central to Paul. "For I determined to know nothing among you except Jesus Christ, and Him crucified" (1 Cor. 2:2).[1]

But what is the Cross? Through the centuries of the Christian era the Cross has become a dramatic symbol that is understandably cherished, respected, revered—and even worshipped. Its use as a sacred emblem on church furniture and in church ritual, and its use for personal adornment, has caused men to lose sight of what the Cross really is. There was nothing attractive about a Roman cross—it was ugly! In the first century it was one of the most cruel and shameful methods of execution devised by the evil mind of man, and was reserved for the most despised criminals. Paul does not attempt to describe the horrors of such a death—this is not his concern.

The Cross simply represents the *manner* of death. In another day or under different circumstances it could have been stoning, a hangman's noose, the gas chamber, or the electric chair. What it depicts is a shameful, disgraceful execution.

At times Paul speaks of the death of Christ in terms of blood. "In Him we have redemption through His blood, the forgiveness of our trespasses, according to the riches of His grace" (Eph. 1:7).[2] When the metaphors of Christ's death are examined below, particularly relating to sacrifice, the significance of this description will be more clearly seen. However, it should be emphasized here that the *total* significance of blood is that it represents the giving of life—or death.[3] Sometimes the Blood has been overdramatized and overliteralized—in both sermon and song—until this central truth is missed.

What has made the Cross such a cherished symbol is that the One who died there was innocent! Christ died on a cross *for* sinful men. "For I delivered to you as of first importance what I also received, that Christ died for our sins according to the Scriptures"

---

1. Cf. 1 Cor. 1:17, 23; Gal. 6:14.
2. Cf. Rom. 3:25; 5:9; Eph. 2:13; Col. 1:20.
3. Cf. Morris, *The Apostolic Preaching of the Cross,* pp. 112-28, in which he concludes with J. Behm's dictum: "'Blood of Christ' is like 'cross,' only another clearer expression for the death of Christ in its salvation meaning."

(1 Cor. 15:3). In this passage, and several others, the Greek very vividly states that Christ died *on behalf of* man (his sins).⁴ This chapter will attempt to explain the teaching of Paul as to what this means. Suffice it to say at this point that when Christ died *for* man He took man's place and suffered the consequences of man's sin. What should have happened to man was suffered by Christ. He died the death that sinful man faces.

When it is realized that such a death is more than physical, the enormity of Christ's loving death is seen, as was pointed out in the previous chapter. On the Cross, Jesus Christ suffered *spiritual* death—separation from His Heavenly Father. This alone can explain His agony in the Garden of Gethsemane (cf. Matt. 26:30-50) and the cry from the Cross: "MY GOD, MY GOD, WHY HAST THOU FORSAKEN ME?" (Matt. 27:46). It was not a shrinking from physical suffering and death, but was the facing of the "hell" of separation from His Father. However, it must be remembered that this separation was two-directional, measuring the love gift of both Father and Son. Yet—thank God—death could not hold Him prey; He was raised triumphant over the grave. In one of the greatest mysteries known to man Christ defeated and destroyed death, hell, and the grave.

Paul used several metaphors to describe the significance and meaning of the death of Christ as it expressed God's love for sinful man. These are illustrations, but they held a wealth of meaning for those to whom Paul wrote. As we see their meaning, our understanding of the divine initiative is greatly enriched.

One of the primary results of sin was the slavery in which it held man (see chapter 5). The old man in sin is helplessly bound and unable to escape from his wretched state. It is against this background that one of Paul's most vivid metaphors of the saving work of Christ on the Cross is seen. Slavery was a familiar fact of life and well known to all. A slave *belonged* to his master, who had *purchased* him, sometimes at great cost. The only possible escape

---

4. The Greek word is *huper*. Cf. its use also in Rom. 5:6, 8; 14:15; Gal. 1:4; Eph. 5:2, 25. Greek scholars generally conclude that there is no significant difference between *huper* (on behalf of) and *anti* (instead of); cf. C. F. D. Moule, IBGNT, p. 64. Cf. the use of *dia* (because of) in Rom. 4:25; 1 Cor. 8:11.

from this bondage was by a payment of this debt or liability, for which there existed little human hope.

However, there was in both Hebrew and Greek thought the concept of escape or deliverance—in terms of *redemption*. In the Old Testament is the never forgotten picture of God delivering His people from Egyptian bondage—"I will also *redeem* you with an outstretched arm" (Exod. 6:6, italics added). God paid the price of deliverance for His enslaved people in Egypt. In the Greek world the custom of "sacral manumission" was well known. By almost superhuman effort, occasionally a slave would manage to earn some change of his own apart from the service of his master. He would deposit this money in a temple. If the slave was able to save enough, the master would be paid the price of manumission and the slave would be set free—*and now was the purchased property of the temple god.*

With this clearly in mind, Paul views the love death of Christ as the purchase price of enslaved, sinful mankind. "Do you not know . . . that you are not your own? For you have been bought with a price" (1 Cor. 6:19-20).[5] Closely tied to the idea of purchase is that of "ransom." Jesus said: "For even the Son of Man did not come to be served, but to serve, and to give His life a ransom for many" (Mark 10:45).[6] The concept of freedom secured or purchased through a ransom is readily understood in modern culture. Paul spoke of the freedom to which such a slave was called, using a technical expression that indicates the purchasing of a slave.[7]

Most vivid of all is the term *redemption (apolutrōsis)* itself. This word sometimes refers to the future hope of the redemption of the body through resurrection,[8] but particularly Paul used it to meaningfully portray the love death of Christ. "In Him [Christ] we have redemption" (Eph. 1:7).[9]

The metaphor is plain to be seen! Man, held fast in sin's slavery, cannot himself possibly pay the purchase price of freedom.

---

5. The Greek term is *agoradzō*, meaning "to buy or purchase." Cf. 1 Cor. 7:23; Gal. 3:13; 4:5.
6. The Greek term is *lutron,* meaning "ransom" or "the price of ransoming." Cf. 1 Tim. 2:6.
7. The Greek phrase is *ep eleutheria*, Gal. 5:13; cf. Gal. 5:1.
8. Cf. Luke 21:28; Rom. 8:23; Eph. 1:14; 4:30.
9. Cf. Col. 1:14; Rom. 3:24.

But "Jesus paid it all!" Through His death on the Cross, Christ assumed the obligation of all men and paid the price for their freedom. He purchased, ransomed, and redeemed every human being with His own precious blood. He released them from the debt they could not pay.

Sin also alienates man and God (see chapter 5). Man's disobedience and rebellion place him in the unenviable position of being an enemy of God. His sin becomes an impassable barrier and the result is separation, estrangement, alienation, and fear, as well as frustration. We will see that one of the glorious aspects of salvation is the restoration of fellowship with God. On the Cross, Jesus made that possible as He broke down every barrier and opened up the way to this fellowship.

The provision that Christ made on the Cross to bring man into fellowship with God is depicted by Paul in the metaphor of *reconciliation*. Alienation and enmity was the accepted and approved attitude of life in the apostle's day. There was open hostility between racial and cultural groups—Greeks vs. Barbarians, Jews vs. Gentiles, freemen vs. slaves. As an obvious result, this characterized relationships between individuals.

The term *reconciliation (katallagē)* is occasionally used with reference to man with man,[10] but it is one of Paul's favorite figures to depict the restoration of relationship between man and God.

> For if while we were enemies, we were reconciled to God through the death of His Son, much more, having been reconciled, we shall be saved by His life. And not only this, but we also exult in God through our Lord Jesus Christ, through whom we have now received the reconciliation (Rom. 5:10-11).

Those who have been reconciled are commissioned to share this ministry of reconciliation.

> Now all *these* things are from God, who reconciled us to Himself through Christ, and gave us the ministry of reconciliation, namely, that God was in Christ reconciling the world to Himself, not counting their trespasses against them, and He has committed to us the word of reconciliation. Therefore, we are ambassadors for Christ, as though God were entreating through us; wo bcg you on behalf of Christ, be reconciled to God (2 Cor. 5:18-20).

---

10. Cf. Acts 7:26; 1 Cor. 7:11.

Sin produces a double alienation—on the vertical and horizontal planes.[11] "But now in Christ Jesus you who formerly were far off have been brought near by the blood of Christ" (Eph. 2:13). As pointed out in chapter 5, this is double reconciliation—between man and man, and man and God. In this passage Paul introduces another idea which enriches the concept of reconciliation. "For through Him [Christ] we both [Jew and Gentile] have our access in one Spirit to the Father" (Eph. 2:18). The idea of "access" (*prosagōgē*) is that of providing a means or way of approach. The term has the technical meaning of introducing one person to another, and even more specifically of bringing one into the presence of a king. Christ, through His love death, opens up the way for all men to approach God.

Man is made for fellowship and friendship with God, but his sin has produced disobedience, rebellion, enmity, and fear. As a result, he is separated from God by the barrier of his own sin. Through Christ's loving death on the Cross the breach is healed and the chasm bridged. A path is opened back to God, and Jesus stands ready to usher man into the presence of God. Man and God are reconciled.

A careful examination of the scripture passages given above will reveal that *God reconciles man to himself*. It most certainly is not a matter of man pacifying or placating God and thus mitigating His wrath or anger. God acts in the love death of Christ as a divine initiative. However, it is *not true* to say that the effect of the Cross was entirely on man and not at all upon God. To be sure, God's attitude toward man has eternally been one of love, as Calvary abundantly demonstrates. However, because of man's sin and in spite of His love, God was estranged from man as well as man from God. The Cross did not change the heart of God—from anger to love—but it did *alone* make possible the expression of love in forgiveness.

This truth, sometimes reverently called the "divine dilemma," is best seen in a third metaphor. The love of God insists that man be forgiven, but the justice of God demands that his sins be

---

11. Cf. Eph. 2:15-17. Cf. also Col. 1:20-22, where the reconciliation extends not only to persons, but to all the creation—even the things in heaven. This is cosmic reconciliation.

punished. God cannot be true to himself and overlook sin—unpunished. So the crucial question is, *How* can God be just and forgiving at the same time? The answer is that, on the Cross, Christ became an Offering or Sacrifice for sin.

In the earliest Church, the death of Christ was viewed as the fulfillment of Old Testament prophecy relating to sacrifice. "For I delivered to you as of first importance what I also received, that Christ died for our sins according to the Scriptures [OT]" (1 Cor. 15:3).[12] In the Book of Hebrews, Christ is presented as the new and better Sacrifice.[13] John presented Christ as the "Lamb of God,"[14] and identifies Good Friday as the day of preparation (for the Passover)—which would picture Jesus being crucified at the very hours the Passover lambs were being slain in the Temple.

Fully in keeping with this understanding of the death of Christ, Paul wrote: "For Christ our Passover also has been sacrificed" (1 Cor. 5:7); and, "Christ also loved you, and gave Himself up for us, an offering and a sacrifice to God as a fragrant aroma" (Eph. 5:2). "He made Him who knew no sin *to be* sin on our behalf, that we might become the righteousness of God in Him" (2 Cor. 5:21). Christ himself became man's Sin Offering.

Most graphic of all is Paul's portrayal of Christ as the Propitiatory Sacrifice. "[Christ] whom God displayed publicly as a propitiation in His blood through faith" (Rom. 3:25). For centuries the term "propitiation" (*hilastērion*) has been a theological battleground. Exactly what is the metaphor? There are two primary difficulties. This is the only time the term is used with reference to Christ.[15] In addition, the grammatical construction is ambiguous —it can be either a noun or an adjective. As a noun, *hilastērion* can mean either "a sacrifice to expiate sin" or "the place where expiation is done and made." The second suggestion finds its meaning in the mercy seat in the Temple, where sacrifice was made. As an adjective, *hilastērion* would mean "able to make expiation for sin."

12. Most NT scholars understand this as a reference to such OT passages as Isa. 53:5-12; cf. Acts 8:32-35.
13. Cf. Heb. 9:14, 28; 10:14.
14. Cf. John 1:29, 36; cf. 1 Pet. 1:19.
15. *Hilastērion* is also used in Heb. 9:5, but there it refers to the mercy seat in the Tabernacle and has no direct reference to the Cross. Cf. 1 John 2:2; 4:10, where a related term, *hilasmos*, is used.

Obviously the concept is tied to the Temple, and all of the above suggestions point to the idea of sacrifice. In keeping with the clear reference to Christ as man's Sacrifice for sin—even the Passover Lamb—this meaning would appear central. However, it is not necessary to make a choice between the possible shades of meaning. Could this be why there is an ambiguity? Christ is all three. He certainly proved *able* to make sacrifice, and He is not only the *Place* of sacrifice, but is *the Sacrifice itself.*

As suggested, it is not a matter of the love death of Christ placating or appeasing the wrath of God. *God* made the sacrifice and not man. Here is where the Old Testament Temple imagery is superseded. However, the New Testament makes it abundantly clear that, in spite of His love, God could not forgive sinful man and still be just. The Cross did something to and for the sin of man. What ought to have happened to man happened to Christ.

As Christ, who knew no sin, "became sin" for man, He therein offered an atoning sacrifice for sin and suffered the consequences of man's sin. Simply stated, the Cross *alone* made it possible for God to forgive sinful man. As William Barclay puts it: "Paul saw in the death of Jesus Christ an action of God Himself, by which God made it possible for the sinner to come home to him, and possible for himself to accept that sinner when he came."[16]

Thus Paul could write, ". . . . that He [God] might be just and the justifier of the one who has faith in Jesus" (Rom. 3:26).

It must be always remembered, however, that the divine initiative stops short of the sovereignty of man. Before the gracious provision of love can become *possession,* man must respond, which is the subject of the next chapter. On the Cross, Christ *purchased* and *redeemed* the enslaved sinner, but man is not set free until the free gift is received. The bridge over the chasm of estrangement has been spanned, and Christ waits to introduce the sinner to a forgiving Father, but man must act. Christ suffered the full consequences of every man's sin and makes it now possible for God to justly forgive, but each man must himself come to that "old rugged Cross." Universal atonement is not universal salvation. God has acted for all men; now every man must act for himself.

---

16. *The Mind of St. Paul* (London: Collins, 1958), p. 82.

Admittedly, much of the significance of these metaphors of atonement is inseparable from the culture of the apostolic age. Modern man knows little—by experience—of slavery and temple sacrifice. However, the imagery of estrangement and reconciliation speaks a universal language. How often modern man—lost, frustrated, guilty, despairing—has asked: How could God ever forgive me? A man who can't forgive himself finds it hard to believe God will forgive him. Certainly man is not worthy of forgiveness—he is guilty and does not deserve forgiveness and fellowship. Equally futile are the attempts to interpret God's love in terms of indulgence—the ignoring of sin. Man doesn't want that kind of God because he can't respect Him. This was one of the fatal mistakes of the insipid liberalism of another generation. Just like a child finds it impossible to truly love a pampering parent, so modern man has said: If God is like that, I can't love Him—and I don't need Him.

But the gospel doesn't proclaim such a God. Instead, the God of the New Testament loves man so much that He does for man what he cannot do for himself. He builds a bridge of reconciliation and restoration. As man looks at the Cross, *that* is what he sees— redeeming, sacrificing, reconciling love. Is it a mystery? Of course it is! But when all is said and done, who can adequately explain love? All that is known for certain is that when one kneels at the foot of the Cross he sees a way opened—all the way to the heart of God! He does not understand how or why, but nonetheless he knows with certainty that God *will* forgive him.

Yet a wise God knows man must have responsibility—to respect himself as well as God. So to this divine initiative there must be a human response.

Chapter 9

The Human Response

One of the greatest revelations in the gospel is that Almighty God—having taken the initiative to save man through the Cross—stops before the sovereignty of man. The Creator and Sustainer of the world, the mighty King of Kings and Lord of Lords, knocks at man's heart door and then waits for the human response. If man is ever saved he must open the door.

For Paul, this human response is *faith*. This was one of his favorite terms[1] and he used it with many meanings. What one believes is called his faith—"He who once persecuted us is now preaching the faith which he once *tried* to destroy" (Gal. 1:23). Often faith relates to the basis for the continuing Christian life—"The *life* which I now live in the flesh I live by faith in the Son of God, who loved me, and delivered Himself up for me" (Gal. 2:20). In addition, faith is pictured as producing miracles— "Does He then who provides you with the Spirit and works miracles among you, do it by the works of the Law, or by hearing with faith?" (Gal. 3:5).

However, the most significant use of the term *faith* is its identification as the human response, to the divine initiative, that brings salvation to man. In the chapters to follow we shall examine

---

1. The noun (*pistis*) is used more than 180 times and the verb (*pisteuō*) is used over 40 times.

salvation from its different perspectives. Here our emphasis is simply to identify faith as the human response.

Exactly what is this faith that is the human response to the divine initiative? An almost automatic answer is that "faith is the assurance of *things* hoped for, the conviction of things not seen" (Heb. 11:1). However, upon closer examination this is seen to be more of a *description* than a *definition* of faith, as it states what faith *does* rather than what faith *is*. This is a common idiom in the English language. For instance, we often say that "water is wet," but this is a description of what water does (makes something wet) rather than a definition of what water is (H2O). The writer in Heb. 11:1 is seeking to emphasize that faith provides or produces assurance and conviction. These are in actuality the witness which comes as the divine response to man's faith.

There is no generic definition of faith in Paul's writings—or in the entire New Testament. It is possible, nevertheless, to distinguish three distinct elements in faith.

1. Faith is mental assent, agreement in mind, or an intellectual persuasion that is normally expressed in English as *belief*.[2] This is clearly seen in Paul's treatment of the delicate problem of food laws and regulations. The key to Paul's counsel is the faith of the one involved (cf. Rom. 14:22-23). The reference is to the mental persuasion of the believer—what he *believes* in his mind—relative to the moral issue of food laws.[3]

2. Yet faith is far more than mental assent; it involves decisive action on the basis of what one is mentally committed to. Faith is the *acceptance of* that which one believes in, which necessitates the surrendering or bowing of the will. Many places in Paul's writings this vital element of faith is emphasized, but nowhere more significantly than in the following:

> If you confess with your mouth Jesus *as* Lord, and believe in your heart that God raised Him from the dead, you shall be saved; for with the heart man believes, resulting in righteousness, and with the mouth he confesses, resulting in salvation. For the

---

2. This is an instance where the English is more definitive than the Greek. The English terms *belief* and *faith* are translations of the same Greek word (*pistis*).
3. Cf. Paul's treatment of eating meat offered to idols (1 Cor. 8:1-13; 10:19-33), where he emphasizes knowledge and the conscience.

Scripture says, "WHOEVER BELIEVES IN HIM WILL NOT BE DISAPPOINTED" (Rom. 10:9-11).

3. There is another dimension of faith that is of vital importance. It is *reliance upon* that which one has accepted because he believes in it. Faith is confidence, trust, dependence. This appears to be the aspect of faith that Paul has in mind when he reminds the Corinthians of the message he had proclaimed among them, "that your faith should not rest on the wisdom of men, but on the power of God" (1 Cor. 2:5). Although it is possible to distinguish these essential elements in Paul's concept of faith, yet—as so often in Paul's thought—his is a composite concept. Rather than using one meaning to the exclusion of the others, there are generally overtones of the other nuances of meaning when one is in the ascendancy.

The full significance of a concept in Paul can many times be seen in its antitheses. Particularly in Romans and Galatians, where Paul is combatting legalism, faith is contrasted with human works.[4]

> Nevertheless knowing that a man is not justified by the works of the Law but through faith in Christ Jesus, even we have believed in Christ Jesus, that we may be justified by faith in Christ, and not by the works of the Law; since by the works of the Law shall no flesh be justified (Gal. 2:16).

This is the context for Paul's repeated emphasis on faith as the basis of the sinner's justification.

> For the demonstration, *I say,* of His righteousness at the present time, that He might be just and the justifier of the one who has faith in Jesus. Where then is boasting? It is excluded. By what kind of law? Of works? No, but by a law of faith. For we maintain that a man is justified by faith apart from works of the Law (Rom. 3:26-28).

When Paul identifies faith as the human response that makes the provision of the divine initiative the possession of the believer, he means man's belief in, acceptance of, and reliance upon God's love expressed in the death of Christ on the Cross. This is in marked contrast to man's dependence upon his own works as the means of salvation.

---

4. As noted above, the law (*nomos*) is primarily equated with human works in these two letters.

One crucial question about faith is whether it is God's or man's activity or work. Without doubt the scripture reference most often alluded to is Eph. 2:8—"For by grace you have been saved through faith; and that not of yourselves, *it is* the gift of God." The difficulty is in the ambiguity of the word "that" in the English translation. Does it refer to grace, faith, or being saved? The margin of the NASB states unequivocally that it refers to salvation.[5] This verse certainly cannot function as a scriptural basis for the teaching that faith is the gift of God.

Paul speaks of the *hearing* of faith. "So faith *comes* from hearing, and hearing by the word of Christ" (Rom. 10:17; cf. Gal. 3:2). Faith is man's response to the word of Christ. It is the preaching of the Cross that the Holy Spirit uses to move man to faith. Yet faith is man's responsible activity.[6] It is his response to the divine initiative of love in the Cross—which makes God's provision his possession. God has faith for no man. It is man's responsibility before God. As just defined, faith is not works,[7] but is simply the responsible reception of that which God has *graciously* provided through the Cross. To make faith the gift or activity of God moves the point of man's responsible choice one step further removed as the condition of receiving God's grace, unless one accepts the untenable doctrine of God arbitrarily bestowing grace upon whom He chooses.

There are, moreover, prerequisites to faith indicated in the New Testament. Perhaps this is the point where the fear might be allayed of those who would deny that faith is the free prerogative of man. Man does not suddenly decide, I am going to have faith in God for salvation. Such an idea completely ignores the nature of

---

5. It is the neuter demonstrative pronoun *touto* and is most literally translated "this thing." It cannot refer to either grace (*charis*) or faith (*pistis*), because both of them are feminine gender, and it would appear to be relating to the whole concept of salvation by grace through faith.

6. There is a sense, of course, in which all of life and human activity is by divine enablement and thus the gift of God. The *ability* to respond in faith is a "gracious" and not a "natural" ability. Man can respond in faith *only* because of God's "prevenient" grace freely given to every man.

7. Faith does not constitute human works in the sense against which the Reformers reacted so strongly—with understandable fear. John Wesley wrestled with the problem and in his sermon on "The Scriptural Way of Salvation" made a distinction between works as *condition* and as *merit* (*Wesley's Works*, 6:43).

sin and the sinner's pitiful predicament as sin's slave. Before a sinner can have saving faith he must repent.[8] In 2 Cor. 12:21, Paul expresses concern about those "who have sinned in the past and not repented of the impurity, immorality and sensuality, which they have practiced." Although the repentance in 2 Cor. 7:9-10[9] has primary reference to the Corinthian believers' attitude toward Paul and not toward God, it does tie repentance to sorrow or grief that is according to God, which works salvation. This godly sorrow is directly contrasted with the sorrow of the world that works out death. Thus both references point to the basic nature of repentance. The Greek word literally means "to change the mind."[10] Such involves a turning *away* from sin and forsaking it (cf. Heb. 6:1), and a turning *to* God (cf. Acts 20:21). Repentance is properly tied to the forsaking of sin, with the genuineness of a man's repentance reflected in his break with sin, at least in attitude of mind. *The truly repentant sinner loathes his sin.*

Paul points to the changed *actions* on the part of the Corinthians because they had sorrowed after a godly manner.

> For behold what earnestness this very thing, this godly sorrow, has produced in you, what vindication of yourselves, what indignation, what fear, what longing, what zeal, what avenging of wrong! In everything you demonstrated yourselves to be innocent in the matter (2 Cor. 7:11).

It was this kind of sorrow which Paul wanted to have displayed toward God (cf. 2 Cor. 12:21).

Before the sinner can experience a godly sorrow that leads to repentance he must be gripped with conviction. This is precisely why a sinner cannot repent at will but only when he is moved to

---

8. It is very interesting that repentance is a minor concept in Paul, as compared with the Synoptics and the kerygma of the Early Church. The only clear references are Rom. 2:4; 2 Cor. 7:9-10; 12:21; 2 Tim. 2:25. A careful examination of these references would seem to indicate that repentance is secondary to the main theme.

9. "Now I rejoice, not that you were grieved, but that you were grieved unto repentance; for you were grieved according to God, in order that you might suffer loss in nothing by us. For the grief according to God works unregrettable repentance unto salvation, but the grief of the world works out death" (lit.).

10. *Metanoeō* is a compound of the word for *mind* (*nous*). Another Greek word (*metamelomai*) means regret more than repentance, indicating a change of feeling more than of mind (cf. Matt. 21:30). It is instructive that Judas *only* regretted (*metamelomai*, Matt. 27:3) and ended up a suicide.

repentance by the conviction of the Holy Spirit. Such conviction, or sense of need, comes in many ways. Paul asks the self-righteous Jews in Rome, who were hypercritical of the Gentile sinners: "Or do you think lightly of the riches of His kindness and forbearance and patience, not knowing that the kindness of God leads you to repentance?" (Rom. 2:4). Many a sinner has been convicted by the goodness or kindness of God. How good God is to all men (cf. Matt. 5:43-48)! Other men are brought to a sense of need through the adversities of life (cf. Luke 15:14-19). In the revealing struggle portrayed in Rom. 7:14-25, conviction is seen as coming through frustration under the law, so that Paul could write elsewhere, "For through the Law I died to the Law, that I might live to God" (Gal. 2:19).[11] Regardless of how it comes—and an all-knowing, all-loving God knows exactly how is best—there must be self-frustration and self-disillusionment before there can be self-realization in Christ. The sinner must see God's face of wrath before he can see His face of mercy.

The human response that makes the provision of the divine initiative of love in the Cross man's possession—is faith. Such faith is the responsible activity of man, but is possible only as man is convicted of his need of forgiveness and in repentance turns from sin and to God.

---

11. It must be remembered that the bondage and slavery of the law thus leading to frustration—in Romans and Galatians—is to be understood in the context of a sinner *seeking to save himself by human works.* Thus there is a proper sense in which he is already a convicted sinner (cf. Rom. 7:14-25), and the concept of law as a *paidagogos* in Gal. 3:22—4:9 must be understood against this background (cf. chapter 6).

Chapter 10

The New Relationship (Union)

What happens when man responds by faith to the divine initiative in the Cross? He enters into a new relationship. His old relationship with sin comes to an end—he is no longer the *old man in sin.* He enters into a new relationship with God through Christ—he is now the *new man in Christ.*

But what exactly is this new relationship? Immediately we think of Paul's words: "Therefore if any man is in Christ, *he is* a new creature; the old things passed away; behold, new things have come" (2 Cor. 5:17). This speaks of the *substance* or *results* of the new relationship, which will be the subject matter for the remaining chapters in this section. In this chapter we will examine the *nature* of this new relationship—what does it mean?

Paul describes the man of faith as being "in Christ." With striking frequency he uses this formula,[1] with minor variations,[2] and it becomes quite obvious that it has a special significance to him. Some scholars have attempted to force this special meaning upon every usage,[3] but it is generally concluded that not more than half of Paul's uses of this formula have such a technical

---

1. "In Christ" (*en Christō*), "in [the] Lord" (*en Kuriō*), "in Him" (*en autō*), etc.

2. Cf. John B. Nielson, *In Christ* (Kansas City: Beacon Hill Press, 1960) for an excellent analysis of Paul's use of this phrase. In Appendix *A* he identifies 95 instances of the phrase with minor variations.

3. Cf. the famous monograph by Adolf Deismann, *Die neutestamenliche Formel in Christo Jesu.*

significance.[4] However, the phrase is used by him with enough frequency, in this special technical sense, that it can be rightly identified as the *key* to his understanding of the new relationship of the man of faith.

Since the time of the Reformation some have seen Paul's teaching on justification by faith as his fundamental understanding of the gospel. However, on closer examination we see that this concept is basically restricted, certainly with any degree of prominence, to Romans and Galatians, where he is combatting legalism as a means of salvation. Even in these letters Paul goes on to emphasize life by the Spirit (cf. Romans 8; Galatians 5). We shall see in the chapters that follow that the *objective standing* that the man of faith has with God, namely, justification by faith, is only one aspect of Paul's gospel. The believer also receives a *subjective experience* with God through Christ, that can be characterized as inward fellowship. Paul's concept of the gospel, summed up in one phrase, is best stated as "union with God." It is such a union that the phrase "in Christ" seeks to express.

Yet when we attempt to explain precisely what Paul means by the phrase "in Christ," the difficulties become apparent. Sometimes man's union with God, as depicted by this phrase, has been understood *sacramentally;* namely, that it is through the sacraments the believer is in Christ—initially in baptism and perpetually in the Lord's Supper. In chapter 14 the significance of the sacraments will be examined, but we can safely conclude here that Paul meant much more than participation in the sacraments when he spoke of being "in Christ." It is in a later development of the Church that the sacraments were given this place of prominence.

In more recent years, with a fuller appreciation of the close tie between the thought of the Old Testament and the New Testament, the Jewish concept of *racial solidarity* has been used to explain Paul's phrase "in Christ." The apostle contrasts the sin and death of man (as the consequence of Adam's trespass) with

---

4. Cf. John Knox (Exegesis), *Interpreter's Bible* (New York: Abingdon-Cokesbury Press, 1951), 9:573; C. F. D. Moule, *The Cambridge Greek Testament Commentary, The Epistle of Paul the Apostle to the Colossians and to Philemon* (Cambridge: The University Press, 1957).

the righteousness and life that come to men because of the love death of Christ.[5] On the basis of this it is pointed out that the old man "in Adam" (in sin) is to be contrasted with the new man "in Christ"; and the "old humanity," in which sin reigns, is to be contrasted with the "new humanity," in which righteousness reigns.[6] An oft quoted scripture is: "For as in Adam all die, so also in Christ all shall be made alive" (1 Cor. 15:22).[7]

But exactly what is meant by *all men being in Adam or Christ*? Taken alone, this could suggest that just as all men *were* in Adam, so all men *shall be* in Christ. Even a casual acquaintance with the teaching of Paul reveals that such a contrast is not valid. All men are *not* made alive in Christ, as all men died in Adam. Paul taught that sin is universal but he certainly did not teach that salvation in Christ is universal!

It is true that all men are included in the *provision* that Christ made on the Cross. This can be considered solidarity and even universalism. But clearly distinguished from this is the *appropriation* (by faith) which makes the universal provision man's particular possession. The relationship of being "in Christ" is the result of faith *appropriation* and does not refer to universal provision. *Not all men are in Christ!*

What does the contrast—"As in Adam all die . . . in Christ all shall be made alive"—mean then? It can only mean that as all men *who are* in Adam share in his sin, so also all men *who are* in Christ share in His righteousness. It is union with Adam or Christ that brings the corresponding results. There is an interesting parallel in how this union takes place. Just as all men are in Adam by *physi-*

---

5. Cf. Rom. 5:12-21; cf. chapter 4.
6. There are those (cf. C. H. Dodd, *The Epistle to the Romans, The Moffatt New Testament Commentary* [New York: Harper and Brothers Publishers, 1932], pp. 100-101) who would deny the historical existence of Adam and consider *Adam* as simply a name that stands for the old corporate personality of mankind. The denial that such a view casts reflections on the historical existence of Christ is hardly convincing. Paul's antithesis, Adam vs. Christ, is too precise. If Adam is but a name, so might Christ be only a name for the new corporate personality of mankind. It is not necessary to thus view Adam to find some truth and value in the concept of solidarity.
7. The contrast is exact in form: "in Adam" *(en tō Adam)* vs. "in Christ" *(en tō Christō).*

cal birth (*Adam* meaning "man" or "mankind"), so all those who are in Christ are so by a *spiritual* birth.

We are still faced with the question of how the concept of racial solidarity gives a meaningful explanation of the phrase "in Christ." Does it do any more than recognize that what happens to (affects) the one (Adam or Christ) happens to all who are united with him? What can solidarity tell us about the *nature* of man's unity with Christ? At best the relationship is described in nebulous and even quasi-mystical terms such as "incorporation in Christ" or "identification with Christ." What experiential meaning do such descriptions provide? In *what way* is the man of faith united with Christ? The concept of racial solidarity does not provide an answer.

Furthermore, the term *racial solidarity* or even *corporate personality* has decisive overtones of pagan pantheism and deification. Paul's view of the individuality and personality of the believer is better seen in an expression such as *inclusive personality,* suggesting the relationship of a person *within* a person.

There is a vital *societary* aspect to salvation in Christ that must not be overlooked, which will be discussed in detail in Chapter 14. Suffice it to point out here that the man in Christ is part of the family of God. He lives in a corporate fellowship although still a full and responsible human being. But the societary reference is exclusively inward—within the Church. There is no corporate relationship with the world. Instead, the world meets Christ only in the lives of individuals as they are nourished and energized by Him and by their relationship to one another.

We must seek further for a more meaningful understanding of the phrase "in Christ." Paul viewed it as a deep consciousness of *oneness with Christ,* a unity of persons resulting in a veritable unification of wills, thoughts, and feelings. The believer and his Lord are attached by spiritual ties until they are one in purpose, aim, emotions, and rational process. They appear to act, even to live, not as two but one person. (In a later chapter this will be analyzed theologically.)

Yet such must not be thought of in metaphysically impersonal terms, like the pantheism and deification taught in pagan mystery cults, where the worshipper sought to become *part* of his god.

Instead, it is the *permeation* of one personality by another until the result is an "inclusive personality."

Where did such a concept come from? Of course, Paul was inspired by the Holy Spirit, but the reality of this new relationship was mirrored in his own experience. He could express the desire "that Christ may dwell in your hearts through faith" (Eph. 3:17) because he could also testify: "I have been crucified with Christ; and it is no longer I who live, but Christ lives in me; and the *life* which I now live in the flesh I live by faith in the Son of God, who loved me, and delivered Himself up for me" (Gal. 2:20).

This new relationship with Christ involved a union so complete that Paul could say: "It is no longer I who live." Instead: "Christ lives in me." The literal word order in the Greek is even more pointed: "I live no longer I, but lives in me Christ."[8] He is saying—I live no longer as I once did, but in a new way—no longer "I," now Christ lives in me—He is the Lord of my new life. Thus he could write elsewhere: "For to me, to live is Christ, and to die is gain" (Phil. 1:21).

Here is Paul's gospel! The new man of faith is in Christ. Although an attempt is made to rationally explain it, when all is said and done it is not explainable to the senses and is not obvious to rational processes. To this extent it has only experiential reality, as the result of the believer's personal faith. It *is* mystically mysterious. Yet it is not nebulous or without spiritual meaning. To the man of faith this relationship of being "in Christ" is spiritual reality.

It is of utmost importance to recognize that this new relationship of being "in Christ" is *by grace,* through faith, as pointed out in the previous chapter. In the immediate context of the grandest passage on salvation by grace is the famous Pauline formula:

> For by grace you have been saved through faith; and that not of yourselves, *it is* the gift of God; not as a result of works, that no one should boast. For we are His workmanship, created in Christ Jesus for good works, which God prepared beforehand, that we should walk in them (Eph. 2:8-10).

---

8. The emphatic first person pronoun (*ego*) could simply emphasize the personal aspect of the statement—and thus be translated: "And I *myself* no longer live." However, in the light of the phrase that follows—"but Christ lives in me" —it would appear to be much more significant, as interpreted above.

Without question the new man is "in Christ" by grace.

Grace is another of the great New Testament words, being used over 150 times with approximately 100 of these found in Paul.[9] But exactly what is grace? The beginning religion student soon learns the classic theological definition: Grace is the unmerited favor of God. Yet that does not communicate very much meaning to most people who lack theological orientation. Much more meaningful is the concept of divine assistance, freely given. Someone has picturesquely described grace as the hand that reaches down to meet the hand that reaches up, or the helping hand of God. In the earliest Church, grace was primarily associated with Jesus Christ because it was supremely manifested in the Cross, and it became the hallmark of the gospel of good news.

Grace was used in the "apostolic blessing"[10] and the "apostolic benediction."[11] Here was the firm foundation of the glorious new way of life. Consequently Paul could triumphantly state: "But by the grace of God I am what I am, and His grace toward me did not prove vain; but I labored even more than all of them, yet not I, but the grace of God with me" (1 Cor. 15:10). It was that by which Paul spoke (cf. Rom. 12:3) and wrote (cf. Rom. 15:15), and was the basis of his apostleship (cf. Rom. 1:5). It is that which enables the Christian to stand (cf. Rom. 5:2), and provides the sufficiency for life (cf. 2 Cor. 9:8; 12:9). This grace of God was always seen as His gift (cf. Rom. 5:15; 12:6).

Most significant to this study is what theologians term "saving grace," defined in *Webster's New International Dictionary* as "the operation of divine love especially as manifested in God taking the initiative toward reconciliation with man in His forgiveness of the repentant sinner." We shall see that all of the *results* of the new relationship of the man "in Christ" are directly tied to grace—divine assistance, freely given. "Where sin increased, grace abounded all the more" (Rom. 5:20). "Being justified as a gift by His grace through the redemption which is in Christ Jesus" (Rom. 3:24). "For this reason *it is* by faith that *it might be* in

---

9. The Greek word *charis* is generally, but not always, translated "grace."

10. "Grace to you and peace from God our Father and the Lord Jesus Christ" (Rom. 1:7*b*).

11. "The grace of our Lord Jesus be with you" (Rom. 16:20*b*).

accordance with grace" (Rom. 4:16). "But if it is by grace, it is no longer on the basis of works, otherwise grace is no longer grace" (Rom. 11:6).

> But God, being rich in mercy, because of His great love with which He loved us, even when we were dead in our transgressions, made us alive together with Christ (by grace you have been saved), and raised us up with Him, and seated us with Him in the heavenly *places,* in Christ Jesus, in order that in the ages to come He might show the surpassing riches of His grace in kindness toward us in Christ Jesus. For by grace you have been saved through faith; and that not of yourselves, *it is* the gift of God; not as a result of works, that no one should boast. For we are His workmanship, created in Christ Jesus for good works, which God prepared beforehand, that we should walk in them (Eph. 2:4-10).

As man responds in faith to the divine initiative of love in the Cross, he enters into a new relationship that Paul graphically decribes as being "in Christ." This is by the grace of God, His divine assistance, freely given, and not by human works.

What significance does this concept of union with God have for us today? Do we all too easily dismiss it as irrelevant—as simply one of the trappings of ancient, superstitious, mythological religions that majored in solidarity with their gods? Can it have any meaning in this enlightened, scientific age? It is one of the strange phenomena of our day that millions of highly educated and sophisticated people are turning to mystery cults that offer thinly disguised variations of the pantheism and deification of the ancient pagan religions.

Could it be that it is because there is innately within man, who is living a lonely and meaningless existence, a *longing* to be near to his God? But an impersonal absorption, regardless of its specific form, fails to satisfy that desire. Man is a person, and when that personhood is violated he is demeaned.

What a gracious and meaningful privilege is ours! We can find union with God *in Christ.* We live in God and God lives in us. Our personality blends with His and finds true fulfillment as we respond to the Master's designing touch.

The substance or results of this new relationship are to be seen in two distinct dimensions: The new man in Christ has a *new status, objectively;* and is a *new person, subjectively.*

Chapter 11

The New Status (Standing)

Once the *nature* of the believer's new relationship is seen, it is necessary to understand the *results* of being "in Christ." In simple terms, what happens? A vital distinction must be made. The man of faith receives *both* a new *status* and a new *state*. His status, or objective standing, is changed; and his state, or subjective spiritual condition, is changed. In this chapter we will look at the believer's new status.

The sinner stands before God guilty and condemned, facing His wrath and judgment. He is under the sentence of death.

> Do you think lightly of the riches of His kindness and forbearance and patience, not knowing that the kindness of God leads you to repentance? But because of your stubbornness and unrepentant heart you are storing up wrath for yourself in the day of wrath and revelation of the righteous judgment of God; who WILL RENDER TO EVERY MAN ACCORDING TO HIS DEEDS: to those who by perseverance in doing good seek for glory and honor and immortality, eternal life; but to those who are selfishly ambitious and do not obey the truth, but obey unrighteousness, wrath and indignation. *There will be* tribulation and distress for every soul of man who does evil, of the Jew first and also of the Greek, but glory and honor and peace to every man who does good, to the Jew first and also to the Greek (Rom. 2:4-10).

This is not too difficult to understand as it relates to the rebel against God who lives in utter disregard of God and His will (cf. Rom. 1:18-32). But it must be remembered that the New Testament has surprisingly little to say about such men. Instead, the New Testament—and specifically Paul in his letters concerning salvation—deals primarily with those who are *concerned* about their relationship with God. Even the Jew, with his holy law, cannot make himself righteous before God. He too is a sinner. This is the burden of Paul's argument in Rom. 2:1—3:20, which climaxes:

> Now we know that whatever the Law says, it speaks to those who are under the Law, that every mouth may be closed, and all the world may become accountable to God; because by the works of the Law no flesh will be justified in His sight; for through the Law *comes* the knowledge of sin (Rom. 3:19-20).[1]

The concerned Gentile also had his "law" by which he sought salvation.

> For when Gentiles who do not have the Law do instinctively the things of the Law, these, not having the Law, are a law to themselves, in that they show the work of the Law written in their hearts, their conscience bearing witness, and their thoughts alternately accusing or else defending themselves, on the day when, according to my gospel, God will judge the secrets of men through Christ Jesus (Rom. 2:14-16).[2]

The possibilities of the above scripture being fulfilled is purely hypothetical. Paul concludes that the Gentile *cannot do* the things of the law—any more than the Jew. He is simply stating that *if* the Gentile is to be justified by the law he would have to obey and keep it (cf. vv. 11-13).

All men—rebellious sinners, concerned Jews, and Gentiles following their "law"—are condemned as sinners. "We have already charged that both Jews and Greeks are all under sin" (Rom. 3:9). It is to such men—condemned sinners—that the gospel of Jesus Christ offers a new status with God as they respond in faith to the divine initiative of love in the Cross. This offer of good news is described by Paul as righteousness.

When Paul describes the status of the new man in Christ as righteous—what does it mean? This has been an area of theological

---

1. There are many such references in Romans and Galatians. Cf. "Now that no one is justified by the Law before God is evident; for, 'THE RIGHTEOUS MAN SHALL LIVE BY FAITH'" (Gal. 3:11).

2. It should be noted that Paul does *not* say the Gentiles *have* the law, or have the law written on their hearts. Rather, they do the *things* of the law and show the *work* of the law written on their hearts. Actually, the concept of "natural law" is a misnomer, as related to Paul. Basically, he reserved the term "Law" *(nomos)* to mean the Jewish law.

controversy since the Reformation. "But to the one who does not work, but believes in Him who justifies the ungodly, his faith is reckoned as righteousness" (Rom. 4:5).

It is unfortunate that there is no *verb* form of the English words *righteous* (adjective) and *righteousness* (noun).[3] As a result it is necessary to use the English words *just* and *justification* as synonyms, thus providing the verb form of "to justify." *Righteousness* and *justification* are translations of the same Greek word (*dikaiōsunē*).

What does Paul mean by righteousness or justification? Is righteousness the result of what man *is* or of what he *does*? Can we properly say a man *is* righteous? There are several references in Paul where the term (*dikaiōsunē*) is directly related to ethical endeavor and human *actions*.[4] However, particularly in the letters where he is combatting legalism as a basis of salvation (Romans and Galatians), Paul uses the term *righteousness* to depict the new status of the believer, and as such it is basically objective in meaning.[5] Here righteousness is *not* descriptive of what man is, but of *how man stands* before God. Man is not righteous *in himself, but in the eyes of God.*

> Therefore having been justified by faith, we have peace with God through our Lord Jesus Christ (Rom. 5:1). Nevertheless knowing that a man is not justified by the works of the Law but through faith in Christ Jesus, even we have believed in Christ Jesus, that we may be justified by faith in Christ, and not by the works of the Law; since by the works of the Law shall no flesh be justified (Gal. 2:16).

We make a serious mistake if we insist on either meaning— objective standing or subjective experience—to the exclusion of the other. As with so many of his concepts, it is preferable to see Paul's meaning as both/and rather than either/or. Often one concept is predominant, but the other still exists in the background. It is

---

3. There actually is such a verb form in Greek *(dikaioō),* but it presents a problem when it is translated into English, because an auxiliary word must be used, such as "to *be* righteous" or "to *make* righteous"—and this has serious theological overtones. (Cf. the discussion which follows.)

4. Cf. Rom. 6:13, 16, 18; 2 Cor. 6:7; 9:10; Phil. 1:11; Eph. 6:14.

5. Cf. Rom. 3:20-21, 26, 30; 4:3, 5-6, 22; 5:1, 9, 17; Gal. 2:16-17, 21; 3:6, 8, 24.

erroneous to suggest, as many have, that this new standing with God is void of moral and ethical significance.

In a splendid article, Leland Jamison examines the conflicting opinions of several representative New Testament scholars about righteousness (*dikaiōsunē*) and concludes that "the vocabulary of *dikaioun* points in both directions, suggesting both a legal status and an ethical metamorphosis."[6] The basic difficulty is that sometimes students of Paul confuse his rejection of human works as a basis for justification with a rejection of all ethical activity. Jamison concludes: "I find no place in his letters where he [Paul] clearly attacks ethical effort as a bad thing."[7]

The believer's new *status* of righteousness does not consist of a previous change within him that *makes* him righteous before God. In a proper sense it is not correct to say he *is* righteous.[8] It is not a matter of man being, or being made, worthy of acceptance with God. The glory of the gospel message is that it is "while we were enemies, we were reconciled to God through the death of His Son" (Rom. 5:10). It is man *as a sinner* who can, by faith in the Cross, stand before God reconciled. To be sure, as we shall see, man does not *remain* a sinner. The grace of God makes a change *within him.* But the order must not be reversed. Too often men feel they must become worthy *before* they can stand uncondemned before God. This is the wonder of the Cross. It is in the Cross that God's love and justice are reconciled, "that He might be just and the justifier of the one who has faith in Jesus" (Rom. 3:26).

The fact is that it is not *man's* righteousness at all, for Paul makes it quite plain that the believing sinner stands before God in *God's* righteousness.

> But now apart from the Law *the* righteousness of God has been manifested, being witnessed by the Law and the Prophets; even *the* righteousness of God through faith in Jesus Christ for all those who believe; for there is no distinction (Rom. 3:21-22).

When God justifies the sinner it is a manifestation of *His* righteousness.

---

6. "*Dikaiosyne* in the Usage of Paul," *Journal of Bible and Religion* 21, no. 1 (Jan., 1953): 98.

7. *Ibid.,* p. 93.

8. As noted in a previous footnote, when an auxiliary word (*is, made, become,* etc.) is used with the word *righteous,* there are serious theological overtones.

For in it *the* righteousness of God is revealed from faith to faith; as it is written, "BUT THE RIGHTEOUS *man* SHALL LIVE BY FAITH" (Rom. 1:17). Whom [Jesus Christ] God displayed publicly as a propitiation in His blood through faith. *This was* to demonstrate His righteousness, because in the forbearance of God He passed over the sins previously committed; for the demonstration, *I say,* of His righteousness at the present time, that He might be just and the justifier of the one who has faith in Jesus (Rom. 3:25-26).

Paul uses Abraham's experience to illustrate that it is the sinner's faith in the Cross that God reckons[9] to him for righteousness.[10]

This concept, which is so strange to modern minds, is understandable only against the background of the search for righteousness through the pursuance of the law. It is in Romans and Galatians that Paul effectively argues that such a search is futile. Man cannot attain to righteousness through the works of the law, but only through faith. "A man is not justified by the works of the Law but through faith in Christ Jesus" (Gal. 2:16).

Without doubt, this basic idea is better understood in a term that Paul used in his later letters, namely, *forgiveness.* "And when you were dead in your trangressions and the uncircumcision of your flesh. He made you alive together with Him, having forgiven us all our transgressions" (Col. 2:13).[11] Men today can grasp the language of forgiveness. As the guilty sinner stands before God in condemnation—in response to his faith in the Cross—the Judge of all the earth pronounces him *forgiven.* The guilt is cancelled. This must not be confused with *acquittal,* because such speaks of innocence, and the sinner is not innocent but guilty. Although he *is* guilty God says: I forgive you because of your faith in the Cross. Here is the secret of the Cross, as it shows man that forgiveness is costly. How readily this is seen on the plane of interhuman relations, and it is no less true between man and God.

Forgiveness is not vindication. Nor is it indulgence. Man could not love or respect a God who demands vindication or offers

---

9. *Logidzomai,* meaning "to count" or "to take into account"; cf. A and G.
10. Cf. Rom. 4:3, 5; 4:6, 9, 22; Gal. 3:6.
11. Cf. Eph. 1:7. Paul goes on to graphically portray this forgiveness in a vivid metaphor—"Having cancelled out the certificate of debt consisting of decrees against us *and* which was hostile to us; and He has taken it out of the way, having nailed it to the cross" (Col. 2:14).

indulgence. But God can and will forgive because of the Cross.

Closely related to the concept of the righteous status of the man in Christ is the portrayal of the believer as *holy*.[12] We shall see later that, even as the word "righteous," so also the term "holy" has a decided ethical and moral content, relating to the subjective experience of the man of faith. However, there is little question that Paul often also used the term to depict the *objective standing* of the man of faith.[13] Because the believer belongs to God, he—like all that belongs to God—is holy. In theology this is called "positional holiness." It is very significant that when the term *holy* is thus used it is always in the plural form, pointing to the fact that it is not the believer as an *individual* who is holy, but only as he is part of the holy *fellowship*.

Not only does the man in Christ have the new status termed righteous and holy, but he is also *reconciled*. One of the devastating consequences of sin is alienation, from both God and men. The Cross makes *provision* for reconciliation. God prepares the way to reconciliation for all men.

> For if while we were enemies, we were reconciled to God through the death of His Son, much more, having been reconciled, we shall be saved by His life (Rom. 5:10). Through Him [Christ] to reconcile all things to Himself, having made peace through the blood of His Cross; through Him, *I say*, whether things on earth or things in heaven. And although you were formerly alienated and hostile in mind, *engaged* in evil deeds, yet He has now reconciled you in His fleshly body through death, in order to present you before Him holy and blameless and beyond reproach (Col. 1:20-22; cf. Eph. 2:15-17).

The man in sin is alienated from God, but the man in Christ stands reconciled with God. The barrier between himself and God is torn down.

As the sinner appropriates the benefits of this reconciliation by faith, he experiences fellowship with God. "God is faithful, through whom you were called into fellowship with His Son, Jesus Christ our Lord" (1 Cor. 1:9). Throughout the New Testament,

---

12. The Greek word is *hagios,* translated "saint" in the KJV.

13. Cf. Rom. 1:7; 8:27; 12:13; 15:25-26, 31; 16:2, 15; 1 Cor. 1:2; 6:1-2; 14:33; 16: 1, 15; 2 Cor. 1:1; 8:4; 9:1, 12; 13:13; Phil. 1:1; 4:22; 1 Thess. 3:13; 2 Thess. 1:10; Eph. 1:1, 15, 18; 2:19; 3:8, 18; 4:12; 5:3; 6:18; Col. 1:2, 4, 12, 26. Cf. also 1 Cor. 6:11; 7:14; Rom. 15:16.

especially against the background of Semitic Palestine, this fellowship between God and man was often pictured in terms of table fellowship.[14] Paul, however, depicts the fellowship of the redeemed sinner in terms of *sonship.* The man in sin is sin's slave, but the man in Christ is God's son.

> For you are all sons of God through faith in Christ Jesus (Gal. 3:26). But when the fulness of the time came, God sent forth His Son, born of a woman, born under the Law, in order that He might redeem those who were under the Law, that we might receive the adoption as sons. And because you are sons, God has sent forth the Spirit of His Son into our hearts, crying, "Abba! Father!" Therefore you are no longer a slave, but a son; and if a son, then an heir through God (Gal. 4:4-7; cf. Rom. 8:14-15; Eph. 1:5; 1 John 3:1-2).

Here is reconciliation on its deepest level! We who were strangers, foreigners, at enmity with God are received as His sons.

This concept of fellowship through sonship takes on an even deeper meaning as it is pictured in terms of adoption. In Roman society an adopted son was not a second-class member of the family, but he shared equally with the children by birth. It is breathtaking to grasp the full significance of Paul's thought. Through faith in the Cross the alienated sinner becomes a full-fledged son of God with all the rights and privileges appertaining thereunto. His old debts are cancelled and the resources of his new Father are at his disposal.

Probably most treasured of these new privileges of sonship is that of *access.*

> Through whom also we have obtained our introduction [access] by faith into this grace in which we stand; and we exult in hope of the glory of God (Rom. 5:2). For through Him we both have our access in one Spirit to the Father (Eph. 2:18). In whom we have boldness and confident access through faith in Him (Eph. 3:12).[15]

---

14. Cf. the parables of Jesus that relate to a feast or dinner (Matt. 22:1-14; Luke 14:7-11, 15-24), the marriage supper of the Lamb (Rev. 19:6-9), and the imagery in Rev. 3:20.

15. The Greek word is *prosagoge*, which had the technical meaning in secular Greek of introducing a speaker or even of introducing a person into the presence of a king (cf. Barclay, *More New Testament Words* [New York: Harper and Row, 1958], pp. 242-45; and NASB translation of Rom. 5:2).

This would have special significance to a Jew, such as Paul, for whom even the name of God was unutterable. Now, through the Cross, he had access to God with the confidence with which a son approaches his father.

Although some of Paul's concepts are foreign to our day and age, we *can* understand the language of reconciliation. We know what it means for an estranged son to be reconciled to his father through forgiving love. It is not a question of rights or even guilt or innocence—*it is acceptance!* And deep within all hearts there is a hunger to be accepted. It is said that when Abrahm Lincoln was asked, as the American Civil War drew to a close, what he would do with the defeated rebels from the southern states, he quickly answered: "I will treat them as if they had never been away." When we today are united with God in Christ, we are accepted— treated as if we had never been away.

As meaningful as is this new status of the man in Christ, even more blessed is the new state, the change man experiences *within himself* by the grace of God—to which this study now turns.

Chapter 12

The New Creation (Person)

It is tragic that from the very beginning the wonderful truth that the new man in Christ stands before God as righteous and reconciled has been, by many, both misunderstood and misrepresented. Some have viewed it as the sum total of the gospel, failing to see that Paul had much to say about the new *state* of the man in Christ. "Therefore if any man is in Christ, *he is* a new creature; the old things passed away; behold, new things have come" (2 Cor. 5:17). There is a dramatic change *within* man as well as in his standing before God.

Paul's critics twisted his message of justification by faith to suggest that the believer is under no moral obligation, while living under grace. In fact, not only was sin pictured as being of no consequence to God, but it was suggested that it would actually provide an opportunity for God's grace to abound. "(As we are slanderously reported and as some affirm that we say), 'Let us do evil that good may come'?" (Rom. 3:8). Sadly, such a travesty on Paul's gospel was not only the taunt of his critics, but appears to have been a serious problem among some of his converts.[1]

Unfortunately this misrepresentation of the glorious truth of salvation by grace through faith has plagued the Church down to

---

1. Paul's rhetorical questions in Rom. 6:1, 15—"Are we to continue in sin that grace might increase?" and "Shall we sin because we are not under law but under grace?"—reflect such a misunderstanding.

this very day, expressing itself in various forms of antinomianism. Such fails to see that Paul's gospel was a proclamation of sanctification as well as justification.

, Paul's reaction to the suggestion that justification carried with it no moral implications was one of abhorrence—"God forbid!"[2] Then he proceeds to ask a crucial question—"Do you not know?"[3] Quite obviously those to whom he was writing did not know or realize the implications of their faith—what had actually taken place when they entered into Christ.

All of Paul's letters are primarily addressed to one question, namely, What are the moral implications of the faith of the man in Christ? (The one possible exception is Philippians, where the word "sin" [hamartia] is never used.) In theology this is generally termed sanctification, which in its fullest sense means to be *made* holy by the removal of sin and the *impartation* of righteousness. In most commentaries Romans 6—8 is classified as sanctification in contrast to Rom. 3:21—5:21, which is termed justification.

In Romans 6, Paul asks:

> Or do you not know that all of us who have been baptized into Christ Jesus have been baptized into His death? Therefore we have been buried with Him through baptism into death, in order that as Christ was raised from the dead through the glory of the Father, so we too might walk in newness of life. For if we have become united with *Him* in the likeness of His death, certainly we shall be also *in the likeness* of His resurrection, knowing this, that our old self was crucified with *Him,* that our body of sin might be done away with, that we should no longer be slaves to sin (Rom. 6:3-6).

---

2. Cf. Rom. 6:2, 15 (KJV). This is an idiomatic (English) statement of the Greek phrase that literally means "Let it not be!" *(mē genoito).* Cf. NASB ("May it never be!"), RSV ("By no means!"), Phillips ("What a ghastly thought!"), NEB ("No, no!").

3. Rom. 6:3—the Greek literally says, "Are you ignorant?" *(agnoeite).* As this study proceeds, it will be seen that this is a constantly repeated question by Paul (cf. Rom. 7:1). Sometimes a different Greek form *(ouk oidate)* is used, literally meaning—"Do you not know?" but it has the same significance (cf. Rom. 6:16; 1 Cor. 6:9).

Through the metaphor of baptism[4] Paul in substance asks: Don't you know and realize the fact that when you entered into Christ you entered into His death? *They had died with Christ to sin* (cf. Rom. 6:8, 11).

What does it mean to die with Christ to sin? What happens in this momentous experience? To understand this we must relate it to the two other ways that death and sin are tied together by Paul. First, the fatal consequence of man's sin is death, as both a present condition and a future state (cf. c. 7). Second, Christ's death was for man's sin (cf. c. 8). When Christ died on the Cross it was more than a physical death. It was a *death in relationship to sin,* a spiritual separation from His Father (cf. Rom. 6:10). But Christ's death was vicarious. It was *because of* man's sin, and *in place of* man's death (cf. 2 Cor. 5:15, 21). Thus, when we, through faith, enter into Christ we enter into His death. This means that the believer appropriates by faith the death that Christ died *for* him. He participates or shares in Christ's death. He dies along with Christ. All men died *provisionally* with Christ when He died on the Cross, but only those who by faith accept that death die *experientially* with Christ.

It is important not to confuse Paul's concept of dying to sin (with Christ) with a psychological separation from sin. We speak today of dying to something, meaning that we separate ourselves from it, but this is *not* what Paul means. Dying to sin does not mean to simply stop sinning! Man cannot die to sin himself by cutting himself off from it, in either action or promise. Death to sin, for Paul, is always related to our identification with Christ's death —by faith.

---

4. When Paul refers to baptism, the *primary* reference is to the rite of Christian water baptism (cf. 1 Cor. 1:13-17; Eph. 4:5), which he (and the earliest Church) considered the *visible* gate of entrance into the Church. Faith was the *invisible* gate. The believer's entrance into Christ could be identified as the time when he either believed or was baptized. Further, baptism carried with it the concept of *burial* into death and *resurrection* to new life (cf. Rom. 6:4-5; Col. 2:12). When Paul speaks of baptism *into Christ,* he has in mind *not only* the rite of water baptism, but the resulting *union with Christ.* Thus, "baptism into death" means "we have become united with *Him* in the likeness of His death" (Rom. 6:5; cf. Gal. 3:27; 1 Cor. 12:13). Baptism is equated with union. The result is that baptism and union can even be equated where water baptism does not exist (cf. 1 Cor. 10:2). The sacrament of baptism will be examined in Chapter 14.

Similarly, crucifixion is *never* used by Paul as a metaphor of self-denial, but *always* relates to Christ's death and our sharing in it. When we fail to realize this, Paul's thought is confusing and we have a serious misunderstanding. Crucifixion denotes the *manner* of death (Christ died), and is a synonym for death (with Christ). This is graphically seen in Romans 6:6: "Knowing this, that our old self was crucified with *Him,* that our body of sin might be done away with, that we should no longer be slaves to sin."

Crucifixion is the way or manner in which Christ died, which death the believer enters into and shares, as seen by the context (cf. vv. 3-10). Paul could have said, "Our old self *died* with Him."

We need to consider what the phrase "our old self" (*ho palaios anthrōpos*) means. It has been the subject of widely divergent interpretations in Wesleyan theological circles.[5] Some understand the phrase to mean the original depravity with which all men are born, thus relating it to the Wesleyan doctrine of entire sanctification. What does the context teach us? Rom. 6:6 is an intricate part of a *list of factual statements* (as seen clearly in the use of the Greek indicative mood) about what *had happened* to these believers *when they entered into Christ.* They had died to sin, been baptized into Christ and into His death, had been buried with Him, etc. (vv. 1-8).

Verses 11 to 13 (cf. v. 19) contain strong exhortations (Greek imperative mood) that are based upon these factual statements, and that *point to* the Wesleyan doctrine of entire sanctification (see c. 20). The only way to identify verse 6 with entire sanctification is to disassociate it from its indicative (factual) context and associate it with the imperative (exhortation) context that begins at verse 11. There is no grammatical support for such a transposition.

In verse 6 Paul states that the *result* of the crucifixion of the old self is that we should no longer be slaves of sin. If there is any question as to *when* this takes place in Christian experience, the discussion that follows makes it clear:

> But thanks be to God that though you were slaves of sin, you became obedient from the heart to that form of teaching to which

---

5. Cf. the discussion in the BBC under Eph. 4:22.

you were committed, and having been freed from sin, you became slaves of righteousness (Rom. 6:17-18).

One of the clearest hermeneutical principles in Paul is that of antithesis. What is the antithesis of the *old self*? Quite obviously it is the *new self*. When does the new self come into being? "Therefore if any man is in Christ, *he is* a new creature; the old things passed away; behold, new things have come" (2 Cor. 5:17). The new self is identified with entering into Christ. The other uses of the old self by Paul (cf. discussion to follow) support the interpretation that it refers to "the man we once were" in sin (Rom. 6:6, NEB).

Thus it seems clear that when Paul in Rom. 6:6 speaks of the old self having died (been crucified) with Christ he is referring to *the sinner dying with Christ to sin.*[6]

But what happens when a man dies with Christ to sin? There is a vital *future* result. When we participate and share in Christ's death, we no longer face death as the result of our own sin. *We have already died*—in Christ.[7] In addition there is a crucial *present* consequence of our death with Christ to sin. *The power of sin is broken in our lives—now!* This thrilling fact is graphically pictured by Paul. The man who dies with Christ to sin *becomes* a *free* man, a *new* man, and a *spiritual* man.

As noted in Chapter 5, sin rules man and brings him under the condemnation of God's judgment. Furthermore, sin alienates man from God and his fellowmen, but the man of faith has the new status of righteousness and reconciliation. This means he is free from the condemnation, the guilt, and the penalty of sin. It also means that his alienation is removed and he is united in fellowship with God and men.

Yet this is far from all! Sin also holds man in bondage and slavery. The sinner is helpless and unable to break the grip of sin. Thus, the believer's freedom in Christ must include freedom from sin's bondage—from its enslaving power.

---

6. When a rigid theological interpretation is superimposed on a term or concept with no regard to the context or its meaning elsewhere, the result is an invalid biblical hermeneutic that destroys scriptural authority.

7. In strict theological concepts this is to be associated with the believer's new *standing* with God. The man who is righteous and reconciled with God does not face judgment and eternal death (cf. c. 11).

This Paul portrays in a graphic metaphor. Sin reigned as a king and ruled as a lord over the helpless sinner. Specifically, this rule was in man's body until it was pictured by Paul as sin's own body (Rom. 6:6), which resulted in total wretchedness and death (cf. Rom. 7:24). Paul categorically says that the purpose[8] of the crucifixion of the old self was that the body of sin might be done away with.[9] As a result man is free from sin and is no longer its slave (cf. Rom. 6:6). Throughout the balance of Romans 6, Paul pictures the man in Christ as a free man.

> But thanks be to God that though you were slaves of sin, you became obedient from the heart to that form of teaching to which you were committed, and having been freed from sin, you became slaves of righteousness (Rom. 6:17-18). But now having been freed from sin and enslaved to God, you derive your benefit, resulting in sanctification, and the outcome, eternal life (Rom. 6:22).

Even more graphically Paul pictures sin ruling man through his flesh, so that a meaningful freedom from sin must be related to the flesh. Paul says that "those who belong to Christ Jesus have crucified the flesh with its passions and desires" (Gal. 5:24). What does it mean to crucify the flesh? The metaphor of crucifixion has a vital significance for Paul, and is not simply a figure of speech. It depicts the believer's identification, by faith, with the death of Christ.[10] As a direct result, the flesh ceases to be an *instrument of sin,* against which man is helpless. The Cross *destroys sin* in the flesh (cf. Rom. 8:3). No longer is the flesh an irresistible or compulsive force for evil in man. The man in Christ is free.

Yet this must not be misunderstood to mean that the flesh is destroyed. No place in Paul, or in the entire New Testament, is

---

8. The Greek construction is a strong purpose construction—a *hina* clause.

9. The Greek word that the NASB translates "done away with" is *katargeō.* Its basic meaning is to make ineffective, powerless, and idle. (Cf. A and G.) Man's body is not destroyed, but sin's power is broken and thus it is no longer sin's body. Man's body, as the unwilling instrument of sin, is done away with.

10. In the strictest sense it is the inner man that is crucified (dies) with Christ and lives again *now* (cf. Gal. 2:20; Rom. 6:2-12; Col. 2:12; 3:3). The outer man (*body* and *flesh*) is consequently freed from the compulsive power of sin (cf. Rom. 6:6). Thus the flesh is referred to as crucified, even as the "world" (the arena of sin) is crucified (cf. Gal. 6:14).

this suggested. The flesh is not sin, but is the *instrument* of sin (in the sinner).

Original sin (self-sovereignty) depraves the inner man, darkening his heart and making his mind reprobate. His heart is often filled with rebellion, enmity, and hatred. This depraved inner man finds expression in the outer man, as his desires and propensities, which are morally neutral *per se,* are illegitimately satisfied and corrupted. When man lives in sin these desires and propensities of the flesh, now inclined to evil, hold him in helpless bondage. Thus the sinner as he lives *according to* the flesh *(kata sarka)* lives *for* the flesh—which is sinful living, as was discussed in Chapter 5.

It is for this reason that Paul speaks of the believer crucifying the flesh *with its passions and desires* (cf. Gal. 5:24). Through his death with Christ the new man is freed from the enslaving grip of *his own* desires and passions. The man of faith must continue to live *in* the flesh, as his sphere of existence (cf. Gal. 2:20). As long as he lives on earth, this is his home—the present, earthly, outer man. He has no other place to live but *in* the flesh. But, unlike the sinner, the new man needs no longer make his flesh his *means* or dynamic of living. He is not *compelled* to satisfy the desires and propensities of his flesh.[11] He is a free man—free from the enslaving grip of sin working through his own flesh. He is free *not* to live according to the flesh.

In a later section it will be seen that the flesh is left weakened by sin and remains, in the new man, as a bridgehead back to sin's slavery. For this reason Paul exhorts the *believers* to "make no provision for the flesh" (Rom. 13:14), to "not *turn* your freedom into an opportunity for the flesh" (Gal. 5:13), and to "not carry out the desire of the flesh" (Gal. 5:16). The flesh is not destroyed, but man's slavery to sin working through the flesh is ended as he dies with Christ to sin. He is a free man!

Man's slavery to sin was also through the law—"The power of sin is the law" (1 Cor. 15:56). Freedom from sin is inseparable from freedom from the law, understood as legalistic requirements. Thus Paul could assure the Romans that "sin shall not be master over

---

11. This is the context for Paul's rare reference to not being or living in the flesh (cf. Rom. 8:8-9, 12; 7:5). Cf. Chapter 3.

you, for you are not under law, but under grace" (Rom. 6:14). Rom. 7:7-13 depicts the law as the unwitting accomplice of sin; and Rom. 7:14-25 pictures total servitude to sin under the law. This important chapter opens, however, with an illustration of the law of marriage.[12] Here Paul is making two simple, but important, points. First, the law—in this case the law of marriage—has jurisdiction over[13] a person as long as he lives. Second, a man is discharged *(katargeō)* or freed from the law only through death. This is true in the case of the marriage law—and all the law. Paul proceeds to make his application from the illustration.

> Therefore, my brethren, you also were made to die to the Law through the body of Christ, that you might be joined to another, to Him who was raised from the dead, that we might bear fruit for God. For while we were in the flesh, the sinful passions, which were *aroused* by the Law, were at work in the members of our body to bear fruit for death. But now we have been released from the Law, having died to that by which we were bound, so that we serve in newness of the Spirit and not in oldness of the letter (Rom. 7:4-6).

Paul's meaning is clear. The believer's death with Christ to sin brought freedom from the law and the slavery it had produced.

Paul used the metaphor of slavery and freedom because it was the common experience of most men, as either victims or victors. It has often been observed that Paul very rarely used the metaphor of cleansing,[14] and this for a very good reason. The concept of cleansing was a Temple metaphor, primarily associated with the sacrificial religion of Judaism. The metaphor of slavery and freedom would be far more meaningful in the Gentile and pagan

---

12. Many attempts have been made to allegorize Paul's illustration of freedom from the law of marriage. Such results in confusion or questionable hermeneutical principles. If it is understood as a simple illustration, such conclusions are unnecessary.

13. The Greek word *(kurieuō)* literally means to "lord it over"; cf. Rom. 6:14.

14. Paul never uses the noun for "cleansing" *(katharismos)*, and uses the verb "to cleanse" *(katharidzo)* only three times (2 Cor. 7:1; Eph. 5:26; Titus 2:14). The word "pure" *(katharos)* is used only once in his primary letters, and that related to meat (Rom. 14:20). The remainder of the uses of "pure" are in the Pastoral Epistles (1 Tim. 1:5; 3:9; 2 Tim. 1:3; 2:22; Titus 1:15*b*).

world where Paul labored.[15] The truth Paul sought to communicate was that through the believer's death with Christ to sin the power and grip of sin was broken. It ceased! It came to an end!

This quite naturally points to the second picture Paul gives of the man in Christ. He is not only a free man—he is a *new man.* The man of faith lives in a new way, because he is a new creature or a new person. "Therefore if any man is in Christ, *he is* a new creature; the old things passed away; behold new things have come" (2 Cor. 5:17; cf. Gal. 6:15; John 3:3, 7). Paul depicts this by the graphic metaphor of spiritual resurrection. In Romans 6, Paul makes it plain that the believer not only enters into Christ's death, *but enters also into His resurrection.*

> For if we have become united with *Him* in the likeness of His death, certainly we shall be also *in the likeness* of His resurrection. . . .
> Now if we have died with Christ, we believe that we shall also live with Him (Rom. 6:5, 8).[16]

The grand design is that "we too might walk in newness of life" (Rom. 6:4). In Col. 2:12 the same connection between death with Christ (baptism) and resurrection is made—"Having been buried with Him in baptism, in which you were also raised up with Him through faith in the working of God, who raised Him from the dead." Although it is less certain, there is good reason to believe that when Paul speaks of knowing Christ and the power of His resurrection and the fellowship of His sufferings, being conformed to His death (cf. Phil. 3:10), he is referring to spiritual resurrection.

What does Paul mean by this vivid picture? The man in Christ is not only freed from sin's grip and power, as he dies with Christ, but he is *made new within,* in heart and mind. He enters a new love slavery to God and men. Paul graphically describes it.

---

15. Sacrifices were a vital part of worship in the Gentile temples, but *not for the purpose of cleansing the worshipper.* Pagan sacrifices were an attempt to appease and placate the gods.

16. As will be seen in later chapters, there is the blessed truth of the future resurrection of the body. Some NT scholars attempt to so interpret these references because they are in the future tense or subjunctive mood. However, v. 11 ("Even so consider yourselves to be dead to sin, but alive to God in Christ Jesus") makes it plain that the new life is logically future in relation to death with Christ. These verses speak clearly of the present, spiritual resurrection of the new inner man.

> If then you have been raised up with Christ, keep seeking the things above, where Christ is, seated at the right hand of God. Set your mind on the things above, not on the things that are on earth. For you have died and your life is hidden with Christ in God (Col. 3:1-3).

Closely related, yet significantly distinct from the concept of spiritual resurrection, is the idea of regeneration. It is ironical that the sinner who is invited to share Christ's death *is already dead.* Immediately following the verse (Col. 2:12) describing spiritual resurrection, quoted above, is the following: "And when you were dead in your transgressions and the uncircumcision of your flesh, He made you alive together with Him, having forgiven us all our transgressions" (Col. 2:13; cf. Eph. 2:1, 5). Actually, when the sinner dies with Christ to sin he is simply exchanging one death for another, but through this new death he finds *newness of life.* The term *regeneration* means literally to make or bring to life, although the term is often used untechnically to refer to the full scope of salvation. This new life will be examined in more detail in the next chapter.

Paul uses a further metaphor to describe the new man in Christ.

> Do not lie to one another, since you laid aside the old self with its *evil* practices, and have put on the new self who is being renewed to a true knowledge according to the image of the One who created him (Col. 3:9-10).[17]

Most New Testament scholars see in this metaphor an allusion to common baptismal practice. As the believer's old garments were stripped off, it was symbolic of the laying aside of the old life of sin. When the convert arose from the baptismal waters he was clothed in a new robe, symbolic of the new life he now entered upon. Of primary importance to this study, this metaphor is graphically

---

17. Cf. the parallel in Eph. 4:22-24. The construction in Col. 3:9-10 uses aorist participles and is clearly an indicative fact, relating to *what was already* the experience of the Colossians—they had already put off the old self and had put on the new self (the aorist participle denotes *antecedent* action). In Eph. 4:22-24 the construction uses aorist infinitives, which are ambiguous—they can be *either* indicative or imperative. It is only good exegesis to interpret the ambiguous passage (Ephesians) in the light of the unambiguous passage (Colossians). Furthermore, the other clear reference to the "old man" (Rom. 6:6) is also unambiguously indicative (cf. above).

descriptive of the fact that the believer is a new man. He is a new person, living a new life.

When a man dies with Christ to sin, he not only becomes a *free* man and a *new* man—he also becomes a *spiritual* man. It is *by the Spirit of God* that a man is free and new. There is a subtle distinction here that is often missed because it is not explicitly stated by Paul. As noted in Chapter 3, Paul uses the term "flesh" *(sarx)* in three relationships to man—as his basis of existence, as his sphere of existence, and as his means or dynamic for living. This same threefold relationship can be seen with reference to the Spirit *(Pneuma)*. All men *are* flesh (their basis of existence), and the new men in Christ *are* spirit (their new basis of existence). Jesus spelled this out to Nicodemus. "That which is born of the flesh is flesh; and that which is born of the Spirit is spirit" (John 3:6). *The new man is both flesh and spirit*—as the basis of his existence.

But there is a distinct difference between *existence* and *living* or between *being* and *doing*.[18] This is seen in Paul's urgent admonition to the Galatians. "If we live by the Spirit, let us also walk by the Spirit" (Gal. 5:25). This distinction is plainer in the Amplified translation. "If . . . we have our life [in God], let us go forward walking in line, our conduct controlled by *the Spirit*." Paul had spoken earlier of the Galatian Christians *receiving* the Spirit,[19] and then he later exhorts them to "*walk* by the Spirit" (Gal. 5:16) and to be "*led by* the Spirit" (5:18). Here is the distinction between existence and living. The same distinction is found in 1 Corinthians, where Paul writes: "Now we have received . . . the Spirit who is from God"[20] and yet he tells these same believers: "And I, brethren, could not speak to you as to spiritual men, but as to men of flesh, as to babes in Christ" (1 Cor. 3:1).

---

18. The third category is the *"sphere* of existence," or *where* a man lives. Mortal man, be he sinner or believer, has only one place to live and that is *in* the flesh. The believer does not live in the spirit in the sense of his sphere of existence. He does not have an unearthly or ethereal existence.

19. Cf. Gal. 3:2; cf. also 3:3—"Having *begun* by the Spirit," and 3:5—"He then who *provides* you with the Spirit" (italics added).

20. 1 Cor. 2:12; cf. also 3:16—"The Spirit of God *dwells in you* [plural]"; and 6:19—"Your [singular] body is a temple of the Holy Spirit *who is in you* [singular]" (italics added).

How is this to be explained? They *were* spiritual men (the basis of existence) but Paul could not speak to them *as to* spiritual men because they were making the flesh, instead of the Spirit, their *dynamic for living.*

Paul's concern about *doing* in contrast to *being* will be considered later, but our concern here is to emphasize that the new man is also a *spiritual* man. He has a totally new basis of existence —by the Spirit.

The experience of becoming a free man, a new man, and a spiritual man, released from the grip of sin and finding a new life of love service to God and men by means of the Spirit, is termed sanctification. "But now having been freed from sin and enslaved to God, you derive your benefit, resulting in sanctification, and the outcome, eternal life" (Rom. 6:22). Strictly speaking, this is *initial* sanctification or the life of holiness begun.[21]

Forgiveness and acceptance with God bring wonderful peace, but the good news of the gospel promises more. You can also *become* a new person in Christ! Although it is difficult for us today to find *experiential* meaning in Paul's concept of death with Christ, the *results* of our faith-union with Christ are very much a reality. We understand what it means to be bound and fettered by sin, and this because we are the veritable slaves of our own appetites and drives. When, through faith in Christ, we are released from their compulsive grip, it is freedom indeed. We discover that we are not only free, but we are new persons—in dramatic contrast to the men we once were! We are alive in a new way. Can we do better than describe it like Jesus did to Nicodemus? We are born again by the Spirit of God.

---

21. This experience can also be identified as "conversion," which literally means to turn around. Paul never used the term *(epistrephō)* in a technical, theological sense; but its basic meaning can be seen in such references as 2 Cor. 3:16; 1 Thess. 1:9. (Cf. Gal. 4:9 for a "reconversion.")

Chapter 13

The New Life

The new man in Christ has a new life and lives in a new way. He is raised to "walk in newness of life" (Rom. 6:4). What is this life—this new spiritual life? A key to understanding Paul's thought is to examine his antitheses, in this case life and death.[1] What does Paul mean by *death*? It is separation or alienation from God because of sin, both in the present and in the future. However, when the barrier of sin is removed, the believer finds life through union and fellowship with God in Christ. This is in full accord with the Johannine concept of life—"And this is eternal life, that they may know Thee the only true God, and Jesus Christ whom Thou hast sent" (John 17:3).

As man responds in faith to the divine initiative of love in the Cross, he enters into a new relationship. He is united to God in Christ. This new relationship gives man a new status, allowing him to stand before God as righteous and reconciled. The believer is also a *free* man, a *new* man, and a *spiritual* man through his death with Christ to sin. All of this can be summed up in one word— *life*. "For to me, to live is Christ" (Phil. 1:21).

Everything Paul associates with salvation—joy, and peace, and power, and progress, and moral victory—is gathered up into one word he uses so constantly, "life." Only those who through

---

1, Cf. Paul's graphic contrast in Rom. 5:15-21; 6:23. The result of Adam's transgression is death, but flowing from Christ's obedience is life; cf. chapters 4 and 7.

Christ have entered into a vital relationship to God are really "alive." Existence outside of Christ is not worthy of the name at all.[2]

In more modern psychological terms, this is vitally related to the *fulfillment* of the individual or his becoming a real person. The man in sin is its slave, which makes personhood impossible. The irony is that the sinner is basically a slave to himself, to his own desires and propensities. Because of this he is unable to realize the full potential of his own existence. On the other hand, the man in Christ is freed from this slavery and the resulting freedom enables him to find life's true meaning.

It is necessary to briefly examine the *content* of the new life found through union with God in Christ. What is its nature? What does it consist of? Actually much of the New Testament is an answer to this question. We shall examine the three greatest terms, and concepts, relating to spiritual life in the New Testament. "But now abide faith, hope, love, these three" (1 Cor. 13:13).

Faith and hope can be studied together because they both depict the same fundamental concept of life, namely, *certainty*. *Webster's New International* defines *hope* as "desire with expectation of fulfillment." However, in common usage the expectation is often lost sight of and hope degenerates to mere desiring or wishing. It is not so in the New Testament. Hope is as certain as faith. A good biblical definition would be: Faith is certainty for the *present*, and hope is a certainty for the *future*.

> Yet, with respect to the promise of God, he did not waver in unbelief, but grew strong in faith, giving glory to God, and being fully assured that what He had promised, He was able also to perform (Rom. 4:20-21). And hope does not disappoint; because the love of God has been poured out within our hearts through the Holy Spirit who was given to us (Rom. 5:5).

The term *faith* has a much more extensive meaning and use than the human response to the divine initiative of the Cross. Faith is one of the fundamental characteristics of the new life. It is a *living* faith as well as a saving faith. The man in Christ *becomes* a man of faith, because faith characterizes his outlook on life. Paul

---

2. James Stewart, *A Man in Christ* (New York: Harper and Brothers Publishers, 1935), p. 192.

wrote to the Romans: "Your faith is being proclaimed throughout the whole world" (Rom. 1:8). He also speaks of the prospect of their encouraging each other by a mutual faith (v. 12). Paul was concerned that the Corinthians' "faith should not rest on the wisdom of men, but on the power of God" (1 Cor. 2:5). Although the technical distinction is not always made, the faith of the man in Christ was based solidly upon His cross and resurrection. "And if Christ has not been raised, then our preaching is vain, your faith also is vain" (1 Cor. 15:14).

Similarly the hope of the new man was based on the promise of the return of Christ. The distinction can be made—faith is certainty based on Christ's resurrection; hope is certainty based on the believer's resurrection. Paul could speak for these earliest Christians—"And we exult in hope of the glory of God" (Rom. 5:2). In fact, Paul could refer to *the* hope—"Not moved away from the hope of the gospel" (Col. 1:23).

Specifically, the hope of the Christian is the promise of the resurrection of the body.

> And not only this, but also we ourselves, having the first fruits of the Spirit, even we ourselves groan within ourselves, waiting eagerly for *our* adoption as sons, the redemption of our body. For in hope we have been saved, but hope that is seen is not hope; for why does one also hope for what he sees? But if we hope for what we do not see, with perseverance we wait eagerly for it (Rom. 8:23-25).

Paul speaks of his earnest desire "that I may attain to the resurrection from the dead" (Phil. 3:11).

As so often is the case, this distinction—between faith (present) and hope (future)—is not always maintained with strict accuracy. There is sometimes a blending of the two concepts. In the passage above, where Paul speaks of the faith of Abraham, he also states: "In hope against hope he believed, in order that he might become a father of many nations, according to that which had been spoken, 'So SHALL YOUR DESCENDANTS BE'" (Rom. 4:18).

Of primary importance for this study is the fact that this certainty of faith and hope created an atmosphere of confidence, assurance, and security in which the earliest Christians lived. This can best be examined by studying the two terms *peace* and *joy*. "Now may the God of hope fill you with all joy and peace in believing, that you may abound in hope by the power of the Holy

Spirit" (Rom. 15:13). Joy is the gladness or happiness that radiates from the life of the man in Christ. It is an *outward expression* of the *inward peace* that indwells the believer. Peace is the absence of anxiety and worry, but much more. It is the positive serenity that results from being and living in a *right* relationship with God, with men and with oneself. "For the kingdom of God is not eating and drinking, but righteousness and peace and joy in the Holy Spirit" (Rom. 14:17).

Joy is the atmosphere of the New Testament, where the term is used over 130 times. Actually, a sad (joyless) Christian is a contradiction. New Testament believers greeted each other with: "Rejoice!" "Peace be with you!" and "Joy be with you!" Joy added lustre to all the Christian virtues and illuminated every experience of life, but nowhere did its glow shine brighter than in adversities. One of the first lessons a neophyte must learn is that joy is not dependent upon circumstances. Rather, joy comes from within, from a man's faith and hope, born of fellowship with God in Christ. Trials are transformed by joy. It is not enough to endure or even overcome adversity. No triumph is fully Christian without joy.

> As sorrowful yet always rejoicing, as poor yet making many rich, as having nothing yet possessing all things (2 Cor. 6:10). That in a great ordeal of affliction their [Macedonians] abundance of joy and their deep poverty overflowed in the wealth of their liberality (2 Cor. 8:2). You also became imitators of us and of the Lord, having received the word in much tribulation with the joy of the Holy Spirit (1 Thess. 1:6; cf. Jas. 1:2-4; 1 Pet. 1: 3-9).

Paul set the example beautifully for his followers as from a Roman prison he wrote:

> But even if I am being poured out as a drink offering upon the sacrifice and service of your faith, I rejoice and share my joy with you all. And you too, *I urge you,* rejoice in the same way and share your joy with me (Phil. 2:17-18). Rejoice in the Lord always; again I will say, rejoice! (Phil. 4:4).

The new man of faith (and hope) was able to meet the adversities, hardships, and suffering of living for Christ—posed by people, problems, and pressures—in joyous victory. He had indeed found newness of life.

> Be anxious for nothing, but in everything by prayer and supplication with thanksgiving let your requests be made known

to God. And the peace of God, which surpasses all comprehension, shall guard your hearts and your minds in Christ Jesus (Phil. 4:6-7).

The third term in the triad of supreme values in the new life is *love (agape)*. The greatest expression of *agape* that the world has ever witnessed was manifested in God's initiative in the Cross. The man of faith, however, is amazed to discover that God not only loves him, but would love *through* him. "Because the love of God has been poured out within our hearts through the Holy Spirit who was given to us" (Rom. 5:5). Properly understood, the love that characterizes the man in Christ is not a human sentiment or emotion, but it has a divine quality. Man cannot create or produce this love; he can only communicate or transmit it. In fact, *agape* is far more than an emotion or a feeling. It involves the total person, including will and intellect.

Basically, *agape* is not affection or even admiration. In this sense "to love" is not necessarily "to like."[3] How much confusion there has been at this point. William Barclay's definition is concise, yet encompassing. *"Agape* is unconquerable benevolence, undefeatable good will."[4]

Such love is a sharing concern or a caring identification with others, that is indifferent to either attraction or worthiness. The one consideration is need. Perhaps the best single word to be used as a synonym is *concern—yet concern that becomes action.*

It is significant that the term *agape* is distinctively Christian, born of necessity to depict the life of the new man in Christ.[5] *Agape*

---

3. As no place else, the poverty of the English language is seen here, with only the one word *(love)* to represent a vast range of concepts. Cf. the standard dictionary definitions of *love.* Barclay writes: "It is said that, in Gaelic, if a lad loves a lass there are twenty different ways in which he may tell her so! In English there is but one word for to love, and that word must do duty for many feelings. But Greek has four words for to love" *(Flesh and Spirit,* p. 63).

4. *Flesh and Spirit,* p. 65.

5. The noun *(agapē),* used first in the LXX (only briefly), is found extensively in the NT. The verb *(agapaō),* though used occasionally in secular Greek, finds its full meaning in the Bible—especially the NT.

is fundamentally a man's attitude and action toward other men, which reflects God's concern for him.[6]

Even as the believer's certainty, born of faith and hope, produces personal peace and joy, so *agape* concern characterizes his relationships with his brethren.

> Let love be without hypocrisy. Abhor what is evil; cleave to what is good. Be devoted to one another in brotherly love; give preference to one another in honor; not lagging behind in diligence, fervent in spirit, serving the Lord; rejoicing in hope, persevering in tribulation, devoted to prayer, contributing to the needs of the saints, practicing hospitality. Bless those who persecute you; bless and curse not. Rejoice with those who rejoice, and weep with those who weep. Be of the same mind toward one another; do not be haughty in mind, but associate with the lowly. Do not be wise in your own estimation. Never pay back evil for evil to anyone. Respect what is right in the sight of all men. If possible, so far as it depends on you, be at peace with all men. Never take your own revenge, beloved, but leave room for the wrath *of God*, for it is written, "VENGEANCE IS MINE, I WILL REPAY, SAYS THE LORD. BUT IF YOUR ENEMY IS HUNGRY, FEED HIM, AND IF HE IS THIRSTY, GIVE HIM A DRINK: FOR IN SO DOING YOU WILL HEAP BURNING COALS UPON HIS HEAD." Do not be overcome by evil, but overcome evil with good (Rom. 12:9-21).

It was Paul who, grasping what Jesus emphasized, saw that this kind of love fulfills the whole Law of God.

> Owe nothing to anyone except to love one another; for he who loves his neighbor has fulfilled *the* law. For this, "YOU SHALL NOT COMMIT ADULTERY, YOU SHALL NOT MURDER, YOU SHALL NOT STEAL, YOU SHALL NOT COVET," and if there is any other commandment, it is summed up in this saying, "YOU SHALL LOVE YOUR NEIGHBOR AS YOURSELF." Love does no wrong to a neighbor; love therefore is the fulfillment of *the* law (Rom. 13:8-10).

More pointedly, *agape* produces the healing remedy of forgiveness.

> And so, as those who have been chosen of God, holy and beloved, put on a heart of compassion, kindness, humility, gentleness, and patience; bearing with one another, and forgiving each other, whoever has a complaint against any one; just as the Lord forgave you, so also should you. And beyond all these things *put on* love, which is the perfect bond of unity (Col. 3:12-14).

---

6. *Agapē* is used of the love of God (and Christ) for men, but only rarely of man's love for God. It is found in Paul only in 2 Thess. 3:5. (Cf. *"agapaō"* in Rom. 8:28; 1 Cor. 2:9; 8:3; Eph. 6:24.)

The life of the new man in Christ is one of patience, long-suffering, and forbearance—with God and circumstances because of his faith and hope, with men because of his love. But *agape* concern is far more than passive forbearance and forgiveness. It expresses itself in a positive generosity, kindness, and goodness. A word often heard today is *involvement.* The new man in Christ cannot live in isolation; the love of God within opens his heart and life to the world around him. He is, in truth, his brother's brother!

What are two of the most often mentioned dimensions of life at its fullest today? Are they not confidence and involvement? If a man is to find life worth the living, he must be freed from destructive fears and face every day with confidence. We are also discovering—often most painfully—that life has societary demands. If we isolate ourselves behind social barriers (curtains?)— of all kinds—life can have no real meaning. We must be involved with our fellowmen in order to truly find life ourselves.

But what is the magic word? What is the answer? Where is confidence to be found? Fears don't depart as they are psychoanalyzed! Insecurities cling to our backs like leeches, draining away our very lifeblood. The simple truth is that we are afraid to become involved! The gospel of Jesus Christ eloquently speaks to man's desperate need for life. In Christ there is wondrous new life. How better can it be expressed: *certainty*, born of faith and hope, and *concern,* as the expression of God's *agape* poured into our hearts?

Chapter 14

The New Fellowship (Church)

There is every evidence in the New Testament that the earliest believers did *not* look at their newfound relationship with God in Christ in an individualistic sense. Salvation was not solitude! A man did not become a believer in isolation. Instead, he became part of a fellowship of believers. The man in Christ entered into a new fellowship.

As so often, dangerous abuses of this truth are to be found at the opposite extremes. In an effort to safeguard the essential fact that saving faith is of necessity personal, evangelical theology has sometimes been mistaken to teach that salvation is totally individualistic, thus missing the corporate aspect of the Christian faith. On the other hand, an overemphasis on the importance of the Church as the mystical body of Christ tends to ignore the clear teaching of the New Testament that every *man* must personally respond to the Cross in faith.

Paul emphasized that the man of faith enters a new fellowship. The word *fellowship (koinōnia)*, which in classical Greek meant an association or partnership, was used by the Early Church with a new significance. There was a fellowship of sharing in the practical necessities of life (cf. Rom. 12:13; 2 Cor. 8:4), of working together for Christ (cf. Phil. 1:5), and even of suffering for Christ's sake (cf. Phil. 3:10). The individual believers were united together through Christ in a close bond (cf. 2 Cor. 6:14), and the inclusion of the Gentiles in this fellowhsip was a miraculous mystery to the Christian Jews (cf. Eph. 3:9). This fellowship was in the

Holy Spirit (cf. 2 Cor. 13:14; Phil. 2:1). "God is faithful, through whom you were called into fellowship with His Son, Jesus Christ our Lord" (1 Cor. 1:9). "The Christian *koinōnia* is that bond which binds Christians to each other, to Christ and to God."[1]

Very early the fellowship of believers was called the *church (ekklēsia)*, a term that is found extensively in Paul.[2] The various uses of the term have been the subject matter for numberless full volumes, so a study of this kind cannot thoroughly treat it.

Sometimes Paul refers to the church as a local assembly (cf. 1 Thess. 1:1; 2 Thess. 1:1; Phil. 4:15), or to a group of churches in a specific area (cf. 1 Cor. 16:1, 19; 2 Cor. 8:1; Gal. 1:2, 22). At other times he speaks of *the* Church universal, even identifying "the church of God which is at Corinth" (1 Cor. 1:2; cf. 2 Cor. 1:1). It appears that Paul's concept of the church developed over the years. Most of the references in his earlier letters were to individual congregations, while in his later letters the vision of the one great universal Church, of which the local congregation is a part, began to clearly emerge.[3] Of course there was a keen awareness that it was the Church of God or Christ, although this was often assumed and unstated as in 1 Thess. 2:14; 2 Thess. 1:4; Rom. 16:16; and 1 Cor. 10:32.

It is vital to remember that in New Testament times the Church had no special buildings,[4] so *ekklēsia* was never used to refer to a building. Instead, the church assembled in homes and thus Paul could write—"Aquila and Prisca greet you heartily in

---

1. Barclay, *More New Testament Words*, p. 174. Cf. his discussion on *koinōnia*, pp. 173-76.

2. The Greek term *(ekklēsia)* has a rich background in Greek and Jewish (LXX) literature. It is used only three times in the Gospels (Matt. 16:18; 18:17), but is found approximately 25 times in Acts and over 40 times in Paul. The term *ekklēsia* literally means the "called-out ones." William Barclay rightly observed that it does not mean to be called in any exclusive sense, but refers to those "who have been summoned out of their homes to come and meet with God" (*More New Testament Words*, p. 70).

3. This is not absolutely the case, because the alternate meanings can be found in both the earlier and the later letters (cf. 1 Cor. 1:2 and Col. 4:16).

4. The earliest church which has yet been excavated and dated with certainty comes from the third century A.D. at Dura in Mesopotamia on the Euphrates River. This was merely a room in a house which had been set apart and furnished as a chapel for worship. Cf. Millar Burrows, *What Mean These Stones?* (New Haven, Conn.: American School of Oriental Research, 1941), p. 207.

the Lord, with the church that is in their house" (1 Cor. 16:19). The point of importance for this study is that Paul makes it plain that the man in Christ was part of a new fellowship, namely, the Church of God. He wanted the believers to be aware of this, and when divisions arose in Corinth he wrote:

> But if one is inclined to be contentious, we have no other practice, nor have the churches of God. But in giving this instruction, I do not praise you, because you come together not for the better but for the worse. For, in the first place, when you come together as a church, I hear that divisions exist among you; and in part, I believe it (1 Cor. 11:16-18).

The corporate consciousness of the new man in Christ was further enhanced by the realization that each individual believer was part of the body of Christ. Indeed, the Church *is* the body of Christ. "And He put all things in subjection under His feet, and gave Him as head over all things to the church, which is His body, the fulness of Him who fills all in all" (Eph. 1:22-23).

Paul speaks in his earlier letters of the unity of believers in terms of the many being one body (cf. 1 Cor. 10:17), and even more specifically: "For even as the body is one and *yet* has many members, and all the members of the body, though they are many, are one body, so also is Christ" (1 Cor. 12:12; cf. vv. 12-27).

This one body is in Christ (cf. Rom. 12:5). But it is in his later letters that Paul develops the concept of the Church as Christ's body, of which He is the Head.[5]

What is the significance of the Church, as the fellowship of believers, being the body of Christ? Ecclesiology has taken incredible flights of fancy at this point, attempting to interpret this beautiful and meaningful concept in mystical terms that are so nebulous that they are totally void of spiritual reality of any kind. To conceive of Paul writing in such meaningless philosophical ideas is to stretch credibility to the breaking point.

What is Paul's whole point? It seems clear that it was to emphasize the unity of the Church, that the individual believer was

---

5. Cf. Eph. 1:22-23; 4:12; 5:30; Col. 1:18, 24; 2:19. There is one earlier reference to the believers' being Christ's body, but there is no direct mention of the Church, although it is clearly implied (cf. 1 Cor. 12:27). Cf. also Eph. 4:4; 4:16; Col. 3:15.

a vital part of a collective whole. The human body offered a vivid metaphor:

> For the body is not one member, but many. If the foot should say, "Because I am not a hand, I am not *a part* of the body," it is not for this reason any the less *a part* of the body. . . . But now there are many members, but one body (1 Cor. 12:14-15, 20; cf. 1 Cor. 12:27).

Although there are several *parts,* their fulfillment could be realized only as they contribute to the *whole.* Further, the body *(sōma)* was that through which the inner reality was expressed. How meaningful and significant to realize that the Church is the body of the glorified Christ, through which the reality of Christ is expressed outwardly to the world! Christ is seen by the world only *through the Church.* So this beautiful metaphor speaks of essential unity and indispensable revelation.

This truth is of vital importance today, especially in the evangelical church. There is a sense in which the individual believer can find his spiritual fulfillment only as a part of that fellowship— as part of the body of Christ. The solitary man in Christ is *not* the body of Christ; he is only so as part of the new fellowship. In this body each has a share and each has a service. Neither is possible alone, but only as a part of the one body.

There is a sense in which fellowship is found as part of the institutionalized Church and, in fact, that is where the man in Christ normally experiences it. But it must always be remembered that *the* fellowship is larger than any institution. An appreciation of the fellowship of believers also places in stark relief the tragedy of division or schism. One of William Barclay's greatest observations is that "a fragmented church is no church at all."[6] Such a "church" is actually a contradiction! To the extent that any fellowship of believers is fragmented by strife or contention, to that extent it forfeits its claim to be part of the body of Christ.

The man in Christ has the objective standing of "holy" before God. But such is *never* viewed in an individualistic sense. The term "holy ones" *(hagiois)* is *always* plural, signifying that the individual is holy only as he is viewed by God as a part of the

---

6. *Flesh and Spirit,* p. 59.

new fellowship; just as, under the old covenant, there was no chosen *man* of God among the Hebrew people—only the nation *as a whole,* made up the chosen people.

It is only against the background of the new fellowship that the New Testament significance of the Christian sacraments can be understood. Christian water baptism was the *visible* gate of entrance into the new fellowship. When it is realized that baptism relates to the Christian Church as circumcision did to the covenant of the Hebrew people, the importance of baptism becomes clear. The male Jew entered into the Abrahamic covenant through the rite of circumcision. This physically offensive rite was superseded in the new covenant by baptism,[7] by which a man entered into Christ.

> Or do you not know that all of us who have been baptized into Christ Jesus have been baptized into His death? Therefore we have been buried with Him through baptism into death, in order that as Christ was raised from the dead through the glory of the Father, so we too might walk in newness of life (Rom. 6:3-4). For all of you who were baptized into Christ have clothed yourselves with Christ (Gal. 3:27).

Water baptism produced *outer* authentication of one's faith in Christ, even as the coming of the Holy Spirit provided *inner* authentication. A Spirit-less Christian or an unbaptized Christian were equally incongruous in New Testament times, being the inner and outer aspects of the one reality.

Many times the significance of water baptism is seen as *our* witness to the world. We are testifying to personal salvation and identifying ourselves with God's people. This certainly is true, but as a sacrament baptism is much more. It is a unique *means of grace* in which *God witnesses to the believer's faith.* Through baptism, the believer's place in the new fellowship is divinely certified.

---

7. Paul speaks on one occasion of the "circumcision of Christ"—"and in Him you were also circumcised with a circumcision made without hands, in the removal of the body of the flesh by the circumcision of Christ" (Col. 2:11). This strange concept is clarified in the succeeding verse, which obviously has a parallel or synonmous meaning—"Having been buried with him in baptism, in which you were also raised up with Him through faith in the working of God, who raised Him from the dead" (Col. 2:12). Cf. also Rom. 2:28-29.

He is part of the family of God. Baptism is thus both the sign and *seal* of our new relationship with Christ.

In spite of technical arguments to the contrary, the New Testament (and the Greek language) does not establish conclusively the mode of baptism (cf. Arndt and Gingrich on *"baptidzō"*). The metaphor of death, burial, and resurrection in Rom. 6:3-5 would strongly suggest immersion and the weight of the argument rests with those who would attempt to deny it.[8] Of primary importance, the *theological* significance of one particular mode, to the exclusion of any other, is a relatively modern development.

It should always be remembered that *water baptism is a sacrament.* Normally, it is not an option. In fact, if we desire to follow the teaching and example of the New Testament, water baptism should be required for membership in His Church. The believer has no choice as to whether or not he should be baptized. But even though baptism may be viewed as a requirement, this does not mean that the sacrament is an intrinsic means or instrument of salvation. One does not become a Christian by simply being baptized.[9] The New Testament makes it clear that there is only one saving response—that is faith. "For by grace you have been saved through faith" (Eph. 2:8). But this *inner* gate of entrance into the Church as the body of Christ is to be complemented by the *visible* gate of water baptism.

The other Christian sacrament is equally related to the new fellowship. It is no accident that it became widely known as "Communion."

> Is not the cup of blessing which we bless a sharing *[koinōnia]* in the blood of Christ? Is not the bread which we break a sharing *[koinōnia]* in the body of Christ? Since there is one bread, we who are many are one body; for we all partake of the one bread. Look at the nation Israel; are not those who eat the sacrifices sharers *[koinōnos]* in the altar? What do I mean then? That a thing sacrificed to idols is anything, or that an idol is anything? No; but *I*

---

8. The writings of the Apostolic Fathers show clearly that all three modes—immersion, effusion, and sprinkling—were in use by the middle of the second century. It is plain that immersion was preferred unless one's physical condition dictated otherwise.

9. In modern theological terms this is called "baptismal regeneration." Contrary to common opinion, very few groups teach this.

> *say* that the things which the Gentiles sacrifice, they sacrifice to
> demons, and not to God; and I do not want you to become sharers
> *[koinōnoi]* in demons. You cannot drink the cup of the Lord and
> the cup of demons; you cannot partake of the table of the Lord
> and the table of demons (1 Cor. 10:16-21).

One of Paul's strongest arguments against Christian participation
in pagan idol feasts was that the participants were sharers
(koinōnoi) in the table of demons. It was inconceivable to Paul that
a Christian believer, who shared the table of the Lord, could share
the table of demons. Here was fellowship at its deepest level—table
fellowship.

The Lord's Supper provided participation *(koinōnia)* in the
body and blood of Christ, the richest of Christian fellowship. Just
as the Jewish priest shared in the sacrifice on the altar over which
he ministered, so the believer—in the priesthood of believers—
shares in the Christian sacrifice. The necessity of separation, at
the level of fellowship, was more clearly drawn.

> Do not be bound together with unbelievers; for what partner-
> ship have righteousness and lawlessness, or what fellowship
> *[koinōnia]* has light with darkness? Or what harmony has Christ
> with Belial, or what has a believer in common with an unbeliev-
> er? Or what agreement has the temple of God with idols? For we
> are the temple of the living God (2 Cor. 6:14-16a).

In the New Testament Church the sacrament was preceded by
the *agape,* or love feast. At this fellowship meal, *on the horizontal
level,* men lovingly shared their food with each other. When this
love feast was desecrated by gluttony, drunkenness, and selfishness (cf. 1 Cor. 11:18-34), the intended fellowship was destroyed.
Paul observes that such made one unworthy to participate in the
sacrament which was to share table fellowship *on the vertical
level* (cf. 1 Cor. 11:27).

Of importance to this study is the fact that the Communion
table was a place of *continuing* fellowship—in a very special sense.
There are many avenues of fellowship, but the sacrament has a
unique function. As the elements, the broken bread and the fruit
of the vine, are taken in thankful and believing remembrance,
and as the words of ritual are reverently spoken, a miracle of fellowship takes place. The believing soul enters into fellowship with
God and with his brethren in a way that is impossible otherwise.
Thus the invitation to the Lord's table is not an option, to be

accepted or refused at will. It is a command performance to dine with the Lord of the Church. Any man who absents himself or enters unfittingly does so with irrevocable loss to his own spiritual life.

The man of faith finds a new fellowship, becoming part of the Church and the body of Christ. This new fellowship is entered through the visible gate of baptism and is maintained through participation in the sacrament of Communion.

There are few things that men today desire more than genuine fellowship and companionship. The disappointing—and often disillusioning—fact is that *merely human* societies and fraternities do not provide this desired fellowship. In spite of constitutions that promise the most idealistic ties of brotherhood, expressions of man's sinfulness such as selfishness, greed, and jealousy make true fellowship veritably impossible. It is true that the Church is a human institution, and often suffers finite limitations; but if it is the Church of Christ it offers vital fellowship to men. To the extent this fellowship is ruptured by divisiveness, it forfeits its right to be the body of Christ.

Summary

In the foregoing chapters an effort has been made to analyze the life and experience of the new man in Christ. Distinctions have been made in logical sequence, but these various aspects of the new life are experientially synonymous.

Of great importance is the fact that the experience of grace depicted by this study is repeatedly described by Paul in the aorist tense. This emphasizes that such is a crisis experience and is an accomplished fact. Repeatedly Paul rejoices with the believers in what God *has done* for them in Christ.

It is essential to keep in proper balance the outward and objective relationship, and the inward and subjective experience. No proper understanding of the life of the new man in Christ is possible without the keeping in balance of these two vital perspectives.

In addition, Paul speaks in three distinct time relationships— the past, the present, and the future. Nowhere is this more vividly seen than in Paul's use of the term *salvation (sotēria)*. Salvation is a fact of the past (cf. Rom. 8:24), a process still going on in the present (cf. 1 Cor. 15:2), and a future prospect (cf. Rom. 5:9).

Yet all of these are in the indicative mood—statements of fact. It is against this background that the full force of Paul's repeated imperatives is seen. It is to these vital imperatives that this study now turns.

PART IV

THE NEW MAN: UNDER AN IMPERATIVE

Chapter 15

The Continuing Concern

All of Paul's writings are letters to new men in Christ, primarily to his own converts.[1] His references to the old man in sin were reflective reminiscences. It is quite easy to distinguish in Paul the "fact of the past" and the "condition of the present." He remembers, with his readers, the life they once had known under the tyranny of sin. He knew well what they had been and from whence they had come. He had confronted them then and there with the good news of the gospel. Paul likewise rejoiced with them over what God had done for them in Christ. Together they praised God for His marvelous grace.

Yet there is another clear note in the letters of Paul—it is concern. In addition to the fact of the past and the condition of the present there is the *challenge of the future*. Repeatedly, with the pastor's heart, Paul expresses a deep concern for a remaining need in the lives of those to whom he writes, and he voices a challenge to meet that need. It is almost impossible to miss this expression of concern by even a superficial reading of his letters.

When the letters of Paul are studied more thoroughly, it becomes clear that there was either some serious lack of understanding or even misunderstanding among those to whom he wrote. His continuing concern is related to this problem of misunderstanding.

---

1. The letter to the Romans is the one exception. Although he had never been to Colossae, the church there was the fruit of his evangelistic labors in Ephesus and the surrounding area.

The gospel of Jesus Christ produces *both* a new *status* (objective standing) and a new *creation* (subjective experience). The new man in Christ *does* have the ethical and moral responsibility to *live* a holy life. Throughout the long history of the Church, the doctrine of grace, strongly emphasized by Paul, has sometimes been either misunderstood or misinterpreted in order to excuse one from the demands of holy living. Evidently this abuse of grace, articulated later as antinomianism, began with some of the converts—certainly the opponents—of Paul. This is part of the apostle's concern.

There was obviously a failure, among some believers at least, to properly appreciate or understand the power of sin. This is not strange, as it has often been the experience of the one who has found new life in Christ. It is easy for the convert, caught up in the rapture of his new relationship with Christ, to almost feel he is immune to sin. Many have suffered the later agony of soul struggle at this point.

Of particular concern to Paul was the failure, by some, to realize the relationship between sin and the flesh. To be sure, the man in Christ is freed from the tyranny of sin working through the flesh. He is no longer sin's helpless victim. Yet his flesh is weakened by sin and as a result it is a constant source of temptation. This temptation, of course, differs in nature and intensity among people, depending in great part on one's former life in sin. Although he must, of necessity, live *in the sphere* of the flesh, the believer dare not live *by means of* the flesh, fulfilling or satisfying its desires. There is the constant threat of being drawn back under the domination of sin. The man in Christ is *not* helpless against the power of sin, as some would suggest, but he must be aware of the weakness of the flesh.

Some of Paul's converts evidently failed to appreciate the power of sin and were not aware of the fact that a victorious life is impossible when a man lives in his own strength—*kata sarka*. A victorious life is possible only as a man lives in the strength God provides—*kata pneuma*.

Of primary concern to Paul was that his converts realize that there is *nothing automatic about victorious living.* The power of sin is compulsive, but man receives the power of God *only by choice.*

It is only as the man in Christ, sensing the power of sin and his dependence upon God's grace, *voluntarily* turns to God that he finds His sufficient power.

In the chapters that follow, this concern of Paul will be examined and explained.

Chapter 16

The Indicative and the Imperative

As the concern of Paul is examined, a crucial and vital distinction can be readily seen. He expresses his concern *in imperative terms*. By contrast the fact of the past and the condition of the present are stated *in indicative terms*. In New Testament Greek this distinction is graphically depicted by two different verb forms, so there is no question about the difference in meaning.[1] Fortunately this distinction is easily understood in English. The indicative mood is a *statement of fact*—that is, was, shall be. The imperative mood is a *command*—this must be. When Paul speaks of what his converts were or are (even shall be) it is the indicative, but when he tells them what they must do or be it is the imperative.

Furthermore, *the imperative is based on the indicative*. It is because of the fact of the indicative that Paul could command the imperative. It was because of what *they were* that Paul could point to what *they must be and do*. As Paul's letters are examined with this in mind, the distinction becomes quite clear.

The rhetorical question of Rom. 6:1 (cf. 6:15): "Are we to continue in sin that grace might increase?" is answered by a series of imperatives that are based upon some stated indicatives. This will be thoroughly examined in the chapters to follow. In the Colossian letter the interplay between the indicative and imperative is graphic:

---

1. The Greek verb forms are called "moods." There are indicative and imperative moods. Sometimes the force of the imperative is expressed by different forms—cf. the hortatory subjunctive and infinitive construction.

As you therefore have received Christ Jesus the Lord [indicative] *so* walk in Him [imperative], having been firmly rooted *and now* being built up in Him and established in your faith, just as you were instructed, *and* overflowing with gratitude (Col. 2:6-7).

Paul was prayerfully concerned about the Colossians:

For this reason also, since the day we heard *of it,* we have not ceased to pray for you and to ask that you may be filled with the knowledge of His will in all spiritual wisdom and understanding, so that you may walk in a manner worthy of the Lord, to please *Him* in all respects, bearing fruit in every good work and increasing in the knowledge of God, strengthened with all power, according to His glorious might, for the attaining of all steadfastness and patience, joyously giving thanks to the Father, who has qualified us to share in the inheritance of the saints in light (Col. 1:9-12).[2]

Such is based on an indicative fact—"For He delivered us from the domain of darkness, and transferred us to the kingdom of His beloved Son, in whom we have redemption, the forgiveness of sins" (Col. 1:13-14). Paul could exhort these believers to "keep seeking the things above" (Col. 3:1) and to "set your mind on the things above, not on the things that are on earth" (Col. 3:2)—*because of the indicative.* "For you have died and your life is hidden with Christ in God" (Col. 3:3; cf. 3:1). In this third chapter of Colossians, Paul's imperatives reach a climax:

Therefore consider the members of your earthly body as dead to immorality, impurity, passion, evil desire, and greed, which amounts to idolatry (Col. 3:5). But now you also, put them all aside: anger, wrath, malice, slander, *and* abusive speech from your mouth. Do not lie to one another (Col. 3:8-9). And so, as those who have been chosen of God, holy and beloved, put on a heart of compassion, kindness, humility, gentleness and patience; bearing with one another, and forgiving each other, whoever has a complaint against any one; just as the Lord forgave you, so also should you. And beyond all these things *put on* love, which is the perfect bond of unity. And let the peace of Christ rule in your hearts, to which indeed you were called in one body; and be thankful. Let the word of Christ richly dwell within you;

---

2. This is not in the imperative mood, but carries the force of an imperative. For example, the infinitive in v. 10 ("so that you may walk") can have imperatival meaning. (Cf. Eph. 1:16-19 with 2:1-10.)

with all wisdom teaching and admonishing one another with psalms *and* hymns *and* spiritual songs, singing with thankfulness in your hearts to God. And whatever you do in word or deed, *do* all in the name of the Lord Jesus, giving thanks through Him to God the Father (Col. 3:12-17).

Again, such a command is possible because of the indicative:

You laid aside the old self with its *evil* practices, and have put on the new self who is being renewed to a true knowledge according to the image of the One who created him (Col. 3:9-10).[3]

Similarly in Ephesians, Paul admonishes his converts:

I, therefore, the prisoner of the Lord, entreat you to walk in a manner worthy of the calling with which you have been called (Eph. 4:1). This I say therefore, and affirm together with the Lord, that you walk no longer just as the Gentiles also walk, in the futility of their mind (Eph. 4:17). And walk in love, just as Christ also loved you, and gave Himself up for us, an offering and a sacrifice to God as a fragrant aroma (Eph. 5:2). But now you are light in the Lord; walk as children of light (Eph. 5:8). Therefore be careful how you walk, not as unwise men, but as wise (Eph. 5:15).

He could require such because they *had learned* in Christ to put off the old self and put on the new self.[4] In even more detail than in Colossians, Paul spells out the imperatives.[5] As in Colossians, so also in Ephesians there are several indicative references in the earlier chapters that provide a broader base for the imperatives.[6]

In Galatians, after reminding the Gentiles whom he had won to Christ that they had been freed from sin and the law through faith in Christ (cf. 3:1—5:12), Paul warned them against an abuse of that freedom. "For you were called to freedom, brethren; only *do* not *turn* your freedom into an opportunity for the flesh, but through love serve one another" (Gal. 5:13). He admonished them

---

3. There are several references to their experience in Christ in the earlier chapters, which give a broader indicative base for the imperative. Cf. Col. 1:2, 4-6, 8, 13-14, 21-23; 2:13-15.

4. Cf. Eph. 4:20-24. Note the argument above that the interpretation of this ambiguous construction in Ephesians should be governed by the unambiguous construction in Colossians.

5. Cf. Eph. 4:25-32. The translation of the opening of v. 25 in the NASB is unfortunate ("Therefore, laying aside falsehood"). The Greek construction is an aorist middle participle *(apothemenoi)* and *indicates antecedent action*. It is much better translated: "Because you have put off from yourself lying."

6. Cf. Eph. 1:3-9, 11, 13-15. Particularly note 2:5-10.

to walk by the Spirit.[7] This would safeguard them from the works of the flesh and provide for them the fruit of the Spirit. This imperative was possible only because they were already free (cf. 5:1, 13) and *had* crucified the flesh with its passions and desires (cf. Gal. 5:24).

Although Paul's first letter to the Corinthians is distinctive in character, dealing with several urgent practical problems, the interplay of the indicative and imperative can be clearly seen. Paul's solution to the disastrous division and strife that fragmented the church was sublimely simple—it was love *(agape)*. After describing this "more excellent way" in the incomparable poem of love in the thirteenth chapter, Paul exhorts these believers in Corinth to pursue love (1 Cor. 14:1). Such was possible *only* because . . .

> Do you not know that the unrighteous shall not inherit the kingdom of God? Do not be deceived; neither fornicators, nor idolaters, nor adulterers, nor effeminate, nor homosexuals, nor thieves, nor covetous, nor drunkards, nor revilers, nor swindlers, shall inherit the kingdom of God. And *such were some of you;* but you were washed, but you were sanctified, but you were justified in the name of the Lord Jesus Christ, and in the Spirit of our God (1 Cor. 6:9-11, italics added).

The imperative is based on the indicative.

In the balance of Paul's letters a similar interplay between the indicative and the imperative can be traced to a minor degree, as other concerns take precedence.[8] This more detailed examination of the indicative and imperative moods in Paul's letters has been made to emphasize that it is absolutely basic to an understanding of his thought. Repeatedly he states, in substance, You *are* a new man who is alive in God, yet you *must* put to death your earthly members and present yourself and your members to God. Further,

---

7. An imperative in 5:16 and a hortatory subjunctive in 5:25.

8. Philippians is unique, as Paul does not have the same concern that is manifested in his other letters. (However, cf. 1:27; 2:3, 14-15.) In 2 Corinthians, Paul's major concern is the defense of his apostleship, but cf. 5:17; 6:1, 6:14—7:1; 12:20-21; 13:9 In 1 Thessalonians, Paul deals with the problems of confusion about the second coming of Christ, disrespect for lay leadership, and an attack on his integrity. In addition he suggests there is a lack in their faith (3:10) and it is the cause for his exhortations to holiness (3:12—4:12). However, he does commend their experience in Christ (cf. 1:3-4, 6-9; 2:13-14; 4:10; 5:5).

you *are* a free man, yet you *must not* continue to live in sin but present your members to God as His slaves—*which you are.* Still further, you *are* a spiritual man, yet you *must not* live by the flesh, but by the Spirit.

This is the most fruitful way to study Paul, carefully distinguishing between the indicative and imperative. It is essential to discern whether Paul is saying "this is" or "this must be" their experience. It can result in nothing but confusion to treat Paul's indicatives as imperatives or vice versa.

Yet, although it is quite easy to identify the indicative and imperative, the relationship between the two is not quite so obvious. We have seen that the indicative is the *basis for* the imperative—but how? For instance, Paul says: "For you have died" (Col. 3:3). Then he goes on to say: "Put to death your members" (Col. 3:5, lit.).[9] What does Paul mean? If we *are* dead, then why must we put our earthly members to death? How can we understand this?[10]

---

9. Note the NASB translation, which is an obvious attempt to resolve what appears to be a paradox—"Therefore consider the members of your earthly body as dead [*nekrōsate*]." The word "consider" is not in the verse, and the verb *(nekroō)* means "to put to death" and not "to consider dead" (cf. A and G).

10. The relationship between the indicative and imperative moods in Pauline thought is one of the most significant issues in NT theology. Some NT scholars simply view the interrelationship of these two moods as an unresolved paradox that must be viewed in constant tension. A familiar German phrase is *"schon und noch nicht"* (already but not yet). This apparent paradox has been described as the intersecting of two aeons or the eternal entering time. However, the paradox seems to be in our understanding rather than in Paul's thought.

Others have attempted to resolve the paradox by the use of philosophical and theological concepts. The indicative, viewed as principle, potential and ideal, is contrasted with the imperative, described as practice, actual and realized. But these concepts do not accurately represent the manner in which Paul understood and stated the relationship.

Sometimes the basic interaction between the indicative and imperative is missed and the imperative is simply viewed as: confirmation, appropriation, growth, or progress. As a result totally un-Pauline ideas emerge, such as: growing out of sin, the beginning of the infinite task of dying, or even fighting sin.

The most extensive consideration of the interaction of the indicative and imperative moods is found in German theology, which produced the famous interpretations *"Werde das was du bist"* (Become what you are) and *"Sei was du bist"* (Be what you are). Although these interpretations reveal an appreciation of the interplay between these two moods, they fail to recognize the basic objective of Paul's imperative. He was not concerned that the man of faith be or become *what he already is,* but rather *something more than he is.*

As the indicative and imperative contrast is closely examined, it will be seen that the imperative is given *because of* the fact of the indicative—or as was noted above, the imperative is based on the indicative. The imperative exhortation of *doing* is based on the indicative fact of *being*. The indicative speaks of what had been *done to* the believer, while the imperative speaks of what *the believer must do* himself because of the indicative. Paul is exhorting the new men of faith to *use what they are and have*. In other words, they should use the *possessed* resources that were theirs because *they were* new men, free men, and spiritual men. What did they have? They had their new life in Christ! Hence Paul's concern. You *have* new life in Christ; what are you going to do with it? You *have* your freedom from sin and the law; now how are you going to use it? You *have* the Holy Spirit; how are you going to let Him live through you?

As the implications of the contrasting indicatives and imperatives are considered, a crucial condition in the new man becomes increasingly evident. Perhaps it can be best understood in terms of the "worlds" in which man lives. The old man lives in the world of sin, under its dominance and control. The indicative clearly states that the man in Christ *no longer* is living in this world under sin. In contrast, the imperative points to another world, where the new man lives under the Spirit, sustained and strengthened by Him. It should be carefully noted that those to whom the imperatives were addressed were *not yet* living in the world under the Spirit.

Quite naturally it can be asked: If the new man is *no longer* living under sin and is *not yet* living under the Spirit—then where is he living? For the want of a better term it can be described as a "no-man's-land" or "twilight zone"—*under self*. He is no longer sin's slave, but is not using the resources *that he already possesses*. Instead of living by the strength of the Holy Spirit he is living in his own strength.

A legitimate question is: *Why?* What is the problem? Why does not the new man in Christ, who has received the Holy Spirit, use the resources that he already possesses? Why is this not as natural as breathing? The answer to this puzzling problem— obviously Paul's concern—is found in a point of theology recognized by practically every classical creed. Original sin remains in the *heart* of the new man in Christ.[11] After a man finds his new status and becomes a new creature, his heart is still depraved. Understandably, in the joy of his newfound life in Christ the believer is not immediately aware of this situation. However, in time, the Holy Spirit reveals the remaining need of his heart. It is at this point that the understanding of original sin as self-sovereignty becomes of special significance. The man in Christ awakens to the fact that he still *holds* the "reins of rule" in his own hands—he is still his own lord.

To be sure, self-sovereignty cannot be *expressed* in rebellion or enmity, because such is overt sin and brings inevitable separation from God. So, within the man who lives in the world under self there is a mortal struggle. Unfortunately this desperate struggle is not *explicitly* depicted by Paul, and can be understood only by implication and as a conclusion drawn from what Paul does state. Yet it is a fact that is too well known by personal experience to be questioned. The man in Christ, who is a free and new person, is still struggling with the depravity with which he was born.

It will be seen that the immediate result of this tragic situattion is that the believer is separated from the essential power of the Holy Spirit. As long as man is sovereign of his own life, the Holy Spirit cannot be sovereign. It is at this point that a common misunderstanding exists. The sinner *receives* Jesus Christ as his Saviour, but the believer must *make* Him his Lord. It is impossible to *receive* Christ as Lord, by the intrinsic nature of lordship or sovereignty. The lordship of the Spirit is over the believer's *new life,* which he does not possess as a sinner. This will be examined further in a later chapter. It is sufficient here to realize that the believer, who still is sovereign of his own soul, has not received Christ as Lord—he is his own lord![12]

---

11. It should be emphasized that original sin remains in the *heart* of the believer; that is, in the inner man. This must not be confused with the results of sinful living in the flesh or outer man.

12. We should not be confused by semantic distinctions. The earliest Christian confession was that Jesus is Lord. Every Christian must acknowledge the lordship of Christ in the sense of submission to that lordship. However, it is only as the believer commences to live the new life that the issue of sovereignty and lordship is fully understood.

Without the enablement that the Spirit brings when the believer lives under His sovereignty, the new man can only face the threat of sin in his own strength, or by self-discipline. This is one of Paul's vital concerns. The new man in Christ must continue to live *in the flesh,* which is a constant source of temptation. His desires, propensities, instincts, feelings, appetites, and habit patterns—so long indulged by self-gratification—now must be disciplined and restructured. They dare not be indiscriminately satisfied or fulfilled. True, the compulsive power of sin working through the flesh is broken, but the attractions remain. The flesh is not destroyed!

To attempt to meet this threat by means of self-discipline is disheartening, if not futile. How well Paul knew this! Victory over sin is possible only by means of the Spirit. "But I say, walk by the Spirit, and you will not carry out the desire of the flesh" (Gal. 5:16). Yet such a *negative* concern—victory over sin—is never the final one for Paul. The believer, struggling against sin in the strength of self-discipline, cannot possibly know the *positive* blessings that are to be found in a life lived under the sovereignty of the Spirit.

Paul, grateful for the indicative, repeatedly points the believer to the possibilities of grace through the imperative. God does promise and provide victory over sin and rich spiritual treasures in the world under the Spirit. The believer need not be a victim; he can be victor. The remedy is found in using the resources that the man in Christ already possesses.

In the chapters that follow, the various aspects of the interplay between the indicative and imperative will be more thoroughly examined. When these two moods were traced above, the vivid contrast in Romans 6—8 was purposely omitted in order that it might provide the scriptural basis for a more detailed study, in logical sequence. First Paul admonishes the Romans to consider the indicative, followed by the strong insistence that sin must be defeated—it must not be permitted to reign in the new man. At this point the believer's relationship to the flesh will be closely examined.

But Paul's imperatives do not stop with a prohibition! The solution to the problem of sin in the life of the believer must include the all-important element of original sin. So the apostle exhorts the believer to present himself, and his members, to God in a new love slavery. This settles the issue of sovereignty! In addition to victory over sin the man in Christ enters the door to fruitful living under the sovereignty of the Spirit.

It has been repeatedly seen that many of Paul's metaphors and descriptions of the new life in Christ had specific significance and meaning to the men of his day. Of necessity these concepts have been stated in terms that the believer today can readily comprehend. Paul's picture of the man in Christ *no longer* living in the world under sin but *not yet* living in the world under the Spirit is, however, all *too* understandable to many who name Christ's name today. How well men remember the deliverance from the enslaving grip of sin which they found when they came to Jesus Christ in saving faith! But, once freed from sin, they have not gone on to live under the sovereignty of the Spirit. They who once rendered, by compulsion, total servitude to sin, now, by choice, give to their new Master such halfhearted allegiance! They are simply not using the resources that they possess. Instead they are in that shadowy no-man's-land under self, attempting to live in their own strength and discipline. Not only is this, in reality, ingratitude—for what is more proper than that a man render his new master the same measure of loyalty and service he rendered his old?—but all too often it leads to sad and even tragic defeat. Paul's corrective has an exciting relevance for the man of faith—today.

Chapter 17

Consider the Indicative

Once the distinction between the indicative and imperative is recognized, it is somewhat surprising to learn where the *logical* beginning of the imperative is. Evidently those in Christ—at least a significant number of them—did not realize the implications of their new faith, as well as several other crucial facts. In most of Paul's letters there is evident an urgent concern about an apparent lack of knowledge or understanding. This concern is expressed in his prayers.

> For this reason also, since the day we heard *of it*, we have not ceased to pray for you and to ask that you may be filled with the knowledge of His will in all spiritual wisdom and understanding, so that you may walk in a manner worthy of the Lord, to please *Him* in all respects, bearing fruit in every good work and increasing in the knowledge of God; strengthened with all power, according to His glorious might, for the attaining of all steadfastness and patience, joyously (Col. 1:9-11; cf. Eph. 1:15-19; 3:14-19; Phil. 1:9-11).

It is very possible that it was this lack of spiritual understanding that Paul is alluding to when he expresses an urgent desire to visit Rome and impart some spiritual gift (cf. Rom. 1:11), and when he earnestly prays that he may complete what is lacking in the Thessalonians' faith (cf. 1 Thess. 3:10). We do know that he exhorted the Corinthians: "Brethren, do not be children in your thinking; yet in evil be babes, but in your thinking be mature" (1 Cor. 14:20).

Repeatedly, particularly in Romans and First Corinthians, Paul pointedly asks: Don't you know? Are you ignorant? Obviously they didn't know or realize some vital things. When Paul sought to solve several practical problems in the Corinthian church he asked this question (Don't you know?), and then proceeded to explain a basic spiritual truth. His answer to the problem of Christians taking each other to a pagan lawcourt was to ask if they didn't know that the saints will one day judge the world (cf. 1 Cor. 6:2-3). He asked those who were attending idol feasts if they didn't know that the sacrificer shares in the altar, with all that this would involve (cf. 1 Cor. 10:18). When Paul sought to correct the abuses arising from the impropriety of some of the women at worship he asked if they did not know that Christ is the Head of every man and a man is the head of a woman (cf. 1 Cor. 11:3). He pointed to the history of Israel and asked if they did not know what happened to them when they disobeyed God.[1]

Several examples have been cited above to emphasize that this concern about the lack of knowledge and understanding makes up a significant part of the general background of Paul's letters. If this was important in the solution of the several practical problems treated by Paul, it is much more so in his most crucial concern of all—victorious living. Paul was disturbed because they apparently did not understand the power of sin:

> Do you not know that when you present yourselves to someone *as* slaves for obedience, you are slaves of the one whom you obey, either of sin resulting in death, or of obedience resulting in righteousness? (Rom. 6:16).

This is his answer, at least in part, to the rhetorical question: "What then? Shall we sin because we are not under law but under grace? May it never be!" (Rom. 6:15). Indeed this was a horrible thought because of the power of sin. They had been once sin's slaves (cf. Rom. 6:17, 20), but had been freed from its slavery (cf. Rom. 6:18, 22). What they evidently did not know or realize was that to continue to sin would result in them again becoming sin's

---

1. Cf. 1 Cor. 10:1. Cf. also 1 Cor. 9:24—"Do you not know that those who run in a race all run, but *only* one receives the prize? Run in such a way that you may win"; also 1 Cor. 12:1—"Now concerning spiritual *gifts*, brethren, I do not want you to be unaware [lit., ignorant]."

slaves. Sin was not something to "dabble" in, but was to be feared because of its power.

Similarly these early believers evidently did not know and appreciate God's total condemnation of sinful living.

> Do you not know that the unrighteous shall not inherit the kingdom of God? Do not be deceived; neither fornicators, nor idolaters, nor adulterers, nor effeminate, nor homosexuals, nor thieves, nor covetous, nor drunkards, nor revilers, nor swindlers, shall inherit the kingdom of God (1 Cor. 6:9-10).

This is not an insignificant or passing reference, but was a repeated and insistent warning of Paul (cf. Gal. 5:21; Eph. 5:5; Col. 3:6). Evidently the believers were being deceived, either by Satan or evil-intentioned men, or possibly both. The sad part was that *they* would be suffering the consequences (cf. Gal. 6:7; 1 Cor. 6:9).

Most critical of all, these new men in Christ did not know or realize the implications of their faith. In fact, *this is the primary purpose of the indicatives throughout Paul's letters—to bring to their attention what God had done for them.* Apparently they had never fully understood and appreciated this fact, or had lost sight of it.

Thus Paul had to ask: "Do you not know that all of us who have been baptized into Christ Jesus have been baptized into His death?" (Rom. 6:3). Then he went on to spell out in graphic pictures the result of this death with Christ, climaxing with: "Knowing this, that our old self was crucified with *Him,* that our body of sin might be done away with, that we should no longer be slaves to sin" (Rom. 6:6). They had to be told anew what *had happened* to them. So also, in the balance of the sixth chapter of Romans, Paul reminded them of what *they had been:* "But thanks be to God that though you were slaves of sin . . . For when you were slaves of sin, you were free in regard to righteousness" (Rom. 6:17, 20). He also called attention to what *they had done:* "You became obedient from the heart to that form of teaching to which you were committed" (Rom. 6:17). Then he stated plainly what *had happened* to them:

> And having been freed from sin, you became slaves of righteousness (Rom. 6:18). But now having been freed from sin and enslaved to God, you derive your benefit, resulting in sanctification, and the outcome, eternal life (Rom. 6:22).

This reiteration of the indicative was to underscore that of which they were evidently not fully appreciative.

Likewise in 1 Corinthians, Paul *reminded* these believers, who were in spiritual danger, of *what they were:*

> Do you not know that you are a temple of God, and *that* the Spirit of God dwells in you? If any man destroys the temple of God, God will destroy him, for the temple of God is holy, and that is what you are (1 Cor. 3:16-17). Do you not know that your bodies are members of Christ? Shall I then take away the members of Christ and make them members of a harlot? May it never be! Or do you not know that the one who joins himself to a harlot is one body *with her?* For He says, "THE TWO WILL BECOME ONE FLESH" (1 Cor. 6:15-16). Or do you not know that your body is a temple of the Holy Spirit who is in you, whom you have from God, and that you are not your own? For you have been bought with a price: therefore glorify God in your body (1 Cor. 6:19-20).[2]

This repeated reference to the indicative, of what God *had done* for them in Christ, and the insistent question: "Don't you know this?" is the essential context for Paul's *first imperative:* "Even so consider yourselves to be dead to sin, but alive to God in Christ Jesus" (Rom. 6:11). This, in logical sequence, is the beginning point of Paul's correction of the problem of sin in the lives of believers.

Paul used a very significant word, which is translated "consider." *Logidzomai* means to reckon or calculate and then, as a result, to evaluate, estimate, consider, or even to ponder and let one's mind dwell on.[3] They *must* realize, recognize, appreciate, or take cognizance of a fact of which they had obviously lost sight. What was that fact? It was that they were dead to sin and alive to God. This *had happened* to them and the cognizance of this was of necessity the foundation of all that would follow.

Sometimes it is suggested that Paul was exhorting the Romans to *let* God do this for them, but such is clearly not the case.

_____

2. The second person pronouns ("you") in 1 Cor. 3:16-17 are plural and refer to the believers as a group in contrast to the verses that follow in which the second person pronouns are singular and refer to the individual Christians. Cf. 1:2, 4-9, 30 for additional clear indicatives.

3. Cf. A and G. Cf. Rom. 8:18; 1 Cor. 13:5; 2 Cor. 10:2a. In these instances *man does the considering.* Elsewhere it is God who does the reckoning, at least by implication (cf. Rom. 4:3-5, 9-11, 22-23).

This *had already happened* and Paul was urging them to recognize and remember it.

Quite naturally the question arises as to why this condition should exist. It would seem that a dramatic change, such as Paul repeatedly describes as happening to them, *ought* to have made such an impression upon these new men in Christ that it would not soon have been forgotten. This is certainly true, which points more intensively to the problem. Although there were obviously many *things* that these believers had to learn, their fundamental problem was undoubtedly not in obtaining information as such. This is strongly indicated by the term used by Paul in Rom. 6:11. He does not exhort them to *learn,* but to *consider* or to take cognizance. There are two ways of knowing. One type of knowledge can leave a man almost stupefied by indifference or preoccupation, while another type of knowledge excites one to action.

It is this latter kind of knowledge that Paul speaks of in 1 Cor. 2:12: "Now we have received, not the spirit of the world, but the Spirit who is from God, that we might know the things freely given to us by God." Such is a knowledge of *appreciation* more than a knowledge of *information.* The former is possible only by the Holy Spirit, which suggests a key to the problem. In all likelihood Paul was giving these men of faith very little *new information;* but, particularly with the indicatives, he was trying to create in them a deeper appreciation of the implications of their faith.

While trying to deal with the problem of attendance at idol feasts, Paul calls attention to the type of knowledge which has been termed above knowledge of information, which is no knowledge at all in the deeper sense.

> Now concerning things sacrificed to idols, we know that we all have knowledge. Knowledge makes arrogant, but love edifies. If any one supposes that he knows anything, he has not yet known as he ought to know (1 Cor. 8:1-2).

It is clear that Paul is not appealing for human knowledge of objective facts, but a spiritual knowledge of appreciation.

Understandably there is a serious question as to whether it can be assumed that a similar problem exists today among those in Christ. Do believers today need to stop and give serious consideration to the indicatives of their lives, or was this a need only among

converts from a primitive, heathen culture? In simple terms—
don't people know better today? Human nature is strikingly the
same. As the imperatives of Paul are further examined—imperatives that most certainly are relevant to the believer today—it
might very well be seen that the man in Christ during the closing
half of the twentieth century needs to *begin* exactly where these
first-century converts did. Perhaps he too needs to see clearly the
power of sin, and God's total condemnation of sinful living. Most
of all, he needs to have a fresh realization of what Christ *has done*
for him.

Chapter 18

Live in Victory over Sin

Although Paul fully recognized the power of sin—probably more clearly than any man before or since—he had no doubt about the gospel of Jesus Christ having power to enable a man to conquer sin. The most systematic presentation that he ever made of the plan of salvation (Rom. 3:21—8:39) stands out in bold relief against the background of the blackest picture of sin's power in the entire Bible (Rom. 1:18—3:20). This is no coincidence. Paul's confidence was: "Where sin increased, grace abounded all the more" (Rom. 5:20).

Sin and grace are opposites and not concomitants. "What shall we say then? Are we to continue in sin that grace might increase? May it never be! How shall we who died to sin still live in it?" (Rom. 6:1-2). A "sinning Christian" is a fallen man! God provides grace to live victoriously over sin.[1]

Having led the believer to a deeper realization of what Christ has done for him, Paul turns to the next imperative—sin must cease!

---

1. There is an area of spiritual struggle that Paul does not explicitly deal with as later NT writers do (cf. 1 John 2:1f.). The man of faith must still do battle with sin and on occasion might fall. But he does not practice or continue in sin. His irrevocable lot in life is *not* to be torn between two equally powerful forces vying for control of his life.

> Therefore do not let sin reign in your mortal body that you
> should obey its[2] lusts, and do not go on presenting the members
> of your body to sin *as* instruments of unrighteousness. . . . For
> sin shall not be master over you, for you are not under law, but
> under grace (Rom. 6:12-14).

While under the power of sin, the believer's body (outer man) was
so dominated by sin that it could be termed "sin's body" (cf.
Rom. 6:6). The helpless victim presented his members as the
instruments of unrighteousness. Now this has all changed. The
believer's body is no longer sin's body; therefore sin must not be
allowed to reign in his body and he must not continue to present
the members of his body to sin as its slave. In dramatic terms Paul
is saying: Sin must cease!

This clear command is often repeated. "Then put to death
those parts of you which belong to the earth—fornication, in-
decency, lust, foul cravings, and the ruthless greed which is
nothing less than idolatry" (Col. 3:5, NEB). Paul is saying: You
must not satisfy your desires and passions in those evil ways that
you once did. Further, you are to:

> put them all aside: anger, wrath, malice, slander, *and* abusive
> speech from your mouth. Do not lie to one another, since you
> laid aside the old self with its *evil* practices, and have put on the
> new self who is being renewed to a true knowledge according to
> the image of the One who created him (Col. 3:8-10; cf. Eph. 4:12
> —5:2).

Paul's warnings about the tragic consequences of sinful living are
given to emphasize that such must cease (cf. 1 Cor. 6:9-10).

How does this direct imperative—Sin must cease—*which lists
specific sins,* relate to law and grace? Does this conflict with Paul's
clear teaching that man is righteous with God on the basis of grace
alone?

It is important to realize that Paul, and the entire New Testament, is not idealistic to the extreme. To be sure, Paul in his
polemic against legalism is strongly opposed to any concept of
moral behavior that is based solely on regulations and rules. Thus
he says: "'All things are lawful for me,' but not all things are help-

---

2. The English is ambiguous. "Its" can refer to either "sin" or "body." The
Greek makes it clear that the reference is to "body" (*auton* is neuter and has case
concord with *sōmati* and not *harmartia*).

ful. 'All things are lawful for me,' but I will not be enslaved by anything" (1 Cor. 6:12, RSV).[3]

The believer's freedom—from the law as works—must be inviolate! Yet in this very context Paul spells out certain basic principles that modify this freedom. He states that the man of faith will be governed by such principles as: (1) that which is helpful (expediency); (2) to not be mastered (enslaved) by anything; (3) the realization of belonging to God as His purchased possession (cf. 1 Cor. 6:19); (4) to glorify God (cf. 1 Cor. 6:20; 10:31); and (5) that which is profitable and edifies (cf. 1 Cor. 10:23). The entire letter (1 Corinthians), which deals with the basic problem of misused freedom, climaxes in the greatest modification of all—love (*agape*, cf. 1 Corinthians 13).

It approaches a travesty when men put into the mouth of Paul such foolish idealism as: "Love God and do what you please." Paul knew better because he knew the power of sin![4] He states emphatically, as repeatedly observed, *there are certain things a man cannot do and enter the kingdom of God.*

This raises a crucial and intriguing question, at least from the modern perspective. (It is doubtful if it ever occurred to Paul.) What *exactly* is Paul commanding? Is he saying: *Stop* committing sin, thus assuming they had continued to do so; or is he saying: You must not *return* to sin? The Greek is ambiguous, so no help is found there.[5] The modern Christian conscience, at least before the present moral revolution, is often scandalized by the

---

3. Cf. 1 Cor. 10:23. Most NT scholars are convinced that Paul is picking up a cliché—probably a corruption of something he had taught—that was being widely used to justify loose living. A similar example—"Food is meant for the stomach and the stomach for food" (1 Cor. 6:13, RSV).

4. Cf. Gal. 5:17—"For the flesh sets its desire against the Spirit, and the Spirit against the flesh; for these are in opposition to one another, *so that you may not do the things that you please.*" Often this has been misinterpreted to mean that the believer is unable to do the things he pleases (or wishes). Such drastically violates the context. Instead Paul is saying that by the Spirit the believer is *enabled to not do* the things that he pleases (in the flesh). The desires of the flesh—what man "pleases"—dare not be fulfilled. (Cf. commentary on Galatians by the author, BBC, Vol. IX, *en loco.*)

5. In Rom. 6:12-13a the imperatives are in the present tense, which can be quite properly translated either to not continue or to commence. In Col. 3:5, 8 the imperatives are in the aorist tense and can mean either to suddenly stop or not to start.

thought that an individual could be a believer and *still* be committing such gross evils. Doesn't a man's new relationship with Christ *automatically* result in the repudiation of such wickedness? Does a person have to be taught such? If so, does it not call into question the genuineness of his faith?

Sadly this is not always so. It must ever be remembered that these earliest believers were drawn from an almost inconceivably evil environment. "For He delivered us from the domain of darkness, and transferred us to the kingdom of His beloved Son" (Col. 1:13). It takes men, accustomed to darkness, a period of time to get their eyes open to see. This is not simply a first-century phenomenon, for many a modern missionary has shared Paul's problem. This is not even restricted to *geographical* heathenism or geographical sins. It is surprising how blind a person can be today in supposedly enlightened and Christian countries.

However, there is an interesting word from Paul that lies *between* the two passages from Colossians referred to above. It must be seen in its context.

> Put to death therefore what is earthly in you: immorality, impurity, passion, evil desire, and covetousness, which is idolatry. On account of these the wrath of God is coming. *In these you once walked, when you lived in them. But now* put them all away: anger, wrath, malice, slander, and foul talk from your mouth (Col. 3:5-9, RSV, italics added).

Note that Paul says, "In these you *once* walked, *when* you lived in them. But *now* . . ." The obvious implication is that they *were not now* living in the things that they *once* had lived in.

This graphically shows a most important viewpoint of Paul. One can distinguish with ease where the believers *once were* (but not now) and where they *must be* (but not yet). This has already been referred to as the "no-man's-land" that lies between the indicative and the imperative. Paul never described or discussed this land in between. He doesn't here, so it can only be conjectured exactly what this condition is. As far as he is concerned, it is no stopping place. The old way is gone. The new way is here. That is what is all-important.

Paul's urgent concern for these new men in Christ points to the fact that *sin is not dead.* The believer has died with Christ to sin, which results in freedom from sin. No longer is sin the ruling, overlording tyrant it had been. Man is now no longer sin's helpless slave and victim. "For sin shall not be master over you" (Rom. 6:14). The compulsive power of sin has been broken. Sin has been condemned in the flesh (cf. Rom. 8:3).

Yet this must not be construed to mean that sin is *destroyed* in the new birth. Its power and control is broken, but it is not destroyed. In terms of classical Wesleyan Theology, sin *remains* but no longer *reigns*. It is a potential threat to the new man in Christ. Otherwise the repeated imperatives of Paul would be meaningless. What is this remaining sin? We have identified it as self-sovereignty.

This condition can be most vividly illustrated by Paul's imperatives associated with the flesh *(sarx)*. Sin rules man through the flesh, making him the slave and victim of his own desires and propensities. Through death with Christ the compulsive grip of sin, working through the flesh, is broken. "Now those who belong to Christ Jesus have crucified the flesh with its passions and desires" (Gal. 5:24). No longer is man the victim of his own desires and propensities—he is free.

However, sin has done something to man's flesh! It is left weakened—in the believer. The years of self-gratification and sinful indulgence have warped and perverted the flesh, so that its instincts, desires, feelings, appetites, etc., are adversely grooved and patterned with a bias toward sin. Thus the flesh, even of the new man in Christ, *cannot be trusted.* He dare not do what he pleases. The flesh must not be indulged and satisfied. It is still vulnerable to sin, because it is what man has made himself under the whiplash of sin.

This is the predicament of the believer. He must live out his new life *in* the flesh *(en sarki),* because this is the only *sphere of existence* that he has. The new inner man can be housed only in the old outer man—awaiting the day of resurrection, which will bring a new outer man. Yet he dare not live *by* the flesh *(kata sarka),*[6] making it the *means of living.* We have observed that Paul speaks of the flesh as the means or dynamic of living *(kata sarka)*

---

6. This use of *flesh (sarx)*, as the means of living, can also be expressed by *en sarki*, when it is a dative of instrument (cf. Chapter 3).

in two distinct senses. It can mean to live *by the flesh,* by means of our own strength and resources, or to live *for the flesh,* to satisfy our own desires and propensities.

In the case of the man who is in the grip of sin, the two meanings of *kata sarka* are inseparable. For him to live in his own strength, to satisfy his desires, is sin. However, through human strength and power the believer *can,* at least for a time, discipline himself so that the desires of his flesh are *not* satisfied or indulged. Yet he is in mortal danger and it is against this danger that Paul gives repeated warning.

> But put on the Lord Jesus Christ, and make no provision for the flesh in regard to *its* lusts (Rom. 13:14). For you were called to freedom, brethren; only *do* not *turn* your freedom into an opportunity for the flesh, but through love serve one another (Gal. 5:13).

In Rom. 8:1-13, Paul warns against living *kata sarka* because the result is to mind the things of the flesh.

> For those who are according to the flesh *(kata sarka)* set their minds on the things of the flesh, but those who are according to the Spirit *(kata pneuma),* the things of the Spirit. For the mind set on the flesh is death, but the mind set on the Spirit is life and peace; because the mind set on the flesh is hostile toward God; for it does not subject itself to the Law of God, for it is not even able *to do so* (Rom. 8:5-7).

There is only one safeguard against such indulgence of the flesh. "But I say, walk by the Spirit, and you will not carry out the desire of the flesh" (Gal. 5:16).

This is the predicament of the believer to whom Paul was writing. He was *no longer* living under the sovereignty (control) of sin, and, as indicated by the imperatives, was *not yet* living under the sovereignty of the Spirit. Then where was he living? We have called it the shadowy "no-man's-land" under the sovereignty of self. This is what makes the believer's position so precarious. Not only is there the attraction of the flesh, but there is original sin remaining in his heart which *prohibits* him from living under the sovereignty of the Spirit.

It was to these new men of faith that Paul spoke the decisive imperative—sin must cease! You must live in victory over sin! Sin must not be allowed to *regain* sovereign lordship over you. Romans 6:16 makes it painfully clear that such was a vital threat.

Do you not know that when you present yourselves to someone *as* slaves for obedience, you are slaves of the one whom you
obey, either of sin resulting in death, or of obedience resulting in
righteousness? (Rom. 6:16).

Paul's concern was primarily motivated by the first law of life,
which is growth and development. Life cannot be *static*—it is by
definition *dynamic*. There is *either* progression or retrogression.
A man cannot live *perpetually* in the no-man's-land under the
sovereignty of self. He must either go forward to live under the
sovereignty of the Spirit or he will fall backward under the sovereignty of sin.

What makes the predicament so acute is that which *results*
from growth. Development in the new life means new light! When
a person begins to live with God, new light comes, and increasingly
he realizes that his new life is only to be understood in the dimensions of love *(agape)*. While he, through self-discipline, can per
haps for a time resist the temptation to gross evil, as the demands
of love come into focus, he increasingly discovers that such *are
possible only by the Spirit*. This is why he cannot live victoriously
in his own strength.

How can a man live victoriously? There is only one way—that
is *kata pneuma* (according to the Spirit). Paul's next imperative
follows naturally.

Chapter 19

Live by the Spirit

Paul's imperative is unmistakable—sin *must* cease and the new man in Christ *must* live victoriously. How is this possible with the handicap of original sin remaining in his heart and the enticements of his own flesh? What is Paul's solution? In identifying the negative (that sin must cease), its positive counterpart has been unavoidable. One of the basic facts of Paul's thought is that *the negative is never the end*. It has its place as one important means; but if one stops there and does not go on to consider the positive dimension, the conclusion is totally un-Pauline. Repeatedly it has been seen that Paul points to the positive solution to the problem. He was perhaps the first to "accentuate the positive," understanding the principle of "the expulsive power of a new affection" long before it became a homiletical example.

Unquestionably Paul's imperative climaxes in the positive command to live by the Spirit. The new man in Christ, for the first time in his life a free man, is faced with a crucial choice. How will he live his new life? How will he use his freedom? He must choose between two ways of living. The mortal danger of living by the flesh has been seen. The other option is to live by the Spirit. In terms of the so-called paradox: Live the life God has given you, or use the resources that you already possess.

Exactly what does it mean to live by the Spirit? *How* does one live by the Spirit? To understand this we must clearly see Paul's distinction between existence and living—with relationship to both the flesh and the Spirit. Although the new man *is* still flesh, and must spend his earthly life *in* the sphere of the flesh, he must not *live by* the flesh. Furthermore, the new man *is* Spirit (as his new basis of existence), but he must *live by* the Spirit (as his new dynamic for living). The imperative is a challenge to active living (doing) which is based on the indicative fact of a new existence (being).

This distinction—between existence and living—explains the *double reference* to the Spirit in Paul. "If we live [have our new existence] by the Spirit, let us also walk [active living] by the Spirit" (Gal. 5:25). Sometimes this deeper dimension of the life of the Spirit is pictured in terms of fullness, as the believer is filled through a second or subsequent *coming* of the Spirit.[1] Instead, Paul views the Spirit as *controlling* the life of the man of faith, as he lives by means of the strength and dynamic of the Spirit.

The understanding of these basic concepts of *being* and *doing* will make clear another fundamental distinction that is often overlooked. Although the new man *has* his new *basis of existence* by the Spirit,[2] he does not necessarily make the Spirit his *means of living*. This is precisely why Paul voices the imperative—*live* by the Spirit. As already observed, Paul recognized that the Galatians were alive (basis of existence) by the Spirit, but they needed to *actively* make the Spirit their dynamic for living (cf. Gal. 5:25).

The clearest imperative to the new man in Christ to live and walk by the Spirit is found in Galatians.

---

1. Actually the concept of being *filled* with the Spirit is not Pauline. In his one reference (Eph. 5:18) Paul uses *plerousthe* (to fill) and in the present imperative, indicating a progressive filling. The dative (*pneumati,* "Spirit")—especially with the preposition *en* ("in" or "by")—is very likely instrumental, which would make the Spirit the *Agent* and not the substance of filling. This agrees with Paul's basic concept of the Spirit filling our lives with His fruit (cf. Gal. 5:22-23; Phil. 1:11). It is Luke who repeatedly speaks of being filled with the Spirit and who exclusively uses another word for "fill" *(pimplēmi),* which has the basic connotation of "to saturate" and thus "to possess" in a metaphorical sense. Furthermore, Luke always uses the aorist tense, indicating a crisis experience (cf. Acts 2:2; 4:31, *et al*).

2. Paul uses such expressions as the Spirit being "given" (Rom. 5:5; 1 Thess. 4:8), "indwelling" man (Rom. 8:11; cf. 1 Cor. 3:16; 6:19), "received" (1 Cor. 2:12; Gal. 3:2). He also told the Galatians they had "begun" in the Spirit (Gal. 3:3). Paul *does not* use the Johannine (John 3:6) and Petrine (1 Pet. 1:3, 23) concept of birth by the Spirit.

But I say walk by the Spirit, and you will not carry out the desire of the flesh (Gal. 5:16). Now those who belong to Christ Jesus have crucified the flesh with its passions and desires. If we live by the Spirit, let us also walk by the Spirit (Gal. 5:24-25).[3]

The context for these metaphors in Galatians 5 is of the greatest importance. The Judaizers had followed Paul into Galatia attempting to force the Jewish law upon his converts, telling them that only thus could they be included in the Abrahamic covenant. Upon learning of this, Paul was deeply disturbed. After establishing the authority for his message and convincingly arguing that salvation is by faith and not through the works of the law, Paul climaxed this letter with the admonition to walk (live) by the Spirit and not by the flesh.

What underlies this controversy with the Judaizers, concerning his converts, is the Judaizers' fear that without the protection of the law the pagan converts would be engulfed by the evil world around them. But Paul insisted on another alternative. In addition to the possible extremes of legalism on one hand and libertinism (license) on the other hand was the alternative of the discipline of the Spirit. In fact, the law could only fail and would lead the Galatians back into a worse bondage than that from which they had been delivered. So with two beautiful metaphors Paul pictures the life lived by the Spirit.

The first word used (*peripateō*, v. 16) is the Greek term generally used for "walking," and pictures two persons out for a walk, journeying through life: hand in hand, arm in arm, and heart to heart. They share all of life's experiences together, in the closest of personal fellowship and companionship.

MY LORD AND I

I have a Friend so precious, so very dear to me.
He loves me with such tender love; He loves me faithfully.
I could not live apart from Him; I love to feel Him nigh.
*And so we **dwell** together, my Lord and I.*

---

3. In v. 16 the present imperative is used, and in v. 25 the first person present subjunctive is found. This latter construction is a hortatory subjunctive that carries with it the same force as the imperative.

Sometimes I'm faint and weary; He knows that I am weak.
And as He bids me lean on Him, His help I'll gladly seek.
He leads me in the path of light, beneath a sunny sky;
*And so we **walk** together, my Lord and I.*

He knows how much I love Him; He knows I love Him well.
But with what love He loveth me, my tongue can never tell.
It is an everlasting love, in ever rich supply;
*And so we **love** each other, my Lord and I.*

I tell Him all my sorrows; I tell Him all my joys;
I tell Him all that pleases me; I tell Him what annoys.
He tells me what I ought to do; He tells me what to try.
*And so we **talk** together, my Lord and I.*

He knows how I am longing some weary soul to win;
And so He bids me go and speak a loving word for Him.
He bids me tell His wondrous love, and why He came to die;
*And so we **work** together, my Lord and I.*

I have His yoke upon me, and easy 'tis to bear;
In the burden which He carries, I gladly take a share.
For then it is my happiness to have Him always nigh;
*We **bear the yoke** together, my Lord and I.*

—Mrs. L. Shorey

This highlights the *central truth* of the life of the Spirit. All too often the coming of the Holy Spirit to the believer's life is *seen as a crisis, climactic experience that changes him and produces a new condition.* This, of course, is true but it is far more than that! The coming of the Holy Spirit is the *beginning of a wondrous new relationship.* The Holy Spirit is a Person, and as always between persons, there is a personal relationship and a living companionship.

This is Paul's climactic imperative and is solidly based on the indicative. The new man in Christ receives the Holy Spirit and this is his new basis of existence. He is a spiritual man. Now he must live in a new way and use the resources he already possesses. He must make the Holy Spirit his means of living. This is what Paul means when he exhorts: Walk by the Holy Spirit!

There is a second imperative in Galatians 5: "If we live by the Spirit, let us also walk [*stoicheō*] by the Spirit" (Gal. 5:25). The believer's walk by the Spirit is not an aimless stroll or meandering through life. Rather, it is a well-laid-out path toward a definite goal. Thus Paul used a different word in verse 25, and that for a very good reason. *Stoicheō* is a military term which means to be kept in line and can best be translated as "march."[4]

The believer is kept in line by the Holy Spirit, which is a vivid metaphor of the disciplined life. This is Paul's answer to the fears of the Judaizers. The believer, walking by the Holy Spirit, lives a disciplined life, under the *link of love* and not needing the *lash of the law*.[5]

What are the results? Pointedly Paul states that this is *the* way *not* to fulfill the desire of the flesh (cf. Gal. 5:16). Consequently this is also the way *not* to produce the tragic works of the flesh (cf. Gal. 5:19-21). The solution to the problem of sin in the life of the believer is not through legalistic regulations and prohibitions, but is in a life lived under the discipline of the Holy Spirit. Yet the results are far greater! A life lived by the Holy Spirit brings forth the harvest of the fruit of the Spirit (cf. Gal. 5:22-23). (Both results will be examined in more detail in the next section.)

The other extended contrast of the two ways of living that are the options of the new man in Christ is found in Romans 8. This passage must also be viewed in its important context. After announcing the gospel of Jesus Christ with its exciting good news that a man can be righteous with God on the basis of faith in the Cross, Paul turned to answer the question of whether or not salvation is also a new condition within man as well as a new status that man has with God. In Romans 6, Paul points to the fact that the new man has died with Christ to sin and has been raised to newness of life. With another metaphor he pictures the believer as an emancipated slave, set free from sin's enslaving grip. His concern

---

4. Cf. Acts 21:24; Rom. 4:12; Phil. 2:16; Gal. 6:16. Note again the Amplified translation: "If . . . we have our life [in God], *let us go forward walking in line, our conduct controlled by the Spirit*" (Gal. 5:25, italics added).

5. This should not be idealized or romanticized as a lessening of discipline. Love disciplines by inward compulsion while law disciplines by outward constraint. Love was the strongest discipline Paul knew (cf. 1 Cor. 8:13—9:27). The discipline of the Spirit through love will be more thoroughly examined in Part V.

in this sixth chapter is that they *live* as men freed from sin, warning that to do otherwise would return them to sin's slavery.

After the illustration of marriage (7:1-6), to show that only death can free one from the law, Paul graphically pictures the impotence of the law against the power of sin, as sin takes opportunity through the commandment to deceive and slay man (7:6-13). Under the law man desires to do the good but is unable to do so as sin enslaves him through his own flesh. His is a state of moral frustration and wretchedness (7:14-25).

By contrast, Christ has done for the man of faith what the law was unable to do. Now the new man faces the option of two ways of living.

> There is therefore now no condemnation for those who are in Christ Jesus. For the law of the Spirit of life in Christ Jesus has set you free from the law of sin and of death. For what the Law could not do, weak as it was through the flesh, God *did:* sending His own Son in the likeness of sinful flesh and *as an offering* for sin, He condemned sin in the flesh, in order that the requirement of the Law might be fulfilled in us, who do not walk according to the flesh, but according to the Spirit. For those who are according to the flesh set their minds on the things of the flesh, but those who are according to the Spirit, the things of the Spirit. For the mind set on the flesh is death, but the mind set on the Spirit is life and peace; because the mind set on the flesh is hostile toward God; for it does not subject itself to the Law of God, for it is not even able *to do so;* and those who are in the flesh cannot please God. However you are not in the flesh but in the Spirit, if indeed the Spirit of God dwells in you. But if anyone does not have the Spirit of Christ, he does not belong to Him (Rom. 8:1-9).

In this passage there is much of the same instruction that was seen before in the passage in Galatians 5, showing the results of the two ways of living. Those who walk by the flesh set their minds on the things of the flesh, which results in what Paul calls in Galatians 5 the works of the flesh. Adversely, when the man of faith walks by the Spirit he sets his mind on the things of the Spirit, which brings a harvest of the fruit of the Spirit. Graphically Paul shows that the aim or purpose of the flesh is hostile to God (cf. v. 7) and can only end in death.

One very important result of walking by the Spirit, that was not stated in Galatians 5, is that in this way of living the just requirement[6] of the law is fulfilled. "He condemned sin in the flesh, in order that the requirement of the Law might be fulfilled in us, who do not walk according to the flesh, but according to the Spirit" (Rom. 8:3-4). The twofold use of the term "Law" *(nomos)* has been examined and it was seen that the Jews had emptied the law of its moral and ethical content as the divine will or standard, and were lost in legalistic regulations. The strongest fear of the Judaizers was that salvation by faith would result in the repudiation of God's law. Paul, a former Pharisee, knew that *the only way God's true law could be fulfilled was through walking by the Spirit.* Some of Paul's interpreters have failed to see this, making *all law* the antithesis of grace. It is only the law *as works,* used as a means of salvation, that Paul sees in conflict with grace. Paul asserted that he was under the law of Christ (cf. 1 Cor. 9:21).

Paul makes it plain *how* the law is fulfilled:

> Owe nothing to anyone except to love one another; for he who loves his neighbor has fulfilled *the* law. For this, "YOU SHALL NOT COMMIT ADULTERY, YOU SHALL NOT MURDER, YOU SHALL NOT STEAL, YOU SHALL NOT COVET," and if there is any other commandment, it is summed up in this saying, "YOU SHALL LOVE YOUR NEIGHBOR AS YOURSELF." Love does no wrong to a neighbor; love therefore is the fulfillment of *the* law (Rom. 13:8-10; cf. Gal. 5:14).

Paul saw, even as his Lord before him (cf. Matt. 22:36-40), that the law as the divine will and standard *can be fulfilled only by love.*[7] Such love is not from man, even living by the legalistic requirements of the law, but is the fruit that comes from walking by the Spirit.

Although these two ways of living are contrasted (with the graphic description of the consequences of each) in Galatians 5, it is in Romans 8 that Paul *emphasizes* that the way of the flesh and

---

6. Cf. Rom. 8:3, RSV. This is an excellent translation of *dikaiōma* as it combines the basic meaning of *requirement* or *ordinance* with the overtones of *righteous* that are intrinsic to the term.

7. Cf. Rom. 10:4, where Paul says "Christ is the end of the law," probably in the sense of fulfillment; and Rom. 3:31, where the law is established by faith and actually becomes the law of faith. This becomes so even in regard to circumcision (cf. Rom. 2:28-29; Col. 2:11).

the way of the Spirit *are alternative choices.* In order to see this
more plainly the key verses will be quoted again:

> He condemned sin in the flesh, in order that the requirement
> of the Law might be fulfilled in us, who do not walk according to
> the flesh, but according to the Spirit. For those who are according
> to the flesh set their minds on the things of the flesh, but those
> who are according to the Spirit, the things of the Spirit. For the
> mind set on the flesh is death, but the mind set on the Spirit is
> life and peace; because the mind set on the flesh is hostile toward
> God; for it does not subject itself to the Law of God, for it is not
> even able *to do so* (Rom. 8:3-7).

As plain as language can state it, Paul says these two ways of living
are *opposite alternatives.* They are totally irreconcilable to each
other. A man can do either—*but certainly not both at the same
time.*

Sometimes Paul is pictured as teaching that the new man is a
split personality,[8] either walking by the Spirit with his new nature
and walking by the flesh with his old nature, or being governed at
one time by the Spirit and at another time by the flesh. A careful
study of Rom. 8:3-7 reveals an entirely different picture.[9] These
two ways of living are strict alternative choices and are not concomitants. The clear portrayal of the choice that lies before the
new man is what makes this passage so central to Paul's thought.
Although he never speaks in imperative terms, as in Galatians 5,
the significance of his vivid contrast can be seen. The believer cannot do both, so he must choose. It is not a matter of adding the
new way of the Spirit to the old way of the flesh. Just as the old
man in sin had to be put off as a condition to his becoming the new
man in Christ, so now *the new man must choose how he will live.*
The antithesis is absolute!

---

8. This is also pictured eschatologically, with the new man described as
straddling two aeons—his new life (from the age to come) overlapping his old life
(in this age).

9. This "two-nature" theory is more often based on Rom. 7:14-25 and Gal.
5:17. It was noted above (cf. Chapter 17) what this writer thinks is the proper
interpretation of Gal. 5:17. It was also argued that Rom. 7:14-25 is a picture of
the enlightened Jew struggling to save himself by the law (autobiographical of
Paul as seen through the eyes of faith) and thus does not describe the new man in
Christ (cf. c. 5). Regardless of how one interprets Rom. 7:14-25 and even Gal. 5:17,
the passage in Rom. 8:3-7 does not depict such a conflict in the new man.

Paul's imperative to live by the Spirit can be easily recognized throughout many of his letters, though in a less direct form. It is primarily expressed in terms of love *(agape)*. Paul's fundamental solution to the various practical problems he had to deal with in the Corinthian church was the imperative: "Pursue love" (1 Cor. 14:1). He writes to the Ephesians:

> Therefore be imitators of God, as beloved children; and walk in love, just as Christ also loved you, and gave Himself up for us, an offering and a sacrifice to God as a fragrant aroma (Eph. 5:1-2).

In a direct imperative he admonishes them further: "And do not get drunk with wine, in which is dissipation, but be filled by the Spirit" (Eph. 5:18, lit.).[10] The Holy Spirit fills the believer's life with His fruit.

Paul exhorts the Colossians: "And beyond all these things *put on* love, which is the perfect bond of unity" (Col. 3:14).

The same basic challenge, although not with a direct imperative, is voiced by Paul in terms of prayer concern. To the Thessalonians he wrote:

> For what thanks can we render to God for you in return for all the joy with which we rejoice before our God on your account, as we night and day keep praying most earnestly that we may see your face, and may complete what is lacking in your faith? Now may our God and Father Himself and Jesus our Lord direct our way to you; and may the Lord cause you to increase and abound in love for one another, and for all men, just as we also *do* for you; so that He may establish your hearts unblamable in holiness before our God and Father at the coming of our Lord Jesus with all His saints (1 Thess. 3:9-13).[11]

---

10. Both the NEB and Phillips follow this interpretation that makes the Holy Spirit the *Agent* that fills the believer's life and not the *substance* with which he is filled.

11. This is spelled out more in detail in the verses that follow: "Finally then, brethren, we request and exhort you in the Lord Jesus that, as you received from us *instruction* as to how you ought to walk and please God (just as you actually do walk), that you may excel still more. For you know what commandments we gave you by *the authority of* the Lord Jesus. For this is the will of God, your sanctification; *that is,* that you abstain from sexual immorality; that each of you know how to possess his own vessel in sanctification and honor. . . . Now as to the love of the brethren, you have no need for *any one* to write to you, for you yourselves are taught by God to love one another; for indeed you do practice it toward all the brethren who are in all Macedonia. But we urge you, brethren, to excel still more" (1 Thess. 4:1-4, 9-10).

It is significant that Paul here identifies the increase of love with the establishment of their hearts unblamable in holiness. This will be examined more closely in the next section. Paul similarly prays that the love of the Philippians "may abound still more and more in real knowledge and discernment" (Phil. 1:9).

What is the source of this love? Without question it is possible *only* as the fruit of the Spirit. Paul would be the first to insist that the love he is concerned that they experience is not of human origin. "The love of God has been poured out within our hearts through the Holy Spirit who was given to us" (Rom. 5:5). So the imperative to experience and express love is simply an indirect imperative to walk by the Spirit.

Paul's imperative, to live by the Spirit, has a startling relevance to the Church of Jesus Christ today. His concern for converts recently emancipated from the grip of the dark, evil world of his day is many times voiced by spiritual shepherds for their flock in this supposedly enlightened age. The church pew is often filled by those who are no longer the victims of sin. Through faith in the Cross they have been set free and now have a new life in Christ. They *are* new men, free men, and spiritual men. It can be said of them that they have a new basis of existence because they, who were once dead, are now spiritually alive.

But, although they no longer live in the world under the sovereignty of sin, they do not live in the world under the sovereignty of the Spirit. Instead they live in that shadowy no-man's-land under the sovereignty of self. They live in their own strength and discipline and consequently all too often are spiritually discouraged and defeated. Of even more far-reaching consequence, they do not experience the power of the Holy Spirit in their lives in its manifold *positive* expressions.

Paul's imperative is very fitting to them. Use the resources that are yours in Christ! You are alive in the Holy Spirit; now let Him be the *means* of your living. Live and walk by the Holy Spirit!

All too often the fears of the Judaizers in Galatia are modernized. No man *wants* to return to the old life in sin, so a legalistic cloak is fashioned as a safeguard and protection. Religion becomes *primarily* a matter of following and defending a set of rules and regulations. The believer is entangled in the web of a *works*-righteousness that very easily becomes a *self*-righteousness.

Paul's warning is solemn and searching. How often in the history of the Church the legalistic "letter" has destroyed the spirit of holiness. A self-righteous, cutting, critical, condemning spirit develops that is in direct opposition to love.

Equally valid is Paul's faith. There is another way besides the alternatives of legalism and license—it is the life under the Spirit. Living by the Spirit and walking under His discipline gives victory over sin and the rich fruitage of His grace.

If this is so, as Paul makes abundantly clear, then why does not the new man automatically live by the Spirit? This too Paul explains in his final imperative, to which this study now turns.

Chapter 20

Present Yourselves

It has been seen that before the new man there is the choice of two ways to live—by the flesh, with its works; or by the Spirit, with its fruit. Only as he lives by the Spirit can he fulfill Paul's imperative to victorious living. It would seem that this choice would be a natural and almost automatic development in the life of the believer. The alternatives are so glaringly obvious that he should, by reason of what has already happened to him, walk right on into the wonderful life under the Spirit, with all that it encompasses. Many of Paul's interpreters assume that this is so and stop their study of his thought at the point arrived at in the last chapter.

Yet such a happy result is clearly not the case. If it were so, then why is Paul so concerned? If it were a natural development, there would be no need for admonition and exhortation, and even warning. The testimony of modern Christian experience is that it simply does not happen that way.

Instead, so often today as in Paul's day, the new man in Christ lives in that shadowy no-man's-land under self. It has been repeatedly seen that Paul does not *explicitly* describe this world under self. However, it can be easily identified, by implication and logical deduction, because Paul makes it very clear where the believer is *not living*. He *no longer* is living in the world under sin and is *not yet* living in the world under the Spirit.

The big issue is: Why? Why does not the new man move right into this wonderful new world under the sovereignty of the Spirit? What is wrong? Furthermore, what can be done about it? What is

Paul's remedy? Most creeds recognize that original sin *remains* in the life of the believer. The major differences arise over the questions of whether or not it *reigns* and when and how it is *removed*. This study is not concerned with a critique of these various theological interpretations. What is important to this study is that in many theologies the remaining original sin is not related to the problem identified here, because original sin is associated with man's flesh (outer man) and not with man's heart (inner man).

When original sin is understood as self-sovereignty, its vital relationship to the problem at hand is readily seen. *In order to live and walk by the Spirit a man must live under the sovereignty of the Spirit.* That is the heart of the matter! The Holy Spirit must *control* the believer who lives under His discipline. Such is impossible unless the Spirit is Sovereign or Ruler of his life. It is not possible to live under the sovereignty of self and the sovereignty of the Spirit at the same time. Only one can rule—not two! It is impossible to fulfill the imperative to live by the Spirit as long as the new man is sovereign of his own soul.

God Almighty respects man's sovereignty, and will not transgress or abuse it. He will no more violate man's sovereignty at the point of commitment, as a believer, than He would at the point of conversion, as a sinner. Man must use his freedom to choose to be saved, and must make an equally free choice in surrendering his sovereignty. This is the point of Paul's final imperative, based on the indicative of what God has already done for the believer in Christ, and on the challenge of allowing God to do much more.

> And do not go on presenting the members of your body to sin *as* instruments of unrighteousness; but present yourselves to God as those alive from the dead, and your members *as* instruments of righteousness to God (Rom. 6:13). I am speaking in human terms because of the weakness of your flesh. For just as you presented your members *as* slaves to impurity and to lawlessness, resulting in *further* lawlessness, so now present your members *as* slaves to righteousness, resulting in sanctification (Rom. 6:19). I urge you therefore, brethren, by the mercies of God, to present your bodies a living and holy sacrifice, acceptable to God, *which is* your spiritual service of worship (Rom. 12:1).

Paul uses a very significant term that is translated above as "present" *(paristēmi)*. In its transitive sense it literally means to stand or place beside and thus means to put at someone's disposal.

It is used to present someone to someone (cf. Acts 23:33; 2 Cor. 11: 2; Luke 2:22).

In Romans 6, Paul pictures sin as a cruel slave master who lords it over the sinner, particularly his body. However, this slavery is *in the past* and believers must not allow sin to reign any longer (cf. v. 12). They had been the slaves of sin (cf. vv. 17, 20), but had been set free in Christ (cf. vv. 18, 20). Furthermore, they had become the slaves of God and righteousness (cf. vv. 18, 22).

It seems strange that Paul should say they *were already* the slaves of God, because the whole object of his imperatives in this chapter is that they might *become* God's slaves. The key is that he is alluding to slavery in at least *two senses*. This is an excellent example of the difficulty that the modern student of the Bible has in grasping the significance of a metaphor taken from a culture completely foreign to his own. However, those to whom Paul was writing would immediately see the significance of his distinction. A man was a slave in two senses—by *ownership* and *servitude*. He not only *was* a slave but *served* as a slave (the distinction between being and doing). Under the slavery of sin there was little practical distinction. *Servitude was compulsive.* Every slave served. However, in Christ it is far different. *Servitude is by choice.* Every believer is God's slave *in terms of ownership;* he belongs to God. He has been purchased by redemption. But, although he is God's slave by ownership, the new man does not necessarily serve as a slave. He is free to serve or not to serve.

This is precisely the sad situation. Although these believers belonged to God as His slaves, they obviously were not serving Him as slaves. This is what so distressed the apostle's heart. They as sin's slaves had given, by compulsion, total servitude; but as God's slaves they were giving, by choice, very little service. This is not right. Their new Master deserves the same wholehearted service that they once gave to their old slave master—sin.

> I am speaking in human terms because of the weakness of your flesh. For just as you presented your members *as* slaves to impurity and to lawlessness, resulting in *further* lawlessness, so now present your members *as* slaves to righteousness, resulting in sanctification (Rom. 6:19).

Paul appeals to their sense of rightness, alluding to what would be fair in the strictly human plane of reference. Just as they had served sin as slaves, so now they should present themselves as slaves to God.

Yet this is precisely the situation all too often today. Men and women who once served sin so *wholeheartedly* and who now are free from that galling bondage, now serve God so *halfheartedly*. The answer lies in Paul's imperative.

Paul exhorts them not to go on *presenting* the members of their bodies as the slaves of sin and as instruments of unrighteousness (cf. v. 13). *The power of sin has been broken and this old servitude must cease.* He therefore admonishes them to *present* themselves to God as those who are alive from the dead and to *present* their members to God as instruments of righteousness (cf. vv. 13, 19). *What is of utmost significance is that Paul changes the tenses of the imperatives in verse 13.* They were to "present no more" (*present* imperative), but they were to "present themselves and their members" (*aorist* imperative). The same aorist construction is repeated in verse 19.

The basic significance of the aorist *aktionsart* (kind of action) is that it depicts a *crisis act* in distinction from a *progressive process*. It is true, as in all grammatical constructions in the Greek New Testament, that the technical meaning of the aorist tense cannot always be demonstrated. However, the *pointed contrast* between the present and aorist imperatives *in the same verse* does underscore a significance that is unmistakable. Paul's imperative calls for a crucial, crisis act of presentation.[1]

Furthermore, as noted by Blass and DeBrunner in their authoritative Greek grammar,[2] the aorist tense indicates activity and the commencement of a way of life. It is the coming about of *conduct* which contrasts with previous conduct. As repeatedly

---

1. Cf. the rules for interpreting the *aktionsart* in the imperative mood when there is a possibility of ambiguity, C. F. D. Moule, *Idiom Book of NT Greek*, p. 136. Roger Hahn, in a seminar research paper that analyzed every Pauline usage of the aorist imperative, concludes: "Paul was very careful in his use of the aorist imperative. With only a few exceptions, the evidence that he purposely chose the aorist imperative to express the full aorist *aktionsart* appeared close by within the context."

2. F. Blass & A. DeBrunner: *A Greek Grammar of the NT and Other Early Christian Literature*, tr. & rev. by Robert W. Funk (Chicago: University of Chicago Press, 1961), p. 173.

noted above, life by the Spirit represents a *marked change in living*. There are the imperatives that indicate *progress* (walking), but it is absolutely necessary to presuppose *a crisis that initiates* these progressive imperatives. Paul uses the aorist imperative here to emphasize the crisis which *commences* the new way of living.

The great significance of the crisis is seen in the metaphor that lies behind it. Paul is calling for the enslavement of servitude. In the year of jubilee every Jewish slave was freed by law. However, it was not uncommon for a slave not to want his freedom, which was now his by law. There was a provision whereby he and his master could appear before the magistrate, where the slave would express his *choice* to remain as a slave although he was *legally* a free man. Such a one was commonly called a love slave. The slave's ear would be pierced by an awl, which was the mark of a love slave (cf. Exod. 21:1-6).

This is the metaphor that lies behind Paul's imperative. He is appealing to these men of faith, now alive from the dead, to voluntarily present themselves to God as His love slaves. Now that they were free from sin's slavery, they could by choice be enslaved as love slaves to God. This would settle the problem of servitude.

The term "present" also is a technical term in the language of sacrifice. It means to present an offering, and it is in this sense that Paul uses the term in Rom. 12:1: "I urge you therefore, brethren, by the mercies of God, to present your bodies a living and holy sacrifice, acceptable to God, *which is* your spiritual service of worship." Here he exhorts[3] the believers to *present* their bodies to God, as a priest makes his sacrifice. Their bodies are living, holy, and acceptable. Such is to be their spiritual service of worship.[4] Again the aorist tense is used, pointing to a crisis presentation, even as the priest offers his sacrifice upon the altar.

Paul is calling for the surrender of the sovereignty that was usurped in the Garden of Eden. This must not be misunderstood as the surrender of freedom.[5] The new man uses his freedom to sur-

---

3. The form is *parastēsai* (aorist infinitive), which is the objective complement of the word of exhortation ("I urge," *parakalō*). It is imperatival in force.

4. The term "spiritual" *(logikēn)* can also mean rational (cf. the margin of the NASB).

5. Sovereignty is the power of *control* and freedom is the power of *choice*.

render the sovereign control of his life to God. As man surrenders his sovereignty—as he *releases* it—God *removes* it. It is vital that this be understood. Too often in evangelical theology this is confused with a decision of dedication or even consecration, *which is strictly a human act.* Nothing could be further from the truth! Original sin, or self-sovereignty, can't be simply laid aside by the act of man. It is too much a part of man. It can be removed only by God, but He will do so only as man releases it by free choice.

This is precisely why, in the fullest sense, Christ cannot be *received* as Lord. The new man must *make* Christ Lord when he surrenders his sovereignty, permitting God to remove it from his heart. Then, and only then, can Christ begin to reign and rule in the believer's life as Lord. The crucial question is: Sovereignty over what? It is sovereignty, not over the old self in sin, but *over the new* man. Only after a man has received this new life can he grasp the full significance of surrendered sovereignty.

When the new man releases his sovereignty so that God may remove it from his heart, one of the greatest of all miracles takes place. With self-sovereignty gone there is a fusion of the human and divine spirits into one spirit.

> Do you not know that your bodies are members of Christ? Shall I then take away the members of Christ and make them members of a harlot? May it never be! Or do you not know that the one who joins himself to a harlot is one body *with her?* For He says, "THE TWO WILL BECOME ONE FLESH." But the one who joins himself to the Lord is one spirit *with Him* (1 Cor. 6:15-17).

Of all sins, immorality appeared the most abhorrent to Paul because the guilty person *became one body* with the harlot. He says this must not be, because their bodies were members of Christ. Even more so: "The one who joins himself to the Lord is *one spirit* with Him." Such is impossible as long as self-sovereignty remains, but once removed by God, this is the glorious result. The union is such—with the Spirit of God indwelling man and man living and walking in the strength and power of the Spirit—that they are one spirit. Christ is truly Lord, as the new man is one spirit with Him.[6]

---

6. This illustrates the importance of understanding Pauline anthropology. The believer is united with Christ *in the inner man* and for him to be united with a harlot *in the outer man* was unthinkable.

It is this oneness of Spirit with the Lord that Paul describes in Gal. 2:20:

> I have been crucified with Christ; and it is no longer I who live, but Christ lives in me; and the *life* which I now live in the flesh I live by faith in the Son of God, who loved me, and delivered Himself up for me.

The result of Paul's crucifixion with Christ is more striking when the word order in the Greek text is literally translated into English: "I live no longer I *[ego]*, but lives in me Christ." The emphatic first person pronoun *(ego)* could simply be a reflexive emphatic construction and thus be translated: "I myself no longer live." However, in the light of what follows, it is much more significant. Paul is saying: I live no longer *as I once did,* but in a new way—*no longer I,* now Christ lives in me—He is the Lord of my new life.

Paul lives "no longer I" because in a crisis capitulation he had surrendered his sovereignty. He *was* "no longer I." Thus he could write elsewhere: "For to me, to live is Christ" (Phil. 1:21).

It is important to recognize that death with Christ encompasses the whole scope of salvation. Every benefit and blessing of the gospel is made possible by the Cross and the believer's identification with it through faith. This includes not only freedom from the *power* of sin, but deliverance from the very *presence* of sin; namely, self-sovereignty.

Without question a study of Pauline thought plainly reveals that his most extensive imperatives are: (1) Sin must cease! and (2) Live (walk) by the Spirit! These emphases have been termed, above, the *continuing companionship.* Undoubtedly they are the predominant imperatives.

The all-important question is: Why? Does this mean that they are all that is important? Many students of Paul form this conclusion and stop with the imperative of Chapter 19—"Live by the Spirit." Is it because the *crisis commitment* is of little importance that it is not spelled out repeatedly?

The results of this study make such a conclusion totally untenable. Instead, two suggested explanations can be given as to *why* Paul's imperative of the crisis commitment is not given more extensively. In the first place, the necessity of such a crisis commitment should be so obvious that it can be properly assumed. Paul's repeated emphasis on living by the Spirit clearly assumes that such is possible only under the sovereignty of the Spirit. It goes without saying that one cannot *live* under the sovereignty of the Spirit until he *surrenders* to the Spirit and makes Him sovereign. Such necessitates a crisis. It cannot, by the very nature of the situation, be a repeated human decision.

In the second place the crisis commitment is *instrumental* in value. The total value of the crisis commitment is to be found in *what it makes possible*. This can be quite easily illustrated. If a valuable treasure was housed in an enclosed room, which had one door as its only means of entrance, that door would be of great value—but only instrumentally. Its total value would be that it was the only way into the treasure room, where the intrinsic values were located. One would certainly not spend a great deal of time talking about the value of the door, but instead would speak of the intrinsic value of the treasure.

So Paul gives major emphasis, not to the instrumental value of the *crisis commitment* which is the way into the treasure, but instead to the intrinsic value of the *continuing companionship* which is the treasure itself. It is true that God removes original sin from the heart of the new man in response to his crisis commitment. But the crucial question is: Why? Does God cleanse a man's heart simply to make it clean—as an end in itself? This would be no more so than for a man to open the door to a treasure room and proudly proclaim: I have the door open! There is only one reason for opening the door and that is to go through it to discover the treasure. If the removal of original sin from the believer's heart was of intrinsic value, then the threat of pharisaical self-righteousness would be irresistible. No! The value of a clean heart is not intrinsic but instrumental—it is what it makes possible.

However, this does not mean for a moment that the crisis commitment has no value. It is of absolutely indispensable value, but not intrinsically. Its value is to be found in what it opens the way to.

The twofold nature of Christian experience is remarkably parallel to a present-day understanding of total self-realization or self-fulfillment. According to this psychological analysis a man can become a real person only by *first* gaining a sense of freedom. To the degree he is enslaved to anyone or anything he is not a real person. This is the struggle of adolescence—to find such freedom.

Then, when freedom is once experienced, personhood can be fully realized only through a *second* step, consisting of the free giving of oneself to others. The attempt to keep to oneself this freedom is to lose it. Is this not exactly what the Master Teacher taught?

> And He was saying to *them* all, "If anyone wishes to come after Me, let him deny himself, and take up his cross daily, and follow Me. For whoever wishes to save his life shall lose it, but whoever loses his life for My sake, he is the one who will save it. For what is a man profited if he gains the whole world, and loses or forfeits himself?" (Luke 9:23-25).

The treasure of life lived under the Spirit is beyond adequate description. When Paul contemplated the treasure and the mystery of God's wisdom in the gospel, he borrowed some thrilling words from Isaiah.

> "THINGS WHICH EYE HAS NOT SEEN AND EAR HAS NOT HEARD, AND *which* HAVE NOT ENTERED THE HEART OF MAN, ALL THAT GOD HAS PREPARED FOR THOSE WHO LOVE HIM." For to us God revealed *them* through the Spirit; for the Spirit searches all things, even the depths of God (1 Cor. 2:9-10).

It is to this rich treasure that the final section turns, examining briefly the new man living under the Spirit.

PART V

THE NEW MAN: LIVING BY THE SPIRIT

A New Enablement
Bearing Spiritual Fruit
Working Out Salvation
Conforming to His Image
Holy yet Human
Finishing the Race

Chapter 21

A New Enablement

Paul's repeated imperatives can perhaps be best summarized as: Use the resources that are already yours in Christ. The new man, living by the Spirit, *does* exactly that! However, it is of crucial importance to emphasize that there is nothing automatic about such living. Life by the Spirit is a *personal relationship* that must be cultivated and maintained. When the new man fails to use the resources that are his, the result can only be existence in his own strength.

The experience of most men reveals the need of constant renewal and revival—it is an essential part of humanity. This is one of the blessed ministries of the Spirit—quickening, awakening, and renewal. When the new man lives in his own strength, he faces the threat of spiritual failure. It *can* result in sin! On the other hand it need not be sin—properly so called. However, as the believer walks with God, he receives more spiritual enlightenment and consequently his spiritual understanding is sensitized and refined. That which one day might have been a point of innocent oblivion often develops into an issue of responsible conscience.

Yet it must be remembered that the crisis of released and removed sovereignty makes a crucial difference in the life of the new man. Christian experience graphically reveals that to lapse into periods of dependence upon human strength, due to preoccupation or even spiritual carelessness, is *distinctly different* than to live in the no-man's-land under the sovereignty of self. It is basically the distinction between *independence* and *insensitivity*.

As long as man lives on earth he will need to be resensitized, and even reawakened by the Spirit.

It is significant that Paul does not appeal to the new man under the Spirit through a direct imperative. He never explicitly says: Live like this! or, Let your life be such! or even, You must grow! The new man is not enslaved by law—even a new law of living. Instead Paul's concern is that the new man maintain a dynamic *personal* relationship with the Spirit—*who is a Person!* Life, totally new and revolutionary, is the natural *by-product* of such a relationship.

Paul has a very special term, *energeō*,[1] to describe this activity of the Spirit in and through the new man. Unfortunately it is often translated as "work," just like the more common term for "to work" *(ergadzomai)*. Instead, *energeō* carries the basic significance of an influence or enablement *from outside of man* and is regularly used by Paul to depict the operation of the Spirit in the new man.[2] The modern transliteration of the term is *energy* and *energize*. The work of the Spirit in the new man is more than an impersonal force or power. *The Spirit energizes man* through a dynamic personal relationship. This is dramatically seen in Phil. 2:12-13. Paul admonished the believers:

> So then, my beloved, just as you have always obeyed, not as in my presence only, but now much more in my absence, work out *[katergadzomai]* your salvation with fear and trembling (Phil. 2: 12).

Then he adds: "For it is God who is at work *[energeō]* in you, both to will and to work *[energeō]* for *His* good pleasure" (Phil. 2:13). Very significantly Paul *changed terms* for "work," in order to emphasize the nature of the work of the Spirit (cf. Gal. 3:5). Paul

---

1. *Energeō* is a distinctively Pauline term. Of the 21 times it is found in the NT, he uses it 18 times. In the Synoptics (Matt. 14:2; Mark 6:14) it is used to refer to the unusual powers of Jesus, whom Herod thought was John the Baptist raised from the dead. Jas. 5:16 is the only other place it is found. The two nouns *(energeia, energēma)* are found only in Paul (18 times) and the adjective *(energēs)* is used twice by Paul and once in Hebrews (4:12).

2. Arndt and Gingrich state that the noun is used "always of supernatural beings," a meaning that is found also in the verb and adjective forms. Even in the reference to the sinful passions "working" (Rom. 7:5), there are the clear overtones of a power greater than man.

uses this significant term several times, and the recognition of the specific meaning greatly increases the understanding of his message. The following two references are excellent examples.

> Now to Him who is able to do exceeding abundantly beyond all that we ask or think, according to the power that works *[energeō]* within us (Eph. 3:20). And for this purpose also I labor, striving according to His power, which mightily works *[energeō]* within me (Col. 1:29).

Specifically the *energizing* of the Spirit results in a life of love. "For in Christ Jesus neither circumcision nor uncircumcision means anything, but faith working *[energeō]* through love" (Gal. 5: 6). The new man is liberated to love, as Paul goes on in this context to describe: "For you were called to freedom, brethren; only *do* not *turn* your freedom into an opportunity for the flesh, but through love serve one another" (Gal. 5:13). The new man lives under the *link of love* rather than the old *lash of the law*.

The question is often asked: What is the vital difference in the life of the new man under the sovereignty of the Spirit? As noted above, it is *not* the total absence of failure. If the new man has at least a measure of faith, hope, and love, with its certainty and concern, *before,* while he is still living under self, then what is the basic difference? It can perhaps best be described as *consistency* and *prospect*.

Nothing is more characteristic of life in the no-man's-land under self than *inconsistency*—repeated defeats, an up-and-down experience. Also, such a life is so preoccupied with gaining victory over the flesh that it is impossible to discover the treasure of spiritual living that God has provided.

The *energy* of the Spirit *through* the life of the new man can be seen in several dimensions. These will be examined in the following chapters, any of which could be expanded into a separate study. Of necessity, the treatment below must be brief.

Chapter 22

Bearing Spiritual Fruit

Paul wrote to the Colossians:

> For this reason also, since the day we heard *of it,* we have not ceased to pray for you and to ask that you may be filled with the knowledge of His will in all spiritual wisdom and understanding, so that you may walk in a manner worthy of the Lord, to please *Him* in all respects, bearing fruit in every good work and increasing in the knowledge of God; strengthened with all power, according to His glorious might, for the attaining of all steadfastness and patience, joyously (Col. 1:9-11).

Later chapters will deal with the matters of the worthy walk and growing, but this chapter is concerned with Paul's prayerful concern that these believers *bear fruit.*

The new life of the man of faith was defined in terms of faith, hope, and love that found expression in confidence and concern. This is basically the fruit of the Spirit and is ever increasingly borne in the life of the new man through the energizing of the Spirit. Yet, as has been stated, the mark of the man still living under the sovereignty of self is a lack of spiritual consistency. He often finds himself defeated and frustrated as the result of living by his own strength, which is all too often only weakness. In contrast, when he moves under the sovereignty of the Spirit, these fruits are harvested in ever increasing supply. They are basically the expression of love *(agape)*—in action.

An exploration of this aspect of the energizing of the Spirit in the believer's life has almost limitless possibilities. We can examine only a few of the more crucial areas of expression.

What is more needed and desired today than *inward strength?* All about are those who go to pieces under the pressures of daily living. It is not a matter of being overwhelmed by outward forces against which they are no match, but the problem lies in an *inner flaw* or weakness. They are simply not equal to life!

Fanaticism at this point is heartless and cruel. Not all sickness is sin, and such a suggestion is both unscriptural and unrealistic. Organic illness is all too real. Sometimes only God knows—and those who have suffered similarly—how real shattered nerves can be.

Further, sometimes the cause for inner weakness is a totally unreasonable work schedule which abuses body, mind, and nerves. God won't compensate for man's foolishness or greed! When such is motivated by an insatiable pursuit of mammon, a man's sense of values acutely needs reexamination.

This is a sad state of affairs for *any* person, but it is no less than tragic for the child of God. It is not God's intention that *any man* find himself unequal to meet the demands and pressures of normal daily living.

Yet, when all of these exceptions are made, still the main reason why so many believers break under the pressure of life, or endure a miserable existence of defeat, is basic inner weakness. This is true of the mother whose work is never done; who faces the pressures of the home, the family budget, sickness, upset plans, unexpected emergencies, problems with children, and a hundred or more other things. Husbands and fathers must face the pressures of working in an evil world; of job security, unreasonable demands, and endless financial obligations. The youth of this day have their own peculiar pressures and problems, which are all magnified by the conviction that the older generation does not understand them.

So, all too often the new man—living in his own strength—lives a life of fret, worry, discouragement, anxiety, fear, impatience, irritability, and spiritual defeat. He is torn apart within, and if this does not result in an outward physical or nervous breakdown, he endures an existence of inner misery.

What makes this so tragic is that God promises and provides inner strength, through the energizing of the Spirit, as the new man lives in a dynamic, personal relationship with Him. *The man of faith can be strengthened!*—"strengthened with all power, according to His glorious might, for the attaining of all steadfastness and patience, joyously" (Col. 1:11).

This is most dramatically depicted in the promise of peace throughout the New Testament. Paul opens Romans with the apostolic blessing (Rom. 1:7) and ends it with the apostolic benediction (Rom. 15:33)—both of which *feature* peace. His earnest wish is: "Now may the God of hope fill you with all joy and peace in believing, that you may abound in hope by the power of the Holy Spirit" (Rom. 15:13). To the Colossians he wrote: "And let the peace of Christ rule in your hearts, to which indeed you were called in one body; and be thankful" (Col. 3:15). The armor of God provides just such a protection:

> Finally, be strong in the Lord, and in the strength of His might. Put on the full armor of God, that you may be able to stand firm against the schemes of the devil. For our struggle is not against flesh and blood, but against the rulers, against the powers, against the world-forces of this darkness, against the spiritual *forces* of wickedness in the heavenly *places.* Therefore take up the full armor of God, that you may be able to resist in the evil day, and having done everything, to stand firm. Stand firm therefore, HAVING GIRDED YOUR LOINS WITH TRUTH, and HAVING PUT ON THE BREASTPLATE OF RIGHTEOUSNESS, and having shod YOUR FEET WITH THE PREPARATION OF THE GOSPEL OF PEACE; in addition to all, taking up the shield of faith with which you will be able to extinguish all the flaming missiles of the evil *one.* And take the helmet of salvation, and the sword of the Spirit, which is the word of God (Eph. 6:10-17).

Even more pointedly, the promise of peace is directly related to living under the Spirit. Peace is one of the fruits of the Spirit (cf. Gal. 5:22), and "the mind set on the Spirit is life and peace" (Rom. 8:6).

But no promise in all of Paul's letters is more meaningfully related to the inward strength that the peace of God's presence brings than the following:

> Be anxious for nothing, but in everything by prayer and supplication with thanksgiving let your requests be made known to God. And the peace of God, which surpasses all comprehension, shall guard your hearts and your minds in Christ Jesus. . . . and the God of peace shall be with you (Phil. 4:6-7, 9).

God's peace *surpasses all comprehension.* It is worth more than all understanding. So often men think that the all-important thing is understanding, but it can still leave frustration and despair within. Instead, peace "guards with a garrison"[1] both the heart and mind of the believer—the inner man.

This inward peace is a fruit borne in the life of the new man as he lives under the Spirit. The energizing of the Spirit produces inner confidence and assurance, a rest of mind and heart, as the man of faith lives under love and not under Law. Harriet Beecher Stowe has put this into verse.

THE PEACE OF GOD

When winds are raging o'er the upper ocean,
And billows wild contend with angry roar,
'Tis said, far down beneath the wild commotion,
That peaceful stillness reigneth evermore.

Far, far beneath the noise of tempest dieth,
And silver waves chime ever peacefully;
And no rude storm, how fierce so e'er he flieth,
Disturbs the Sabbath of that deeper sea.

So to the soul that knows Thy Love, O Purest,
There is a temple peaceful evermore;
And all the babble of life's angry voices
Dies hushed in stillness at its sacred door.

Far, far away the noise of passion dieth,
And loving thoughts rise ever peacefully;
And no rude storm, how fierce so e'er he flieth,
Disturbs that deeper rest, O Lord, in Thee.

O rest of rest! O peace serene, eternal!
Thou ever livest, and Thou changest never;
And in the secret of Thy presence dwelleth
Fullness of joy, forever, and forever.

---

1. This is one of Paul's most vivid metaphors. The Greek word *(phroureō)* alludes to the Roman practice of guarding or securing a captured city with a garrison or military guard (cf. 2 Cor. 11:32). Thus God's peace is a garrison.

With such peace the new man of faith, living under the Spirit, faces each day in the confidence that "my God shall supply all your needs according to His riches in glory in Christ Jesus" (Phil. 4:19).

A second area in the life of the new man where he experiences the energizing influence of the Spirit is that of *dynamic power*. Not only must the believer possess inward strength, but his life should also evidence the power of God in outward influence.

The power of evil is vivid and spectacular. It can be seen on every hand in the growth of crime, the decadence of moral values, widespread dishonesty and deceit, the breakdown of family life, juvenile *and* parental deliquency, drunkenness and drug addiction. This period in history is witnessing an immoral revolution of shocking proportions.

In striking contrast to the power of evil is the weakness and impotence of the Christian witness—individual and collective. Exactly how much influence does the Christian Church have in modern society? Is her voice *really* heard in the affairs of the community, the state, the nation, and the world? Even more pointedly, what influence does the individual believer have in his neighborhood, at work, in the school?

History shows unmistakably that this need not be so. The exploits of a handful of dedicated disciples in Acts, the impact of Luther in Germany, of Calvin and Zwingli in Switzerland, of Knox in Scotland, of Wesley in England, and of Finney and Moody in America—all give eloquent testimony of the dynamic power of God working through the lives of men. To these could be added numberless multitudes of unknown men of faith who have influenced their world for God and righteousness.

God would energize men who are weak in themselves and make them powerful against the forces of evil.

> For consider your call, brethren, that there were not many wise according to the flesh, not many mighty, not many noble; but God has chosen the foolish things of the world to shame the wise, and God has chosen the weak things of the world to shame the things which are strong, and the base things of the world and the despised, God has chosen, the things that are not, that He might nullify the things that are (1 Cor. 1:26-28).

Men of faith today need a new realization that all things are theirs in Christ.

So then let no one boast in men. For all things belong to you, whether Paul or Apollos or Cephas or the world or life or death or things present or things to come; all things belong to you, and you belong to Christ; and Christ belongs to God (1 Cor. 3:21-23).

Paul's understanding of the power that God has ready to exert on man's behalf staggers the imagination.

I pray that the eyes of your heart may be enlightened, so that you may know what is the hope of His calling, what are the riches of the glory of His inheritance in the saints, and what is the surpassing greatness of His power toward us who believe. *These are* in accordance with the working of the strength of His might which He brought about in Christ, when He raised Him from the dead, and seated Him at His right hand in the heavenly *places,* far above all rule and authority and power and dominion, and every name that is named, not only in this age, but also in the one to come. And He put all things in subjection under His feet, and gave Him as head over all things to the church, which is His body, the fulness of Him who fills all in all (Eph. 1:18-23).

This power that God used to raise Christ from the dead is not only *experienced in* spiritual resurrection from the death of sin, which Paul proceeds to describe (cf. Eph. 2:1-10), but is also *exercised through* the life of the man of faith. Paul's prayer that God "would grant you, according to the riches of His glory, to be strengthened with power through His Spirit in the inner man" (Eph. 3:16) is based on the conviction that God "is able to do exceeding abundantly beyond all that we ask or think, according to the power that works within us" (Eph. 3:20). The believer today needs to hear again Paul's exhortation to Timothy, his son in the gospel.

And for this reason I remind you to kindle afresh the gift of God which is in you through the laying on of my hands. For God has not given us a spirit of timidity, but of power and love and discipline (2 Tim. 1:6-7).

One cause of impotence is the failure to appreciate the manner in which the dynamic power of the Spirit is received. All too often this power is viewed as a gift that God dramatically deposits in the heart of man in some climactic experience, and from then on he is empowered by this supernatural energy cell within. Nothing could be further from the truth. The power of the Spirit *cannot be stored up* for the simple reason that it *is dynamic.* Just like the electrical power that energizes great cities cannot be stored up, but is available only as the great power cables are attached to the huge dynamos that supply it, so the power of the Spirit is experienced only as man lives in a dynamic personal relationship with the Spirit. As the new man lives under the Spirit, he will know this power in his life.

The third area of expression of the energizing of the Spirit in the life of the new man is seen in the fruit of a *compelled witness*. It is highly questionable if Paul ever used the term and concept of *fruit (karpos)* to refer to the winning of converts to Christ,[2] but the compassion that motivates the witnessing, resulting in such soul winning, is certainly a fruit.

As the believer becomes preoccupied with the needs and problems of his own life, it is very easy to be indifferent and even callous to the needs of others. We have seen that the life of the new man in Christ is characterized by *agape* concern, specifically toward the brethren. If this is so, then why is it that the heart of the believer is often without compassion? Certainly the New Testament makes it abundantly clear that God expects men to have compassion like their Lord. The difficulty must be in the failure to understand that a heart of compassion is not created or maintained by man. Instead, it is one of the fruits of living under the Spirit. As noted earlier, love *(agape)* is the specific manner in which the Spirit energizes the new man. Faith works through love (Gal. 5:6)! There is a sense in which all of the fruits of the Spirit are love in action.

> Now if your experience of Christ's encouragement and love means anything to you, if you have known something of the fellowship of his Spirit, and all that it means in kindness and deep sympathy, do make my best hopes for you come true! Live together in harmony, live together in love, as though you had only one mind and one spirit between you. Never act from motives of rivalry or personal vanity, but in humility think more of one another than you do of yourselves. None of you should think only of his own affairs, but each should learn to see things from other people's point of view (Phil. 2:1-4, Phillips).

---

2. Such references as Gal. 5:22; Rom. 6:21-22; Eph. 5:9; Phil. 1:11; Rom. 7:4-5; Col. 1:10 all clearly refer to spiritual qualities within the life of the believer. In Rom. 1:13 and Col. 1:6 the meaning is unclear, but probably should be understood by the clear usage of the term elsewhere.

The result of the experience of Christ's encouragement and love and the fellowship of His Spirit is that men live together in harmony and love. There is a oneness of mind and spirit between them. This is because they "do not *merely* look out for their [your] own personal interests, but also for the interests of others" (Phil. 2:4). True humility is put to the test when others are regarded as superior to yourself (cf. v. 3.). It cannot be too strongly emphasized that the compassion which makes this possible is from the experience of Christ's love and the *fellowship of His Spirit.* Concern for others comes directly from companionship with the Spirit.

But the believer's compelled witness is not only within the circle of those of like faith. Flowing from the love of Christ in his heart, the new man living under the Spirit has a compelling concern for those outside of Christ.

> For if we are beside ourselves, it is for God; if we are of sound mind, it is for you. For the love of Christ controls us (2 Cor. 5:13-14). Therefore from now on we recognize no man according to the flesh. . . . Therefore if any man is in Christ, *he is* a new creature; the old things passed away; behold, new things have come. Now all *these* things are from God, who reconciled us to Himself through Christ, and gave us the ministry of reconciliation, namely, that God was in Christ reconciling the world to Himself, not counting their trespasses against them, and He has committed to us the word of reconciliation. Therefore, we are ambassadors for Christ, as though God were entreating through us; we beg you on behalf of Christ, be reconciled to God (2 Cor. 5:16-20).

Paul was beside himself with concern for lost men. The love of Christ had full control of him and was the very spring of his actions (cf. 2 Cor. 5:14, Phillips). He viewed men in a new light, not in outward appearance, but as the new creatures they could become in Christ. God had invested Paul—and all new men in Christ—with the ministry of reconciliation. The follower of Christ is to be His ambassador, through whom God can entreat men to be reconciled to himself, Christ.

As the new man lives under the Spirit, his heart will be moved to compassion for lost men—just like his Lord, when He confronted lost men. He has a compelled witness, due to the inner compulsion of love.

If Paul used the term *fruit* basically to refer to the spiritual qualities within the believer's own life, he most certainly related *gifts* to the outreach witness of the man of faith.

Now there are varieties of gifts, but the same Spirit. And there are varieties of ministries, and the same Lord. And there are varieties of effects *[energēma],* but the same God who works *[energeō]* all things in all *persons.* But to each one is given the manifestation of the Spirit for the common good. For to one is given the word of wisdom through the Spirit, and to another the word of knowledge according to the same Spirit; to another faith by the same Spirit, and to another gifts of healing by the one Spirit, and to another the effecting *[energēma]* of miracles, and to another prophecy, and to another the distinguishing of spirits, to another *various* kinds of tongues, and to another the interpretation of tongues. But one and the same Spirit works *[energeō]* all these things, distributing to each one individually just as He wills (1 Cor. 12:4-11; cf. 1 Cor. 12:28-31; Rom. 12:6).

We have seen that Paul uses his distinctive terms *(energeō, energēma)* for the energizing of the new man by the Spirit. It is through this enablement that the man of faith can effectively witness. The Holy Spirit operates through these gifts to reach other men. Still the more excellent way is the way of love (cf. 1 Cor. 12:31; 13:1-13). It is this way of love that is to be pursued (cf. 1 Cor. 14:1).

Of utmost significance to this study is the recognition and remembrance that the fruit, the gifts, and particularly the excelling way of love are *all* the result of the *energizing* of the Spirit as the new man lives under His sovereignty in a dynamic, personal companionship.

Chapter 23

Working Out Salvation

In the previous chapter the energizing of the Spirit in the life of the believer was emphasized. Now the other aspect of the dynamic relationship must be considered. As previously observed, Paul, in his letter to the Philippians, beautifully expressed the vital synthesis between man and the Spirit working through man:

> So then, my beloved, just as you have always obeyed, not as in my presence only, but now much more in my absence, work out your salvation with fear and trembling; for it is God who is at work in you, both to will and to work for *His* good pleasure (Phil. 2:12-13).

It must be emphasized that it is a synthesis—neither the Spirit *nor* man acts alone.

This must not be misunderstood to mean that it is human works *per se*. In the dynamic relationship, the Spirit so works through man that it can be accurately concluded that it is not man's work, but God's. The works are really the fruit of the indwelling Spirit in those who are obedient unto righteousness. Yet man does have a fundamental responsibility to *work out* his salvation.

The synergistic nature of salvation, with both man and the Spirit at work, is nowhere seen so graphically as in the area of *growth and development*. It is erroneous to suggest that immediately upon entrance into life under the sovereignty of the Spirit the new man will bear spiritual fruit *to a full and complete degree*. Paul's letters abound with metaphors of progress and development.

As suggested earlier, Paul does not *command* growth. Instead he sees growth as the by-product of the dynamic relationship between the new man and the Spirit. "We pray that you may bear fruit in active goodness of every kind, and grow in the knowledge of God" (Col. 1:10, NEB). Paul writes to the Thessalonians that he is thankful to God "because your faith is growing abundantly" (2 Thess. 1:3, RSV; cf. 2 Cor. 10:15). In a collective sense, the believer, as a part of the Church, grows. This Paul vividly describes in such passages as Eph. 2:21; 4:15-16; Col. 2:19.

In addition to these specific terms for growth,[1] Paul uses some graphic metaphors to portray the concept of growth. There are three that are closely related to each other in basic meaning, depicting a crescendo of ideas. First there is the term "to increase" *(pleonadzō)*, then the term "to fill" *(pleroō)*, and finally "to abound or overflow" *(perisseuō)*. Although these three terms are not generally used in direct relationship to each other, they will be examined in this manner in order to clearly show the basic concept of growth and development.

Not only is Paul thankful because the faith of the Thessalonians is growing but also because "the love of every one of you for one another is increasing" (2 Thess. 1:3, RSV). He prays that the Lord may "cause you to increase *[pleonadzō]* and abound *[perisseuō]* in love for one another, and for all men, just as we also *do* for you" (1 Thess. 3:12). Here the increase is related to abounding or overflowing.

Paul often speaks of growth in terms of the believer being filled or filled up *(pleroō)*, which in intrinsic meaning is an advance beyond simply increasing. He is concerned that the believer be filled with knowledge (Rom. 15:14), specifically of God's will (Col. 1:9). The man of faith will be sincere and blameless at the *Parousia* because he has "been filled with the fruit of righteousness which *comes* through Jesus Christ, to the glory and praise of God" (Phil. 1:11). The measure is to be "filled up to all the fulness of God" (Eph. 3:19).[2] Further, the Spirit is the *Agent* of filling in the life of

---

1. *Auxanō, auxēsis, huperauxanō.*
2. This translation captures the proper meaning of *eis* with the accusative. It should be translated "unto" rather than "with" (cf. Robertson and Davis, *A New Short Grammar*, pp. 224 f., and the ASV).

the believer, with Paul directly admonishing the believers to be filled by the Spirit (cf. Eph. 5:18).

Paul associated *fill* and *abound* in Rom. 15:13, when he writes: "Now may the God of hope fill you with all joy and peace in believing, that you may abound in hope by the power of the Holy Spirit." As observed above, Paul is concerned that the love of the Thessalonians both increase and abound (cf. 1 Thess. 3:12). He even more pointedly exhorts them: "For indeed you do practice it [love] toward all the brethren who are in all Macedonia. But we urge you, brethren, to excel [abound] still more" (1 Thess. 4:10). His prayer for the Philippians is that "your love may abound," which will result in "real knowledge and all discernment" (Phil. 1:9). Here a growth in knowledge is related to abounding love, which certainly is similar to being filled with knowledge, as seen above.

In one of his most graphic pictures of the result of growth, Paul states that the joy of the Macedonian believers had overflowed, along with their poverty, causing them to give liberally to assist the destitute saints in Jerusalem (cf. 2 Cor. 8:2). Thus Paul urged the Corinthians, who abounded in faith, utterance, knowledge, earnestness, and love, to also abound in this contribution, following the example of the Macedonians. It is out of the overflow that fullness of growth and development is found. "And God *is* able to make all grace abound toward you; that ye, always having all sufficiency in all *things,* may abound to every good work" (2 Cor. 9:8, KJV).

One additional metaphor of growth used by Paul is generally translated in the King James Version as "to edify" *(oikodomeō)* or "edification" *(oikodomē).* It is better understood as "to build" or "building." Paul wrote to the Colossians that the result of walking in Christ is that, among other things, they will be built up (Col. 2:7). The Romans were encouraged to "pursue the things which make for peace and the building up of one another" (Rom. 14:19; cf. Rom. 15:2; 1 Thess. 5:11).

Paul considered his apostolic authority to be a means of building up his converts (cf. 2 Cor. 10:8; 13:10) and viewed them as God's field and God's building in which he and God were fellow workers (cf. 1 Cor. 3:9). Thus he justified the defense of his apostleship as being for their edification (2 Cor. 12:19). The criterion for determining proper activity and conduct is not whether or not it is lawful, but whether or not it edifies (1 Cor. 10:23). It is love, of course, which edifies and this is of primary importance (cf. 1 Cor. 8:1; 13:1-13; 14:3 f.).

It is apparent that Paul did not view the life of the new man under the Spirit as one that bore fruit in maturity or was full-grown. Instead there was to be growth and development in knowledge, righteousness, thanksgiving, liberality, joy, peace, faith, and hope. Of supreme importance was the believer's growth in love *(agape).*

Quite similar to the concept of growth is Paul's concern that the man of faith become *established,* which can conceivably be viewed as an aspect of growth. It certainly is part of the process of working out salvation.

Sometimes the term "to be established" *(steridzō)* is used. Paul, who had not been to Rome, wrote to the church there, saying, "I long to see you in order that I may impart some spiritual gift to you, that you may be established" (Rom. 1:11). He closes the Roman letter with the following benediction: "Now to Him who is able to establish you according to my gospel and the preaching of Jesus Christ" (Rom. 16:25). Paul's expressed reason for sending Timothy to Thessalonica was "to establish you in your faith" (1 Thess. 3:2, RSV). But it is God who actually establishes the heart of the believer (cf. 2 Thess. 2:17; 3:3). Like so many concepts already examined in this and the previous chapter, the believer's establishment is directly related to love. This is not surprising, because it has been repeatedly seen that love is the *primary* result of the energizing of the Spirit in the life of the new man.

> And may the Lord cause you to increase and abound in love for one another, and for all men, just as we also *do* for you; so that He may establish your hearts unblamable in holiness before our God and Father at the coming of our Lord Jesus with all His saints (1 Thess. 3:12-13).

In the Ephesian and Colossian letters, the concept of establishment is depicted in agricultural ("rooted," *ridzoō*) and architectural ("founded" or "grounded," *themelioō*) metaphors. As the believer walks in Christ he is rooted as well as built up (cf. Col. 2:7), and if he continues in the faith he will be founded (cf. Col. 1:23). The two figures are brought together in Paul's prayer for the

Ephesians. "So that Christ may dwell in your hearts through faith; *and* that you, being rooted and grounded in love . . ." (Eph. 3:17).

In addition Paul uses a variety of other metaphorical terms to depict the basic concept of establishment. The term "confirm" *(bebaioō,* 1 Cor. 1:8) at times is translated as "establish" (cf. 2 Cor. 1:21; Col. 2:7). The terms "steadfast" *(hedraios)* and "unmoved" *(ametakinētos)* are used together (cf. 1 Cor. 15:58; Col. 1:23). There are a few times when the common word for "to stand" *(histēmi)* is used in this metaphorical sense of establishment (cf. Rom. 5:2; 1 Cor. 15:1). Finally, the believer must "continue" or abide *(epimenō)* (cf. Rom. 11:22; Col. 1:23).

It was pointed out that probably the primary characteristic of life under the sovereignty of the Spirit was consistency or establishment, in contrast to the up-and-down experience of the believer living in the no-man's-land under self. But it must be clearly seen that such is a matter of *becoming* and is part of working out salvation.

A specific area of establishment in the life of the new man under the Spirit can be identified as *victorious living.* As seen in the last section, this *begins* with victory over sin working through the flesh. Thus Paul promises: "But I say, walk by the Spirit, and you will not carry out the desire of the flesh" (Gal. 5:16). But such is *only* the beginning! Nothing could be more erroneous than the suggestion that when the believer walks by the Spirit he is spared temptation and adversity. This is simply not so!

The terms "temptation" *(peirasmos)* and "to tempt" *(peiradzō)* are often seriously misunderstood. In modern English, a synonym for *temptation* is *enticement*—obviously to evil. When the KJV was written this was not so, hence the confusion. The Greek term means basically to test or try, and only in a secondary and minor sense to entice to evil. Thus all enticement to evil is *peirasmos,* but the opposite is not true.

Of course, the new man living under the Spirit is tempted in the narrow sense of enticement to evil. There is no hope or prospect of escape from such in this life. But the believer's greatest—and most successful—defense is to live and walk by the Spirit.

However, the new man living under the Spirit is also faced by temptation in the larger meaning of test and trial. This comes as a shock to some people, because the gospel of Jesus Christ has been presented to them in a manner that suggested escape from the tests and adversities of life. It is most unfortunate, because there is no thought of such in the Scriptures. God promises victory over life's trials, but never escape.

One of the greatest verses in the Bible, and the favorite of the author, vividly spells out four fundamental truths about trials.

> So far you have faced no trial beyond what man can bear. God keeps faith, and he will not allow you to be tested above your powers, but when the test comes he will at the same time provide a way out, by enabling you to sustain it (1 Cor. 10:13, NEB).

In the First Corinthian letter Paul dealt with several practical problems, including those that involved idolatry and immorality. The tenth chapter opens with the warning that all of the Israelites received the same marvelous, miraculous ministry in the desert, but most of them perished. This was because they committed the very same sins the Corinthians were indulging in. This happened as an example to them, and "if you feel sure that you are standing firm, beware! You may fall" (1 Cor. 10:12, NEB). Paul then antici- pates that these Corinthians, living in their evil environment, might feel that the test was beyond their power to resist. So Paul, in one tremendous verse, explains four eternal truths about trials.

First, there is a basic *perspective*. Trials are a normal part of human experience and there is nothing unusual or unique about experiencing them. Second, is the *foundation*—that God keeps faith. It is essential to realize and remember that in every test God is faithful to minister to the one undergoing the trial. Third, there is the *confidence* that every test is controlled by God, who has guaranteed that no trial will be beyond what that man can bear by His grace. Finally, in the midst of every trial there is the *expec- tation* that God is providing a way out, which enables the tried man to sustain the test.

These truths about trials are what make it possible for the man of faith to live victoriously.

> Who shall separate us from the love of Christ? Shall tribula- tions, or distress, or persecution, or famine, or nakedness, or peril, or sword? Just as it is written, "FOR THY SAKE WE ARE BEING PUT TO DEATH ALL DAY LONG; WE WERE CONSIDERED AS SHEEP TO BE SLAUGHTERED." But in all these things we overwhelmingly conquer through Him who loved us. For I am convinced that neither death, nor life, nor angels, nor principalities, nor things present,

nor things to come, nor powers, nor height, nor depth, nor any other created thing, shall be able to separate us from the love of God, which is in Christ Jesus our Lord (Rom. 8:35-39).

It cannot be emphasized too strongly that life under the Spirit is not the promise of escape from adversity and even suffering.

We are afflicted in every way, but not crushed; perplexed, but not despairing; persecuted, but not forsaken; struck down, but not destroyed; always carrying about in the body the dying of Jesus, that the life of Jesus also may be manifested in our body. For we who live are constantly being delivered over to death for Jesus' sake, that the life of Jesus also may be manifested in our mortal flesh (2 Cor. 4:8-11).

Somewhere, probably as a subtle attack of Satan, the idea began that all suffering is evil, *per se*. This is certainly not the teaching of the New Testament, and particularly of Paul. His counsel to the Philippians is not an exception, but reflects his basic attitude. "For to you it has been granted for Christ's sake, not only to believe in Him, but also to suffer for His sake" (Phil. 1:29). Suffering is as much the gift of God's grace as the privilege of faith! In suffering, the believer finds a precious level of fellowship with Christ (cf. Phil. 3:20), "if indeed we suffer with *Him* in order that we may also be glorified with *Him*" (Rom. 8:17).

There is a vital perspective in suffering that the new man under the Spirit discovers.

For I consider that the sufferings of this present time are not worthy to be compared with the glory that is to be revealed to us (Rom. 8:18). And we know that God causes all things to work together for good to those who love God, to those who are called according to *His* purpose (Rom. 8:28). We look not at the things which are seen, but at the things which are not seen; for the things which are seen are temporal, but the things which are not seen are eternal (2 Cor. 4:18).

Thus suffering is borne in faith and hope.[3]

This is not an ethic born of persecution psychology. Certainly it is not a matter of *seeking* suffering, as was later practiced among some Apostolic Fathers when a cult of martyrdom developed. Rather, it is recognizing that suffering is transformed into a spiritual blessing in the hands of God. When the believer, who is called

---

3. Cf. the repeated instances in Acts, of which 5:40-42 is typical. Cf. also Jas. 1:2-4; 1 Pet. 1:6-9.

upon to suffer, immediately cries for escape and deliverance he loses the treasures of darkness that God would graciously provide. Only eternity will reveal the spiritual loss due to a wrong attitude toward suffering.

It is the responsibility of the new man living under the Spirit to work out his salvation. Such is not his works, but is possible only through the energizing of the Spirit, with whom he lives in a dynamic relationship. Growth and development result as his life increases, fills, and overflows with the fruit of the Spirit. He becomes established as he continues in God's love, rooted, grounded, and made steadfast. In the tests and adversities of life he finds God's grace sufficient to make him victorious.

Chapter 24

Conforming to His Image

It has been seen that in the life under the Spirit there is growth, development, and establishment. Now the questions arise —To what? In what? What is the norm, the standard, the goal, the pattern? It most certainly is more than a negative victory over sin. *Nowhere in Paul's writings is there the suggestion that the new man grows in sinlessness!* Such is a biblical misnomer.

Paul does set forth some definite standards relative to the life of the man of faith. The believer is to *behave properly*.

> The night is almost gone, and the day is at hand. Let us therefore lay aside the deeds of darkness and put on the armor of light. Let us behave properly as in the day, not in carousing and drunkenness, not in sexual promiscuity and sensuality, not in strife and jealousy. But put on the Lord Jesus Christ, and make no provision for the flesh in regard to *its* lusts (Rom. 13:12-14).[1]
> And to make it your ambition to lead a quiet life and attend to your own business and work with your hands, just as we commanded you; so that you may behave properly toward outsiders and not be in any need (1 Thess. 4:11-12).

Further, in the verse considered in previous chapters as it relates to bearing fruit and growth (increase), Paul also speaks of a worthy walk.

> So that you may walk in a manner worthy of the Lord, to please *Him* in all respects, bearing fruit in every good work and increasing in the knowledge of God (Col. 1:10).

---

1. The fact that it was the reading of these verses that precipitated the conversion of the sainted Augustine has given them a special place in the hearts of believers from that day to this.

He is very careful to emphasize that it is the believer's *walk* or manner of conduct that is to be worthy.

> I, therefore, the prisoner of the Lord, entreat you to walk in a manner worthy of the calling with which you have been called (Eph. 4:1). Only conduct yourselves in a manner worthy of the gospel of Christ; so that whether I come and see you or remain absent, I may hear of you that you are standing firm in one spirit, with one mind striving together for the faith of the gospel (Phil. 1:27). So that you may walk in a manner worthy of the God who calls you into His own kingdom and glory (1 Thess. 2:12).

Unfortunately this has often been misunderstood. Paul is not suggesting for a moment that a human being is deserving and personally worthy of the love and grace of God bestowed through Christ on the Cross. This would contradict his basic theological conviction. *All men are undeserving and unworthy!* Instead Paul is emphasizing that the manner in which the new man lives should be such that it is a fitting reflection of what God has done for him in Christ. That is why Paul emphasized walk and conduct and not intrinsic worthiness. There is a great difference between *walking* worthy and *being* worthy.[2]

As seen above in Col. 1:10, the worthy walk is specifically to please Him in all respects. Paul also writes:

> Finally then, brethren, we request and exhort you in the Lord Jesus that, as you received from us *instruction* as to how you ought to walk and please God (just as you actually do walk), that you may excel still more (1 Thess. 4:1).

This clearly shows that the new man's walk is worthy as it *pleases* his Lord, which is certainly not a matter of personal worthiness.

---

2. In each of the verses above, the *adverb* "worthily" *(axiōs)* is used. Although the *adjective* "worthy" *(axios)* is used several times in the NT, it is *never used* by Paul relative to the believer being worthy of Christ. The closest is his single use of the verb "to consider worthy" *(axioō)*—"To this end also we pray for you always that our God may count you worthy of your calling, and fulfill every desire for goodness and the work of faith with power" (2 Thess. 1:11). The context makes it plain that it is *conduct* he is referring to. The matter of partaking of the sacrament of Communion "unworthily" (1 Cor. 11:27) has too often been tragically misunderstood. The context clearly shows that Paul is not speaking of personal worthiness, but of improper horizontal relationships (with the brethren) making one undeserving of the vertical relationships experienced in Communion.

Only those who walk by the Spirit can please God (cf. Rom. 8:1-9), because "those who are in the flesh cannot please God" (Rom. 8:8).

Proper behavior, which is worthy and pleasing conduct, certainly includes sincerity. Paul was concerned that the Philippians be "sincere and blameless until the day of Christ" (Phil. 1:10). Sincerity and hypocrisy are direct opposites, in their basic scriptural meaning. Sincerity is *singleness,* and thus purity, of motive; while hypocrisy is *doubleness,* and thus duplicity, of motive. The basic meaning of the Greek term *(eilikrinēs)* is "unmixed."

The English term *sincerity* is made up of two Latin words that mean "without" *(sine)* "wax" *(cera),* alluding to the practice of camouflaging imperfections in a piece of art sculpturing with wax. Paul likens sincerity to unleavened bread, which is dough that is unmixed with leaven (cf. 1 Cor. 5:8). Thus the life of the new man under the Spirit is pure in motive. Mixed or ulterior motives of duplicity can have no place in his life. He is sincere and not hypocritical (cf. Rom. 12:9).

But the standard of the life of the new man under the Spirit is more than inward motive, as important as that is. It is significant that the concept of good works and doing good is found *extensively* in all of Paul's letters. As an understandable reaction to the erroneous teaching of righteousness being achieved by man's works, sometimes Paul is pictured as depreciating *all* efforts of man, including good works. Instead, however, he saw the works of the new man as the fruit of the indwelling Spirit, under whose sovereignty the believer lived. The Spirit energizes man, operating or working through him. Paul speaks of the Philippians being "filled with the fruit of righteousness which *comes* through Jesus Christ, to the glory and praise of God" (Phil. 1:11; cf. Gal. 5:22-23).

Paul writes to the Romans: "Let love be without hypocrisy. Abhor what is evil; cleave to what is good" (Rom. 12:9). At the close of his detailed explanation of what love in action is, he exhorts them: "Do not be overcome by evil, but overcome evil with good" (Rom. 12:21). His practical advice is that there is no cause to fear those in authority if one does good; in fact such conduct will call forth their praise (cf. Rom. 13:3). One of Paul's closing words to the Roman church was "I want you to be wise in what is good, and innocent in what is evil" (Rom. 16:19).

Goodness will be the issue on the day of judgment. "For we must all appear before the judgment-seat of Christ, that each one may be recompensed for his deeds in the body, according to what he has done, whether good or bad" (2 Cor. 5:10). The result of the abounding grace of God in the life of the believer is that they "may have an abundance for every good deed" (2 Cor. 9:8). Paul admonishes the Galatians: "So then, while we have opportunity, let us do good to all men, and especially to those who are of the household of the faith" (Gal. 6:10; cf. 1 Thess. 5:15). Even more pointedly he writes to the Ephesians: "For we are His workmanship, created in Christ Jesus for good works, which God prepared beforehand, that we should walk in them" (Eph. 2:10).

It cannot be emphasized too strongly that, instead of depreciating a life of good works in the believer, Paul viewed it as one of the norms or standards in the life of the new man under the Spirit. This concern is central, rather than being minor or inconsequential. Yet it must always be remembered that good works are the fruit of the Spirit, and thus provide no basis of man's self-righteousness.

When the believer lives by the Spirit, the just requirement of the law is fulfilled. There is a vital sense in which the law, as the divine will, is the *standard* for the new man living under the Spirit. It has been repeatedly seen that the Spirit energizes the new man—specifically in terms of love *(agape)*. This love, which is the only way that the divine standard is brought to its full validity and effectiveness, is the norm or standard of the newness of life under the Spirit.

Another standard of the life of the new man under the Spirit is that he is to be *blameless*. Although Paul uses four different adjectives, and the adverbial form of one of them, to describe this norm,[3] the four terms are practically synonymous in meaning, as can be seen in the various English translations.

> Just as He chose us in Him before the foundation of the world, that we should be holy and blameless *[amōmos]* before

---

3. *Anegklētos* means "irreproachable" or "beyond reproach"; *amōmos* means "unblemished"; *amemptos* means "faultless"; and *aproskopos* means "undamaged" and "without offense" (cf. A and G).

Him (Eph. 1:4). That you may prove yourselves to be blameless *[amemptos]* and innocent, children of God above reproach *[amō-mos]* in the midst of a crooked and perverse generation, among whom you appear as lights in the world (Phil. 2:15).

The imagery is clearly sacrificial, related to the unblemished animals used in Temple worship. Yet this does not mean that Paul's concept of blamelessness was either an inactive or an intrinsic morality. As he applies the vivid metaphor, Paul makes it clear that it is the power of the Spirit that *preserves* the believer blameless in the midst of the evil world in which he must live.

It is significant that the concept of blamelessness is often related to the *Parousia.*

Who shall also confirm you to the end, blameless *[aneg-klētos]* in the day of our Lord Jesus Christ (1 Cor. 1:8). Yet He has now reconciled you in His fleshly body through death, in order to present you before Him holy and blameless *[amōmos]* and beyond reproach *[unegklētos]* (Col. 1:22).

Paul was concerned that the man in Christ be able to bear the scrutiny of his Lord's presence without rebuke. It has already been stated that one standard of life under the Spirit was sincerity or purity of motive. Equally so must the standard be blamelessness of conduct, *not before the eyes of men,* but as he stands before his Lord. He can thus stand void of offense only through the energizing of the Spirit.

Paul's association of the standard of blamelessness with the *Parousia* must not be misunderstood through hindsight. It should always be remembered that for Paul, particularly in his earlier letters, the coming of Christ was not an event in the long distant future, but was as close as the dawn of a new day. He wanted his converts presented to Christ as blameless. This was true, not only of the individual convert, but of the Church as a whole (cf. Eph. 5: 25-27).

The new man, living under the Spirit, is not only to be blameless, but also holy. The term "holy" *(hagios)* is found in three of the five references related to blamelessness cited above. The *objective status* of the man in Christ is many times identified as holy, but always in a collective sense, as part of the holy fellowship. This is only *one way* the concept of holiness is used by Paul. It is clear that this is another term that he uses to depict the standard of life under the Spirit. In fact the concept of holiness ties together the various terms that Paul uses to describe the norm for the life of the new man.

The concept of holiness is complex and needs to be examined from several perspectives. In addition to the several references to the believers as holy ones (*hagioi,* "saints"), which were treated in an earlier chapter, Paul refers to the men of faith as the "holy *[hagios]* Temple" (cf. 1 Cor. 3:17; Eph. 2:21). In theological terminology this is called "positional sanctification"[4] and is descriptive of the believer as part of the *holy* fellowship, the Church of Jesus Christ.

Not only does Paul use holiness in the sense of the believer's objective status, but also with a meaning that clearly indicates a *subjective state* or condition. He recognizes that God's precreation purpose for the believer is that he be holy. "According as he hath chosen us in him before the foundation of the world, that we should be holy and without blame before him in love" (Eph. 1:4, KJV).[5] The fact that this holy state is identified with blamelessness *(amōmos)* and love makes it plain that Paul is referring to *active* holiness. Similarly he associates sanctification by the Spirit with God's purpose of salvation for man.

> But we should always give thanks to God for you, brethren beloved by the Lord, because God has chosen you from the beginning for salvation through sanctification by the Spirit and faith in the truth (2 Thess. 2:13).

Even more pointedly Paul states that the new man "in *the likeness of* God has been created in righteousness and holiness *[hosiotēs]* of the truth" (Eph. 4:24).[6]

---

4. There is no basic difference between sanctification and holiness. In the KJV they are translations of the same word (cf. 1 Thess. 4:3, 7). The term *hagiasmos* basically relates to the "*state* [italics added] of being made holy more often than a process" (A and G). *Hagiōsunē* and *hagiotēs* primarily relate to a *quality* of character rather than a *state,* with the two terms possibly coming from two different schools of Greek philosophy (cf. A and G). *Hosiotēs* means more the idea of piety or devoutness. The verb *hagiadzō* means simply to make holy.

5. It is an open question whether "in love" goes with v. 4 or v. 5. Cf. the discussion in BBC, *en loc.,* with the conclusion that it is better understood with v. 4.

6. It should be observed that Paul does not use one of the cognates of *hagios* here, which is the basic term for *holy,* but rather a term that means more piety or devoutness (cf. A and G).

It is clear that Paul considered the new man to be a sanctified or holy man, not only in objective status but in subjective state. Theologians have identified this as *initial* sanctification or the life of sanctification *begun.*

However, for the specific emphasis of this study, it is significant to recognize that Paul saw the life of sanctification essentially related to the imperative that he addressed to the new man. This imperative was seen to climax in terms of crisis presentation. It is important that the *results* of that presentation are, at least in part, described by Paul in terms of sanctification.

> So now present your members *as* slaves to righteousness, resulting in sanctification *[hagiasmos]* (Rom. 6:19). But now having been freed from sin and enslaved to God, you derive your benefit, resulting in sanctification *[hagiasmos]*, and the outcome, eternal life (Rom. 6:22).

The relationship between sanctification and the crisis imperative in the life of the believer is further seen in Paul's more extensive teaching in the First Thessalonian letter.

As repeatedly shown above, this letter is addressed to believers of an exemplary nature.

> For our gospel did not come to you in word only, but also in power and in the Holy Spirit and with full conviction; just as you know what kind of men we proved to be among you for your sake. You also became imitators of us and of the Lord . . . so that you became an example to all the believers in Macedonia and in Achaia. . . . how you turned to God from idols to serve a living and true God (1 Thess. 1:5-9).

Yet Paul was concerned about a remaining need in their lives. "We night and day keep praying most earnestly that we may see your face, and may complete what is lacking in your faith" (1 Thess. 3:10). He then proceeds to address himself to this need in terms of *sanctification.*

> And may the Lord cause you to increase and abound in love for one another, and for all men, just as we also *do* for you; so that He may establish your hearts unblamable in holiness *[hagiō-sune]* before our God and Father at the coming of our Lord Jesus with all His saints (1 Thess. 3:12-13).

It was suggested that Paul's use of the term "holiness" ties together several concepts that he uses to describe the norm or standard of the life of the new man under the Spirit. This can be vividly seen here. Paul's concern about growth, establishment, and blamelessness *(amemptos)* are all to be related to holiness. The believers' *growth* was to be specifically in love, which in turn would *establish* their hearts *unblamable* in holiness *(hagiōsunē)*. *Holiness is the quality of their blamelessness.* It is further significant that this growth in love is the *direct result* of living under the sovereignty of the Spirit.

Paul continues on in the next chapter to develop and further explain this concern about holiness in the life of the new man.

> For this is the will of God, your sanctification *[hagiasmos]*; *that is,* that you abstain from sexual immorality; that each of you know how to possess his own vessel[7] in sanctification *[hagiasmos]* and honor, not in lustful passion, like the Gentiles who do not know God (1 Thess. 4:3-5).

Although Paul makes an immediate application to sexual purity, which was a vital problem in that day, it is a mistake to understand Paul's concept of holiness as *only* that. The context clearly relates holiness to the life of love of which the proper discipline of the body is a necessary part (cf. 3:12-13; 4:9 f.). Paul goes on to say:

> For God has not called us for the purpose of impurity, but in[8] sanctification *[hagiasmos]*. Consequently, he who rejects *this* is not rejecting man but the God who gives His Holy Spirit to you (1 Thess. 4:7-8).

We have seen that Paul directly relates the sanctification of the believer with the imperative that he present himself and his members to God in a crisis commitment. Sanctification is the *result* of this presentation. The crucial problem is seen in the next logical question. What is the nature of this sanctification? Is it a process or a state? Paul does use primarily the term *hagiasmos,*

---

7. Many have questioned whether "vessel" *(skeuos)* refers to *body* or *wife* (cf. NASB margin, RSV). To interpret this as *body* appears to be more interpretation than translation (cf. the parallel use in 2 Cor. 4:7, where it is clearly *body*). Actually, the interpretation of *wife* would basically relate to a man's control of his own body, so there is really no great difference in meaning.

8. Paul uses a most unexpected preposition *(en),* which is normally locative (in, on, at) or instrumental (by means of), but neither fits the verse very well. The context suggests that *hagiasmos* is the *object* of the call, thus the KJV translation "unto." Moule suggests it might be adverbial, thus relating to the nature of the call—a "holy calling."

which Arndt and Gingrich specifically say relates to "the state of being made holy more often than a process." Although he does not explicitly say so, this would certainly suggest that Paul is speaking of a crisis experience of sanctification as he writes to the Thessalonians.

Paul closes the first Thessalonian letter with a prayerful wish (optative) for these believers:

> Now may the God of peace Himself sanctify *[hagiadzō]* you entirely; and may your spirit and soul and body[9] be preserved complete, without blame *[amemptos]* at the coming of our Lord Jesus Christ (1 Thess. 5:23).

Here again is the tie between holiness and the norm of blamelessness. The plain implication is that the believer will be kept or preserved complete and without blame until the *Parousia,* because he has been *entirely* sanctified.[10] It is of particular significance that, after using the present tense, which depicts progressive action, five times in verses 19 through 22, Paul carefully uses the aorist tense in verse 23. This decisive change of tenses would seem to identify God's sanctifying work as a crisis act. This definitive construction would clarify the less definite references in chapters 3 and 4. Paul's concluding word would seem to be addressed to any possible question that might arise. "Faithful is He who calls you, and He also will bring it to pass" (1 Thess. 5:24).

One further reference, which is to the sanctifying of the Church rather than the individual, gives support to the foregoing interpretation.

> Christ also loved the church and gave Himself up for her; that He might sanctify *[hagiadzō]* her, having cleansed her by the washing of water with the word, that He might present to Himself the church in all her glory, having no spot or wrinkle or any such thing; but that she should be holy *[hagios]* and blameless *[amōmos]* (Eph. 5:25-27).

---

9. Any effort to find anthropological significance in this single instance where Paul distinguishes between spirit, soul, and body misses the main point. Paul is simply concerned about the *whole man* being entirely preserved.

10. This single Pauline reference to being *entirely* sanctified or sanctified *wholly* should not be confused with the theological idea of *final* sanctification (i.e., glorification). This is understood in Wesleyan theology to refer to the *entire removal of original sin* (cf. Chapter 4) and not to the end of the process of sanctification.

Again the elements of blamelessness *(amōmos)*, holiness *(hagiad-zō, hagios)*, and the day of Christ are tied together. In verse 26 the NASB has quite properly noted the important fact, missing in the KJV, that the cleansing of the Church *preceded* the sanctifying of the Church.[11] It is generally agreed that Paul is referring to the Church being cleansed by the washing of regeneration, with an apparent allusion to baptism. It is *following* this that the Lord would sanctify the Church, in order to present it to himself as holy and blameless. The term "to sanctify" *(hagiadzō)* is in the aorist tense, which indicates a crisis act rather than a process.

Without question the sanctification that characterizes the new life of the believer under the Spirit also involves a process. After all, it is *a life* and *living.* The sanctification that is *begun* when the sinner becomes a new man in Christ is most certainly *continued* as he lives under the sovereignty of the Spirit. Thus there is *initial* sanctification and *progressive* sanctification. However, Paul also refers to sanctification in terms of a state of being that is the result of the believer's crisis presentation of himself and his members to God. It is true to Pauline thought to witness: I *am* sanctified as well as I *am being* sanctified. It is an accomplished *state* as well as a *process.*

It is of great importance to emphasize that such a state of sanctification is *not* the result of human works, but is the *act of God* in response to the believer's crisis commitment and faith. When the new man *releases* his sovereignty, God *removes* it, cleansing him from original depravity. Wesleyan theologians identify this as entire sanctification, with specific reference to 1 Thess. 5:23. This *does not* suggest that the process of sanctification is complete, but rather that the *original depravity* is entirely removed. There still remains the continuing process of sanctification which will be more definitively examined in the next chapter.

Of primary importance to the subject matter of this chapter is the question of how holiness relates to the standard of the life of the new man living under the Spirit. The norm has been identified

---

11. The word "having cleansed" *(katharisas)* is an aorist participle, which indicated action that is antecedent to the main verb ("sanctify," *hagiasē)* (cf. BBC, *en loc.*).

as proper behavior, worthy and pleasing conduct, sincerity, good works, the fulfilling of the law through love, blamelessness, and holiness. There is a proper sense in which holiness unites the other concepts into a cohesive unity, particularly when holiness is understood in terms of love *(agape)*.

Yet it is possible to view the many aspects of the standard of life under the Spirit in a purely *impersonal* manner—which is a serious mistake. If Paul had been asked directly: "What is the norm of life lived under the Spirit?" he probably would have had a very simple answer: "The norm or standard is nothing other than Jesus Christ!" Although Paul had little to say about the earthly life of Jesus, there is no doubt that he was as concerned as Peter that the believer walk "in His steps" (cf. 1 Pet. 2:21).

Having set before the Philippians the challenge of living in love and humility,[12] Paul admonished them: "Have this attitude in yourselves which was also in Christ Jesus" (Phil. 2:5). The description that follows of the attitude that was in Christ is the famous "kenosis passage."[13]

Even more directly Paul wrote to the Ephesians: "Therefore be imitators of God, as beloved children; and walk in love, just as Christ also loved you, and gave Himself up for us, an offering and a sacrifice to God as a fragrant aroma" (Eph. 5:1). This is in the midst of his most extensive imperative to right living (cc. 4—6) and is the key exhortation. It is to be an imitator of God, particu-

---

12. "Now if your experience of Christ's encouragement and love means anything to you, if you have known something of the fellowship of his Spirit, and all that it means in kindness and deep sympathy, do make my best hopes for you come true! Live together in harmony, live together in love, as though you had only one mind and one spirit between you. Never act from motives of rivalry or personal vanity, but in humility think more of one another than you do of yourselves. None of you should think only of his own affairs, but each should learn to see things from other people's point of view" (Phil. 2:1-4, Phillips).

13. "[Christ Jesus] who, although He existed in the form of God, did not regard equality with God a thing to be grasped, but emptied Himself, taking the form of a bond-servant, *and* being made in the likeness of men. And being found in appearance as a man, He humbled Himself by becoming obedient to the point of death, even death on a cross. Therefore also God highly exalted Him, and bestowed on Him the name which is above every name, that at the name of Jesus every knee should bow, of those who are in heaven, and on earth, and under the earth, and that every tongue should confess that Jesus Christ is Lord, to the glory of God the Father" (Phil. 2:6-11).

larly of the love that was demonstrated in the Cross. Paul commends the Thessalonians: "You also became imitators of us and of the Lord, having received the word in much tribulation with the joy of the Holy Spirit" (1 Thess. 1:6). He further challenges his converts to follow his example (as in Gal. 4:12; Phil. 3:17; 4:9; and 2 Thess. 3:7), and even to imitate him (as in 1 Cor. 4:16). This was because he could further say: "Be imitators of me, just as I also am of Christ" (1 Cor. 11:1). Christ is *the* Example and Pattern.

But Christ is more than an Example of how the new man is to live and walk! It is breathtaking to read: "For whom He foreknew, He also predestined *to become* conformed to the image of His Son, that He might be the first-born among many brethren" (Rom. 8: 29).

Conformed to His image! To put it into other terms—to be like Christ! The natural desire of the new man living under the Spirit is: "Oh, to be like Thee!" He is *the* Standard and Character of newness of life. Yet this must not be viewed as attainable in some climactic moment of either surrender or endeavor. Instead, conformity to Christ is the grand goal of the new life.

Paul makes it crystal-clear that conformity to Christ is a process. "But we all, with unveiled face beholding as in a mirror the glory of the Lord, are being transformed into the same image from glory to glory, just as from the Lord, the Spirit" (2 Cor. 3:18). Similarly he writes: "And [we] have put on the new self who is being renewed to a true knowledge according to the image of the One who created him" (Col. 3:10). The key words are *transformed* and *renewed.* Transformation *always* depicts a continuing process and *never* a completed act.[14] The believer, living under the sovereignty of the Spirit, is being gradually transformed into the image of Christ. Further, it is the *inner man* that is being transformed. "Therefore we do not lose heart, but though our outer man is decaying, yet our inner man is being renewed day by day" (2 Cor. 4:16). In the next chapter the discipline of the outer man will be examined, and in the final chapter the promise of receiving a new

---

14. The Greek word is *metamorphoō,* which has been transliterated *metamorphosis* or to *metamorphize.* It *always* depicts a gradual change (cf. the metamorphosis of a butterfly). The Greek term is always in the present tense, indicating process, and it is a misnomer to speak of instantaneous transformation.

outer man at the resurrection will be seen. However, at the present the new inner man is being transformed, through a day-by-day renewal (cf. Col. 3:10). Even more specifically this transformation process takes place by the renewing of the mind.

> I urge you therefore, brethren, by the mercies of God, to present your bodies a living and holy sacrifice, acceptable to God, *which is* your spiritual service of worship. And do not be conformed to this world, but be transformed by the renewing of your mind, that you may prove what the will of God is, that which is good and acceptable and perfect (Rom. 12:1-2).

Again this is directly tied to the crisis commitment examined in Chapter 20. As the believer makes a crisis presentation of himself (body) to God as a living, acceptable, and holy sacrifice, he finds a protection from the pressures of the world and enters upon a process of transformation by the renewing of his mind. "Don't let the world around you squeeze you into its own mold, but let God remold your minds from within" (Rom. 12:2, Phillips). In this way we *prove* that God's will is good, acceptable (satisfying to us), and perfect.

As the believer is conformed to the image of Christ, he measures up to the standard and norm of the new life lived under the Spirit. Under the sovereignty of the Spirit he seeks to live a life that is proper, worthy, pleasing, sincere, good, lawful, blameless, and holy. However, it is never to be understood in terms of impersonal standards, but rather as the outward expression of his increasing conformity to Christ.

Chapter 25

Holy yet Human

One of the most serious problems that the new man faces as he lives under the sovereignty of the Spirit is to reconcile God's clear standard of holiness with the obvious limitation, weakness, and failure that are a *normal* part of his life. As examined in the previous chapters, in response to his faith in the Cross, God has done wonderful things for the new man. He enters into a new relationship, giving him a new status, making him a new person, living a new life as part of a new fellowship. Through a crisis presentation of his new life to God he enters into a personal companionship with the Spirit. Yet this great treasure is housed in an earthen vessel. "But we have this treasure in earthen vessels, that the surpassing greatness of the power may be of God and not from ourselves" (2 Cor. 4:7).

The adjective "earthen" *(ostrakinos)* depicts that which is made of clay; a piece of brittle, kiln-baked pottery. The metaphor is clear, picturing that which is fragile and breakable. Paul goes on to say: "*We are* afflicted in every way, but not crushed; perplexed, but not despairing; persecuted, but not forsaken; struck down, but not destroyed" (2 Cor. 4:8-9). As Paul faced the intense pressures and persecutions of early missionary life he marvelled at how God preserved him, and likened his daily deliverance to an entering into the resurrection power of Jesus.

Always carrying about in the body the dying of Jesus, that the life of Jesus also may be manifested in our body. For we who live are constantly being delivered over to death for Jesus' sake, that the life of Jesus also may be manifested in our mortal flesh. So death works in us, but life in you (2 Cor. 4:10-12).

The human house, or earthen vessel, is the outer man, and it *is* fragile and weak. Sometimes this fragility is seen as the new man meets the tests and trials of life. Although they are not of the same nature that Paul faced, they are nonetheless very real. However, this is by no means the only way the weakness of the outer man is revealed. One of the most difficult aspects of the problem is that Paul did not *explicitly* deal with human limitations and weaknesses. This is not surprising because there are many practical matters he did not specifically treat while under the pressure of missionary evangelism and probably because of his expectation of the imminent *Parousia.* Yet it is possible to project what his answers might have been to these questions as suggestions are *implicit* in the various principles he enunciated.

The human house shows its fragility by its age. Paul plainly suggested this. "Therefore we do not lose heart, but though our outer man is decaying, yet our inner man is being renewed day by day" (2 Cor. 4:16). The human body—physical and psychological—*does* progressively decay and there are the unmistakable effects of physical infirmity, loss of faculties, failing memory, lessening understanding, lack of judgment, unreasonable demands, impatience, and even harshness of words and spirit.

However, the most crucial point of human infirmity does not come in trials, or even advanced age. The deeply sensitive and sincere believer finds his greatest struggle with spiritual failure, weakness and limitation, lack of judgment, and any of a score more problems *that arise from personality or temperament.* No two people have quite the same struggle. How often the beleaguered soul pleads with God to change him or to remove the difficulty—only to learn that *God does not change a man's personality as an intrinsic part of salvation.*

The crucial question is how the man of faith is to reconcile this *actual* fact of human infirmity with God's clear *ideal* of holiness. Can there be a reconciliation of the idealism and realism? Unfortunately this is all too seldom dealt with from pulpit or with pen. Perhaps this is because of all areas of thought this lends itself least to dogmatism and most to misunderstanding. Yet there is no area of Christian truth where rugged honesty and realism are more needed.

A few people fail to see, at least to acknowledge to themselves, the problem that is so glaringly visible to others, and the result is that they live on a superficial spiritual plane. Others face the problem and battle it alone, without the help and understanding they need.

Much is said about relevance in religion today, with some ridiculing its importance and others bowing at its shrine. The simple fact is that for an alarming number of people—young and old—Christianity has become irrelevant, as God is systematically excused from their lives. One probable cause is the lack of spiritual reality, which turns to denial as a defense mechanism. There are many practical reasons for a lack of spiritual reality, but failure, which is too often branded hypocrisy—and it must be remembered that inconsistency and hypocrisy are not synonymous—is certainly one of the chief ones.

When something "doesn't work" it is easy to conclude it isn't necessary! Inconsistency in other people has always created problems in the Church, but the neophyte must learn early that his example is Christ—not men. The man of faith must leave people with God, and His just judgment. Yet what about failure and inconsistency *within oneself?* It is the writer's increasing conviction that the major cause for spiritual apostasy is the frustration and disillusionment resulting from the disparity between the ideal and actual *within the apostate himself.* To be sure, there are many smoke screens to cover his own disillusionment, but they are only defense mechanisms.

The man of faith who takes seriously the clearly defined ideal of holiness in the New Testament is most vulnerable to this crucial threat. He needs to understand how a man can be holy and yet human. Such an understanding must begin with a clear insight into what the New Testament, and specifically Paul, teaches about the ideal.

It is most unfortunate that the Christian ideal is identified, by all too many, with a totally nonbiblical concept of holiness and perfection. The first thing that the believer must do is to disassociate from his thinking these modern theological ideas about holiness that are both unscriptural and unrealistic. As an example, nowhere in the thought of Paul is there the remotest suggestion of holiness or perfection being attained through progressive growth toward sinlessness. Such an idea would totally contradict his basic theological concepts.

What is Paul's concept of perfection?[1] The first and most important thing to understand about Paul's—and the entire New Testament's—idea of perfection is to recognize that *it is a relative concept.* Its basic meaning, according to Arndt and Gingrich, is "to complete," "to finish," "to attain its end or purpose." Its meaning is *totally dependent* upon the nature of the goal or object that is being completed. There is a vital sense in which the distinction between *absolute* perfection and *relative* perfection is an artificial one. All perfection, in its New Testament sense, is relative—related to whom or what is being perfected. The distinction between absolute and relative is in the *goal* and not in the *degree* of attainment.

Perfection is the completion of either a stated or obviously assumed goal. This goal can be either temporal (obtainable in this life) or eternal (obtainable only at the end of this life or in the life to come). Growth and development are *not* perfection; only completion is perfection.

Paul counsels the Corinthians: "Brethren, do not be children in your thinking; yet in evil be babes, but in your thinking be mature *[teleios]*" (1 Cor. 14:20). Here the contrast is clearly between being childlike or grown-up—specifically in their thinking. He is concerned that he might "present every man complete *[teleion]* in Christ" (Col. 1:28). In this context, the perfection Paul was concerned about was to be fully informed—"teaching every man with all wisdom." Later in this letter Paul refers to *agape* (love) as the bond of completeness, meaning that love binds completely together all of the other virtues, even as an outer cloak (cf. also Col. 3:14). Several times Paul uses the term *epiteleō* to depict the completion of that which has been already begun. "Are you so foolish? Having begun by the Spirit, are you now being perfected *[epiteleō]* by the flesh?" (Gal. 3:3; cf. 2 Cor. 7:1; 8:6).

The above references are clearly *temporal* in significance. There are at least two passages where Paul uses *perfection* with an

---

1. The basic terms are the adjectives *teleios* (perfect) and its cognates *teleiotēs* (perfection), *teleioō* (to perfect), and *epiteleō* (to complete).

eternal significance. In 1 Corinthians 13, Paul is contrasting love (along with faith and hope), as a value which will *remain,* with prophecy, knowledge, and tongues, as values which will *cease.* He states that, at present, knowledge and prophecy are *partial,* even like an indistinct image in a mirror, "but when the perfect *[teleion]* comes, the partial will be done away" (1 Cor. 13:10). He goes on to explain that this perfection is face-to-face knowledge. "For now we see in a mirror dimly, but then face to face; now I know in part, but then I shall know fully just as I also have been fully known" (1 Cor. 13:12). Such perfection is obviously attainable only after this life.

The other passage to be examined is the best-known perfection passage in Paul, namely, Phil. 3:12-15. In this chapter, Paul plainly states his objective or goal, *which provides the key to his meaning of perfection.*

> More than that, I count all things to be loss in view of the surpassing value of knowing Christ Jesus my Lord, for whom I have suffered the loss of all things, and count them but rubbish in order that I may gain Christ, and may be found in Him, not having a righteousness of my own derived from *the* Law, but that which is through faith in Christ, the righteousness which *comes* from God on the basis of faith, that I may know Him, and the power of His resurrection and the fellowship of His sufferings, being conformed to His death; in order that I may attain to the resurrection from the dead (Phil. 3:8-11).

His objective is *to gain Christ, to be found in Him, to know Him* and the power of His resurrection, *to be conformed to His death,* and *to attain to the resurrection from the dead.* It is this to which he refers when he goes on to say:

> Not that I have already obtained *it,* or have already become perfect, but I press on in order that I may lay hold of that for which also I was laid hold of by Christ Jesus. Brethren, I do not regard myself as having laid hold of *it* yet; but one thing *I do:* forgetting what *lies* behind and reaching forward to what *lies* ahead, I press on toward the goal for the prize of the upward call of God in Christ Jesus (Phil. 3:12-14).

Here in unmistakable terms is perfection, in its eternal sense, and the present attitude toward it.

An examination of this passage reveals that it has *absolutely nothing* to say about progressive sinlessness or development in moral stature. Paul's goal is to finish the Christian race and attain to the resurrection of the dead. This perfection is to complete the race. It is a most serious error to inject here any idea of gradual, moral development and growth.

What has complicated the passage is the verse that follows the verses quoted above: "Let us therefore, as many as are perfect, have this attitude; and if in anything you have a different attitude, God will reveal that also to you" (Phil. 3:15). The expression "as many as *are perfect"* is almost universally interpreted as *maturity,* referring to perfection in the entirely different sense of temporal perfection, understood as a maturity of knowledge and experience (cf. discussion above). Yet it is a deep mystery why Paul would inject such a totally foreign concept into this passage.

It is instructive that in this controversial verse (v. 15), in the crucial phrase, "as many as are perfect," *there is no verb form.*[2] The Greek literally reads: "Let us, as many as perfect, have this attitude." The copula or linking verb (to be) is assumed. According to very old rules of ellipsis[3] the most fundamental principle is that the meaning must be *readily assumed from the context or from customary usage,* and the assumed copula *cannot introduce a new element.* The inserting of the present indicative form of "to be" *(eimi),* namely, "are," as is universally done, most certainly *does* introduce the totally new concept of present, possessed perfection, as the exegetical history of this passage eloquently substantiates. There is absolutely nothing in the context that remotely suggests such a present experience, and there is nothing in the context to define the goal of such present perfection.

Instead the unmistakable argument of the context would dictate the *future* form of the assumed verb. This verse, which is actually a summary, would then read: "Let us therefore, as many as *shall be* perfect, have this attitude." Such a translation integrates verse 15 into the entire context, which relates to the future completion of the Christian race. (Cf. a similar example of ellipsis in Rom. 8:29.)

---

2. This is called an ellipsis and is commonly used in the Greek NT *where the meaning is obvious* and can be readily assumed. It is a type of Greek shorthand probably in part motivated by the exorbitant expense of writing materials.

3. Cf. George B. Winer, *A Grammar of the Idiom of the New Testament* (Andover, Mass.: Warren F. Draper, 1897), pp. 580 f.

Paul's teaching on perfection has been examined in some detail in order to clearly demonstrate the fact that he does not, in any manner, relate perfection to gradual sinlessness. Instead, whether used in the temporal or eternal perspective, perfection is the *attainment* of a clearly defined goal and does not relate to any degree of growth or development. An understanding of this is essential to the man of faith who takes seriously the New Testament ideal of holiness.[4]

If the ideal of holiness in Paul, and the entire New Testament, is *not* to be understood in terms of progressive sinlessness, then how is it to be understood? The answer to this question has been repeatedly alluded to. Throughout the foregoing chapters the energizing of the Spirit that brings forth fruit, the basis of growth and development, and the standard of holiness have *all been defined in terms of love (agape)*. It is likewise here that the reconciliation of the ideal and the actual can be seen. The disparity between the holy and human is bridged through love. This is found in the teaching of Jesus (Matt. 5:38-48; 22:36-40) and of John (1 John 4:15-21).

Holiness is not progressive sinlessness, which would limit it basically to a negative concept (the absence of sin), but it is the conquering power of Christ through love. But what exactly does that mean? In love there is the *realization* of the standard of the new life, while there is at the same time *anticipation* in terms of increase and growth. Here the paradox of the ideal and the actual is resolved, "just as the perfection of the bud shares in the glory of the perfect flower, and the opening theme in a symphony participates in the beauty of the final movement."[5]

The new man must not only understand the Pauline concept of the ideal of holiness in terms of love, but he must also *understand himself*. A surprising degree of confusion and despair arises from a failure to relate the promise of salvation to the fundamental nature of man. This is the basic reason why the opening section

---

4. Often discussions on perfection are not based on NT *terms* but on theological *concepts* that identify perfection with conformity to the image of Christ— becoming sinless like Christ is sinless. Paul *never* identifies such conformity as perfection (cf. Chapter 24).

5. Vincent Taylor, *Forgiveness and Reconciliation* (London: Macmillan and Co., 1956), p. 170.

of this study attempted to depict the Pauline view of man. It was seen that man is twofold, with the inner man of the heart (mind) finding expression and present realization through the outer man of the body (flesh).

It is necessary first to understand, at least in some measure, how the inner man and the outer man are formed. The inner self is formed by three things: namely, heredity, environment (including his training), and the depravity or original sin with which man was born. Together these three influences "create" the inner self, determining the qualities of character, convictions, and ideals that reflect what a person really is. Often the inner self is hidden and unseen, except by God and the person himself.

The outer self—the human house—is made up of the members and organs of the physical body, the brain, the amazing and intricate network that is called the nervous system, *and* the basic human instincts.

These instincts, drives, and urges[6] are shaped into an outward personality pattern of behavior tendencies, disposition, and temperament—*by the inner self.* The outer self, particularly the personality temperament, reflects what a man is within. This is why people "act" like they do![7] Very significantly, the outer self reflects the depravity of the inner self, as desires are illegitimately satisfied and even satiated, and the normal human capacities are scarred and hardened into patterns of distinctive behavior.

Not only is there this important distinction between the inner and outer self, but if the believer is to understand himself he must recognize that human activity is of *two distinct types or kinds.* Sometimes a man's thoughts, words, and deeds are *directed* by the inner self. In New Testament terms this is activity *from the heart,* which is identified in more modern psychological terms as moral activity that *involves knowledge and will.* The activity of the new

---

6. The basic human instincts are sex, fear, anger, curiosity, love of beauty, ambition, gregariousness (friendship), and self-esteem.

7. This is seen in the following extremes and all the shades in between: moody—even tempered; happy-go-lucky—serious; gay—solemn; sensitive—callous; fussy—sloppy; stubborn—changeable; humorous—sober; friendly—distant; excitable—calm; talkative—quiet; impulsive—deliberate; thoughtful—unthinking; procrastinating—prompt; argumentative—agreeable; etc.

man that comes from the heart is governed by love if he is living under the Spirit. It is not this kind of activity that poses the crucial problem.

However, much of human activity is *not* on the level of conscious will. Instead it is instinctive and involuntary and simply a "mechanical" *reaction* to environmental stimuli. The precise nature of such involuntary activity is determined by the basic personality and temperamental disposition. This can be readily illustrated by the widely varying reaction to such stimuli as a loud noise, the appearance of a mouse, a flash of lightning or clap of thunder, the hearing of tragic news or the witnessing of a scene of horror, etc. The response is totally involuntary, determined by the individual's personality temperament.

It is of vital importance to realize that salvation, in this life, relates basically to the inner man. "Therefore we do not lose heart, but though our outer man is decaying, yet our inner man is being renewed day by day" (2 Cor. 4:16). The inner man is transformed into the image of Christ through the renewing of the mind. But what about the outer man? Paul, as do the rest of the New Testament writers, points to the day of resurrection as the time when the new outer man will be received. (This will be examined in the next chapter.) But until that day the *new* inner man can be expressed only through the *old* outer man.

Many believers are confused, and even discouraged and defeated, when they discover that all of the old desires were not destroyed when they became new men. Unfortunately, a large share of the blame for this situation is to be borne by careless and unscriptural preaching. God does not destroy basic human desires or appetites, although He does replace the *wish* to satisfy them in the wrong way with the *wish* to satisfy them in the right way.[8] It is

---

8. A great cause of confusion is the failure to recognize that our desires (propensities, drives, urges, etc.) are part of the *outer man,* and thus are *not* intrinsically involved in *present* salvation. This means we do *not* receive new desires when we become new men. We shall see, in the discussion that follows, that instead our old desires can and must be disciplined. However, the believer does experience a new motivation in the inner man that can be described as *wish, purpose,* or *intent.* This new inner motivation is sometimes termed *desire,* but it should not be confused with the desires of the outer man (cf. discussion, Chapter 5).

imperative to realize that *desire in itself is not sin,* but is the avenue of temptation. Desire or temptation only becomes sin when joined by the will.[9]

Paul repeatedly dealt with this problem with his imperatives to the new man relative to the flesh. The flesh, with its desires and propensities, although morally neutral in its original state, is left adversely affected by years lived in sin. Sin has done something to man's desires as he lived by the flesh, illegitimately satisfying his desires on forbidden fruit. Habit patterns were built, which are not destroyed in salvation. This is the significance of Paul's graphic contrast of the desires of the flesh with the desires of the Spirit in Gal. 5:17, climaxing with the words "so that you may not do the things that you please." The new man dares not freely satisfy his own desires.

This causes consternation to some believers because they fail to anticipate this struggle with the old habit patterns caused by sinful living. But, contrary to the theology of some, the new man *can* live victoriously. Living under the sovereignty of the Spirit, he can destroy these old habit patterns. "For if you are living according to the flesh, you must die; but if by the Spirit you are putting to death the deeds of the body, you will live" (Rom. 8:13). One of the results of living by the Spirit is that the *deeds*[10] of the body, or outer man, are being put to death. In a graphic metaphor of the discipline necessary to successfully compete in the Greek athletic games, Paul describes in these words the necessity of disciplining the body:

> Do you not know that those who run in a race all run, but *only* one receives the prize? Run in such a way that you may win. And everyone who competes in the games exercises self-control in all things. They then *do it* to receive a perishable wreath, but we an imperishable. Therefore I run in such a way, as not without aim; I box in such a way, as not beating the air; but

---

9. This is graphically pictured in Jas. 1:14-15: "But each one is tempted when he is carried away and enticed by his own lust. Then when lust has conceived, it gives birth to sin; and when sin is accomplished, it brings forth death." The word "lust" *(epithumia)* is the basic Greek word for *desire*. It is when desire *conceives*—is united to will—that sin is born.

10. The Greek word is *praxis,* and is the closest term to the English concept of *habit* (cf. interpretation by Vincent, *Word Studies, en loc.*).

I buffet my body and make it my slave, lest possibly, after I have preached to others, I myself should be disqualified (1 Cor. 9:24-27).

Paul says that he buffets or bruises (*hupōpiadzō*, "give a black eye to") his body in order to make it his slave. The old habit patterns, in spite of the dissipation of years in sin, *can* be broken by the strength and power of the Spirit.

But Paul's final word is never negative! It is not enough to break old habits. It is of vital importance to realize that *every* human desire and propensity has a holy and right purpose and fulfillment, which can be discovered under the leadership of the Spirit. Every work of the flesh depicted in Gal. 5:19-21 is a corruption of a potentially good and holy desire—without exception. God will teach the new man the right and normal expression of human desire. The *right* expression is the *normal* expression.

All habit patterns remaining from the old life in sin are not related to desire and thus are not dealt with at the level of conscious will. In fact, the disparity between the ideal and the actual is most acutely experienced in the area of involuntary or instinctive behavior, which is governed by basic personality characteristics.

As suggested above, the same influence that shaped the old inner man, producing character, also shaped the outer personality, forming behavior tendencies, disposition, temperament, etc. It is of great importance to see that the instinctive and involuntary habit patterns that make up the outward expression of personality were built up and deeply ingrained by years in sin, when there was no desire or intent to glorify God. Instead, the sinner lived to satisfy the dictates of his own sinful heart. When such a man is saved, these personality patterns are *not* immediately changed. Without a doubt, every sincere and sensitive believer has often wished that God would have remade his personality when He saved his soul. Certainly every pastor has!

Is it any surprise that even with the best of intentions from a holy heart, a personality left warped by sin—moody, sensitive, fussy, stubborn, explosive—gives the wrong impression, is misunderstood, and poorly expresses what is in the heart? There are countless specific manifestations, but undoubtedly the most commonly distressing personality problem is related to impatience, irritability, and anger. When for years this has been the involuntary response to pamper and protect a sinful heart, a habit pattern is created. Even after God's grace has come to the new man, it is all too easy to instinctively follow this habit pattern and respond with an indignant word or act—*most often to those genuinely loved the most. It is not moral behavior,* as it does not come from the heart. It is an involuntary response to environmental stimuli. It is totally unrealistic—and grossly injust—to identify one personality expression, such as anger, as sinful, and excuse other personality traits, such as sensitivity, stubbornness, pugnaciousness, etc., as human flaws or weakness.

The crucial question is—What can be done about personality problems? Can they be solved? Is it right for a believer to simply say: "That is the way I am and I can't do anything about it"? Can personality problems be reconciled with the ideal of holiness? This is the urgent question of the sensitive soul who realistically faces the facts of his personal life *and* God's clearly defined standard of holiness. The same principle of discipline under the Spirit can be applied here. The old habit patterns of personality behavior *can* be broken and new habit patterns created. There are some basic principles that will assist the earnest believer.

At the outset, there is no substitute for personal integrity— only God and the individual himself know whether or not an action comes from the heart. As no place else, one must be hard on himself and easy on others. The believer *must* face the facts of his life with total honesty. Deception here can be only *self*-deception. The problem must be identified for what it is with no attempt to minimize or excuse it. It must be dug out of the inner closet and faced with rugged honesty and courage. The amazing thing is that often everyone else sees the problem before the person does himself. Whatever the personality or temperament problem, God will reveal it if the individual *wants* to see it.

Next the problem must be seen in all of its ugliness. One must realize how it hurts others, dishonors God, and compromises his witness for Christ. The new man must grieve over it and unashamedly weep *before God*—not necessarily before men. However, the believer should be humbled; and, if he has hurt someone, then that person's forgiveness must be sought. *It is amazing how quickly a humbling apology will break up a habit pattern!* Finally, the problem should be made the subject of daily, earnest prayer. There is nothing in this world that God desires more than to help the earnest soul.

It should always be remembered that God promises and provides victorious grace, in spite of the dissipation of years in sin. This includes power to break the old habit patterns and the creation of new ones, as the man of faith lives under the Spirit. When God promises that He "will not allow you to be tempted beyond what you are able" (1 Cor. 10:13)—which certainly includes the testings caused by the old outer man—this involves what can be termed spiritual healing. There are many times when the effects of the past life in sin leave the outer man so weakened and bent toward sin—in both desires and personality traits—that the new man would be helpless against evil. In such cases God graciously brings spiritual healing to the beleaguered soul—instantly and miraculously. Sometimes it is the healing of a dissipated desire and not uncommonly a personality quirk. But it must always be remembered that such is healing and *is not intrinsic to the experience of grace.* Tragically, some who are thus healed have called into question the reality of the spiritual experience of others who have been left to discipline the difficulty from which the questioner was instantly delivered (for example, the habit of alcohol or nicotine).

God's purpose and plan are plain. It is His stated purpose that the new man glorify Him, *while still living in the flesh.*

> Or do you not know that your body is a temple of the Holy Spirit who is in you, whom you have from God, and that you are not your own? For you have been bought with a price: therefore glorify God in your body (1 Cor. 6:19-20). Always carrying about in the body the dying of Jesus, that the life of Jesus also may be manifested in our body. For we who live are constantly being delivered over to death for Jesus' sake, that the life of Jesus also may be manifested in our mortal flesh (2 Cor. 4:10-11).

Contrary to the teaching of those who picture the new man as the helpless victim of his outer man, the new man living under the Spirit is *guaranteed* sufficient grace by God.

> And because of the surpassing greatness of the revelations, for this reason, to keep me from exalting myself, there was given me a thorn in the flesh, a messenger of Satan to buffet me—to keep me from exalting myself! Concerning this I entreated the

Lord three times that it might depart from me. And He has said to me, "My grace is sufficient for you, for power is perfected in weakness." Most gladly, therefore, I will rather boast about my weaknesses, that the power of Christ may dwell in me. Therefore I am well content with weaknesses, with insults, with distresses, with persecutions, with difficulties, for Christ's sake; for when I am weak, then I am strong (2 Cor. 12:7-10).

Under the discipline of the Spirit, working through the outer man, the believer can glorify God and actually praise Him for his trials because when he is weak, then he is strong. To the extent that this victory necessitates spiritual healing, it is graciously provided by God. Nevertheless the believer, like Paul, is left with all he can handle by the grace of God.

God's standard of holiness *can be* reconciled with the fact of human frailty and infirmity. The new man must understand that the New Testament does not teach a perfection of gradual sinlessness that always leaves him short of his goal, but rather teaches perfection in terms of love that is both realized and yet anticipates growth and development. When he understands the distinction between the expression of that love at the level of conscious will and as the involuntary response of his personality temperament which is brought under the discipline of the Spirit, *then* he can reconcile the ideal and the actual in his own life. The commitment of his life is to see the great change, brought to the inner man, *inwrought* in character and *outwrought* in conduct.

Chapter 26

Finishing the Race

What does Paul say about the consummation of the life that is lived under the sovereignty of the Spirit? As noted earlier, in more than one instance he alluded to life in the metaphor of a race, with his own valedictory given in this image:

> I have fought the good fight, I have finished the course, I have kept the faith; in the future there is laid up for me the crown of righteousness, which the Lord, the righteous Judge, will award to me on that day; and not only to me, but also to all who have loved His appearing (2 Tim. 4:7-8).

Even the term *salvation* has an essential future dimension: "For now salvation is nearer to us than when we believed" (Rom. 13:11; cf. Rom. 5:9; 1 Thess. 5:9). What is the prize at the end of this race? What awaits the believer when he arrives at the goal?

In theology this is termed *eschatology,* properly understood as the doctrine of future things. Yet the term *eschatology* has been given a developed meaning in much of modern New Testament study which almost entirely divorces it from any reference whatever to the future. Instead, *eschatology* is used to express in a timeless sense the ultimate issues of life. This is understandably confusing, particularly to the student not trained in these technical disciplines. However, in this study, the term will be used in its less sophisticated sense of relating to future events. Even in this simpler sense it is impossible in this closing chapter to treat the subject with any degree of adequacy. Instead, it will be possible to make only a few of the more obvious observations.

Before we examine the *future* dimension of life under the Spirit, it is necessary for us to see clearly the all-important *present* consequences of our hope in Christ. It is quite natural for us to speak of the privileges and blessings that are ours *now* because of our faith in Christ—hence all that has been examined thus far. But we must always remember that *all of this is in faith.* That which makes any of it possible is both the *faith* and the *hope* of resurrection. It is *faith* in the resurrection of Christ and *hope* in our own resurrection.

> But if there is no resurrection of the dead, not even Christ has been raised; and if Christ has not been raised, then our preaching is vain, your faith also is vain. Moreoever we are even found *to be* false witnesses of God, because we witnessed against God that He raised Christ, whom He did not raise, if in fact the dead are not raised. For if the dead are not raised, not even Christ has been raised; and if Christ has not been raised, your faith is worthless; you are still in your sins. Then those also who have fallen asleep in Christ have perished. If we have only hoped in Christ in this life, we are of all men most to be pitied (1 Cor. 15:13-19).

Throughout the New Testament, and particularly in Paul, there is this all-important future perspective—relating to salvation *now.* Everything is dependent upon our future resurrection, which alone can bring total vindication of both our faith and our hope in Christ. That is why salvation is always *coming* as well as being present and past.

> Much more then, having now been justified by His blood, we shall be saved from the wrath *of God* through Him. For if while we were enemies, we were reconciled to God through the death of His Son, much more, having been reconciled, we shall be saved by His life (Rom. 5:9-10).

The assurance of *present* justification gives us the certain hope that *we shall be saved.* But we can't be saved without that future triumph, when we are raised from the dead and receive our new *outer man.*

It is important to recognize that Paul—as the rest of the New Testament—is basically Jewish in his eschatology. For the Jew, time was divided into two ages: the *present* age, which was entirely wicked and evil and under the control of the forces of evil; and the *future* age, which would be characterized by splendor, glory, and righteousness. The transition from the present evil age to the future age of glory would be brought about by the "day of the Lord," or the coming of the Messiah. Paul's eschatology can be understood only in relation to this basic Jewish world-view.

It will not be necessary to reexamine Paul's view of the present evil age, as this has already been discussed here. His exhortation to the Philippians is representative.

> Do all things without grumbling or disputing; that you may prove yourselves to be blameless and innocent, children of God above reproach in the midst of a crooked and perverse generation, among whom you appear as lights in the world (Phil. 2:14-15).

Paul graphically contrasts the coming future age with the present evil age, a contrast as distinct as light and darkness, and night and day.

> And this *do,* knowing the time, that it is already the hour for you to awaken from sleep; for now salvation is nearer to us than when we believed. The night is almost gone, and the day is at hand. Let us therefore lay aside the deeds of darkness and put on the armor of light. Let us behave properly as in the day, not in carousing and drunkenness, not in sexual promiscuity and sensuality, not in strife and jealousy (Rom. 13:11-13; cf. 1 Thess. 5:4-8).

The future age will be one of glory.

> For I consider that the sufferings of this present time are not worthy to be compared with the glory that is to be revealed to us (Rom. 8:18). It [the body] is sown in dishonor, it is raised in glory; it is sown in weakness, it is raised in power (1 Cor. 15:43). Christ in you, the hope of glory (Col. 1:27; cf. Rom. 2:7; 5:2; 1 Tim. 3:16).

This glory will be *eternal.*

> For momentary, light affliction is producing for us an eternal weight of glory far beyond all comparison (2 Cor. 4:17). That they also may obtain the salvation which is in Christ Jesus *and* with *it* eternal glory (2 Tim. 2:10).

Here is reflected another aspect of Paul's view of the future age—it is eternal. The basic concept of eternity is depicted by the Greek word for *age (aiōn),* from which is taken the English term *aeon.* There are several expressions that can be properly translated as *eternity* or *forever,* as is found in most English translations.[1] The important concept is the *endlessness* of the coming age.

In addition, Paul often uses the adjective *eternal (aiōnios),* to depict the same concept. Above it was seen that Paul speaks of eternal glory. In contrast to the things that are seen, which are temporal, the things that are not seen are eternal (cf. 2 Cor. 4:18). This is certainly what Paul is emphasizing when he climaxes the poem of love with the words: "But now abide faith, hope, love, these three; but the greatest of these is love" (1 Cor. 13:13). They have an eternal dimension (cf. 2 Thess. 2:16). One of the most assuring facts about the believer's resurrection body, which will be discussed shortly, is "that if the earthly tent which is our house is torn down, we have a building from God, a house not made with hands, eternal in the heavens" (2 Cor. 5:1). Indeed, one thing that makes the future age of greatest appeal is its eternality.

Undoubtedly most significant are Paul's repeated references to eternal life. He takes one of the most important Greek words for *life (zōē)* and modifies it with the adjective *"aiōnios"* (eternal).

> But now having been freed from sin and enslaved to God, you derive your benefit, resulting in sanctification, and the outcome, eternal life. For the wages of sin is death, but the free gift of God is eternal life in Christ Jesus our Lord (Rom. 6:22-23). For the one who sows to his own flesh shall from the flesh reap corruption, but the one who sows to the Spirit shall from the Spirit reap eternal life (Gal. 6:8; cf. also Rom. 2:7; 5:21; 1 Tim. 1:16; 6: 12, 19; Titus 1:2; 3:7).

Just as sanctification is the *present result* of the believer's life under the sovereignty of the Spirit, so the *future benefit* is eternal life. It is instructive that, although eternal life is depicted in John as a present reality which biblical theologians call "realized eschatology," in Paul eternal life is always viewed as part of the future age.

---

1. The term *eternity* has sufficient theological overtones that *forever* is a preferable translation. Cf. the following: "of the ages" *(ton aiōnōn),* Eph. 3:11; 1 Tim. 1:17—probably better translated adjectivally as "eternal"; "into the ages" *(eis tous aiōnas),* Rom. 1:25; 9:5; 11:36; 2 Cor. 11:31; "into all the generations of the ages" *(eis pasas tas geneas tou aiōnas),* Eph. 3:11; and "into the ages of the ages" *(eis tous aiōnas tōn aiōnōn),* Rom. 16:27; Gal. 1:5; Phil. 4:20; 2 Tim. 4:18—better translated as "forever and ever."

Closely tied to the concept of eternal in the age to come is that of "immortality." Two Greek words are translated as "immortality" in the English versions. Twice, in the crucial "resurrection chapter" (1 Corinthians 15), the term *athanasia* (immortality) is contrasted with *thnētos* (mortal).[2]

> For this perishable must put on the imperishable, and this mortal must put on immortality. But when this perishable will have put on the imperishable, and this mortal will have put on immortality, then will come about the saying that is written, "DEATH IS SWALLOWED UP IN VICTORY" (1 Cor. 15:53-54).

In these same verses the word *aphtharsia* (imperishable) is used, in direct contrast to *phthora*, which means "corruptible" in the specific sense of perishing through decay and disintegration. It is plainly seen that *incorruptible* does not basically mean that which is uncontaminated, but rather that which does not perish or deteriorate. This same term *(aphtharsia)* is used in other contexts as a synonym for *immortal (athanasia):* "But now [God's purpose] has been revealed by the appearing of our Savior Christ Jesus, who abolished death, and brought life and immortality *[aphtharsia]* to light through the gospel" (2 Tim. 1:10; cf. Rom. 2:7).[3]

The close association between *immortality (athanasia)* and *incorruption (aphtharsia)* provides a clue to the meaning of *immortality*. As related to man, it clearly refers, not simply to his longevity, but to the fact that the future age holds the promise of man being imperishable. This becomes of further significance when it is realized that, with reference to man, immortality *always related to man's body and never to man's soul.* It was seen above that the word *immortality (athanasia)* is *used only* in the context of the resurrection of the body (1 Corinthians 15), and in the other references to immortality (cf. Rom. 2:7; 2 Tim. 1:10)—which are ambiguous and could refer to man's body—the other term *incorruptible (aphtharsia)* is used. It is clear that Paul, and the rest of

---

2. It is significant that *athanasia* (immortality) *is a noun,* in contrast with *thnētos* (mortal), *which is an adjective.* The adjective *athanatos* (immortal) is never found in the NT. In 2 Cor. 5:4, *mortal* is contrasted with *life.*

3. The adjective *incorruptible (aphthartos)* is used to refer to the incorruptible God (Rom. 1:23), an imperishable wreath (1 Cor. 9:25), and immortal God (1 Tim. 1:17).

the New Testament, do not conceive of immortality in terms of the Greek concept of an immortal soul.

Early in the history of the Church, the theologians, influenced by their Greek philosophy, made such an association (between immortality and the soul), which has vitally affected Christian thought down to the present day. Only in recent years have New Testament scholars succeeded in reconstructing the basic biblical view of immortality—*of the body and not the soul.*

In the basic Greek view of salvation, the soul, imprisoned in the body, seeks escape and deliverance. Only in some nebulous type of disembodied existence can the soul find its full realization and fulfillment. The key concept is *release* from the body. In one passage in particular, some New Testament scholars feel that Paul approached this fundamental Greek concept.

> For we know that if the earthly tent which is our house is torn down, we have a building from God, a house not made with hands, eternal in the heavens. For indeed in this *house* we groan, longing to be clothed with our dwelling from heaven; inasmuch as we, having put it on, shall not be found naked. For indeed while we are in this tent, we groan, being burdened, because we do not want to be unclothed, but to be clothed, in order that what is mortal may be swallowed up by life (2 Cor. 5:1-4).

There is without question some element of release in this passage, but not to permanent inactivity, which is the Greek idea. It is, rather, an entry into life and service: "In order that what is mortal may be swallowed up by life" (2 Cor. 5:4). Further, Paul makes it plain that "we do not want to be unclothed [as the Greeks], but to be clothed" (2 Cor. 5:4). He speaks of longing "to be clothed with our dwelling from heaven; inasmuch as we, having put it on, *shall not be found naked*" (2 Cor. 5:2-3, italics added).

Instead of the foregoing passage depicting the Greek idea of a disembodied spirit (or soul), it instead strongly emphasizes the basic Semitic concept of *somatic existence,* referred to in Chapter 2. In order for there to be life and existence in the future age there must be a new body, an outer self, that will be adapted to the new age. This is the significance of Paul's well-known observation:

> It [body] is sown a natural body, it is raised a spiritual body. If there is a natural body, there is also a spiritual *body* (1 Cor. 15:44). Now I say this, brethren, that flesh and blood cannot

inherit the kingdom of God; nor does the perishable inherit the imperishable (1 Cor. 15:50).

This does not mean that man's resurrected body will be *composed* of Spirit, but rather just as the natural body is adapted to the present flesh-and-blood existence, so the new body will be adapted to the new life of the Spirit. Life is inconceivable to Paul without a body or outer self, as otherwise he would be naked or unclothed.[4]

It is clear that the promise of the future age is fundamentally dependent upon the resurrection of the body. This alone makes possible the consummation of life under the Spirit. It was seen that in the present age the new man is renewed in the inner self, unto the image of Christ, and the outer self is disciplined through the Spirit. The believer looks with anticipation to the glorious day when he will receive a new outer man. Thus Paul writes:

> That I may know Him, and the power of His resurrection and the fellowship of His sufferings, being conformed to His death; in order that I may attain to the resurrection from the dead. Not that I have already obtained *it,* or have already become perfect, but I press on in order that I may lay hold of that for which also I was laid hold of by Christ Jesus. Brethren, I do not regard myself as having laid hold of *it* yet; but one thing *I do:* forgetting what *lies* behind and reaching forward to what *lies* ahead, I press on toward the goal for the prize of the upward call of God in Christ Jesus (Phil. 3:10-14).

The prize Paul sees as his goal is "that I may attain to the resurrection from the dead" (Phil. 3:11).

The future resurrection of the body, which alone makes possible the glories of the future age, is described by Paul in four vivid metaphors.

First, man's body will be *redeemed.*

> And not only this, but also we ourselves, having the first fruits of the Spirit, even we ourselves groan within ourselves, waiting eagerly for *our* adoption as sons, the redemption of our body (Rom. 8:23).

The concept of redemption has already been examined (Chapter 8). This not only includes the present redemption of the

---

4. It is interesting that Paul suggested a "cosmic" resurrection as well as a personal, bodily resurrection (cf. Rom. 8:19-23).

inner man, but also the future redemption of the body. Only thus is salvation complete.

Second, Paul pictures the resurrection as an *exchange* of bodies. "For we know that if the earthly tent which is our house is torn down, we have a building from God, a house not made with hands, eternal in the heavens" (2 Cor. 5:1). The present earthly tent will on the day of resurrection be exchanged for the house not made with hands.

Third, viewed from another perspective, man's body will be *changed* through resurrection.

> So also is the resurrection of the dead. It is sown a perishable *body*, it is raised an imperishable *body;* it is sown in dishonor, it is raised in glory; it is sown in weakness, it is raised in power; it is sown a natural body, it is raised a spiritual body. If there is a natural body, there is also a spiritual *body* (1 Cor. 15:42-44). Behold, I tell you a mystery; we shall not all sleep, but we shall all be changed, in a moment, in the twinkling of an eye, at the last trumpet; for the trumpet will sound, and the dead will be raised imperishable, and we shall be changed. For this perishable must put on the imperishable, and this mortal must put on immortality. But when this perishable will have put on the imperishable, and this mortal will have put on immortality, then will come about the saying that is written, "DEATH IS SWALLOWED UP IN VICTORY" (1 Cor. 15:51-54).

We shall all be changed! A perishable, natural, mortal body of weakness and dishonor will be *changed* into an imperishable, spiritual, immortal body of power and glory.

Finally, this earthly body will be *transformed.* "The Lord Jesus Christ . . . will transform the body of our humble state into conformity with the body of His glory, by the exertion of the power that He has even to subject all things to Himself" (Phil. 3:20-21). The key Greek term is *metaschēmatidzo,* which means "to change the form of" or "to transform." Of greatest significance, the believer's body will be transformed *into conformity with the body of His glory.* Man's body will not only be changed, but it shall be like His body!

Repeatedly Paul terms this prospect of the believer enjoying the glories of the future age as his hope.

> For we through the Spirit, by faith, are waiting for the hope of righteousness (Gal. 5:5). *I pray that* the eyes of your heart may be enlightened, so that you may know what is the hope of His

calling, what are the riches of the glory of His inheritance in the saints (Eph. 1:18). Because of the hope laid up for you in heaven, of which you previously heard in the word of truth, the gospel (Col. 1:5; cf. Rom. 5:2; Col. 1:23; 1 Thess. 1:3; 4:13-18; 5:8; 1 Tim. 1:1; Titus 3:7).

As noted earlier, the biblical concept of hope must not be confused with the modern usage of the term. Hope is *certainty* of the future. It was this hope that enabled the earliest believers to be faithful, even unto death.

As was seen at the beginning of this chapter, in the Jewish world-view it was the "day of the Lord" that would usher in the future age. Quite naturally Paul, and the rest of the New Testament writers, saw the second coming of Christ as the event that would bring in the future day of hope and resurrection.[5] "Looking for the blessed hope and the appearing of the glory of our great God and Saviour, Christ Jesus" (Titus 2:13).

Paul's writings abound with references to the hope of Christ's return, or the *Parousia*. It would be impossible in this study to attempt an exhaustive analysis of the references. He speaks of the coming of Christ.

For as in Adam all die, so also in Christ all shall be made alive. But each in his own order: Christ the first fruits, after that those who are Christ's at His coming (1 Cor. 15:22-23). For who is our hope or joy or crown of exultation? Is it not even you, in the presence of our Lord Jesus at His coming? (1 Thess. 2:19). For this we say to you by the word of the Lord, that we who are alive, and remain until the coming of the Lord, shall not precede those who have fallen asleep. For the Lord Himself will descend from heaven with a shout, with the voice of *the* archangel, and with the trumpet of God; and the dead in Christ shall rise first. Then we who are alive and remain shall be caught up together with them in the clouds to meet the Lord in the air, and thus we shall always be with the Lord (1 Thess. 4:15-17; cf. 1 Thess. 5:23).

Similarly the Second Coming is termed the "day of Christ."

Our Lord Jesus Christ . . . shall also confirm you to the end, blameless in the day of our Lord Jesus Christ (1 Cor. 1:7-8). *For*

---

5. Although there is in the gospel the clear teaching that the *first* coming of Christ inaugurated the future age, which His *second* coming will consummate, there is no such comparable emphasis in Paul. However, as will be seen below, Paul does use the concept of the kingdom of God in this twofold sense, but he does not directly relate the *present* kingdom of God to the coming of Christ.

I am confident of this very thing, that He who began a good work
in you will perfect it until the day of Christ Jesus (Phil. 1:6). For
you yourselves know full well that the day of the Lord will come
just like a thief in the night (1 Thess. 5:2; cf. 1 Cor. 5:5; 2 Cor.
1:14; Phil. 1:10; 2:16; 2 Thess. 2:2).

Even the term *day* has the specific significance of Christ's return.
"Each man's work will become evident; for the day will show it, because it is *to be* revealed with fire; and the fire itself will test the
quality of each man's work" (1 Cor. 3:13; cf. Rom. 13:12).

There is little question that in his earliest letters Paul expressed confidence that Christ would return in his lifetime. He
wrote to the Thessalonians: "That *we who are alive,* and remain
until the coming of the Lord . . ." (1 Thess. 4:15, italics added).[6] He
expected to be alive when the momentous event took place.
There is a spirit of expectancy reflected in many of his letters
which is nowhere better characterized than in his closing word to
the Corinthians. *"Marana tha—*Come, O Lord!" (1 Cor. 16:22,
NEB).[7] It is true that there is little if any reference to the *Parousia*
in Ephesians and Colossians, which are his latest general letters.[8]
The reason for this lack of emphasis on the *Parousia* in these
letters is not clear, but it is not necessary to conclude that Paul
ceased to expect Christ to return.

One possible explanation of what appears to be a lessening
emphasis on the *Parousia* is that his letters reflect a deepening
understanding of the believer's resurrection. There is no question
that Paul always saw that the new man's hope (with certainty) of
personal resurrection was totally dependent upon his faith in the
resurrection of Christ.

Now if Christ is preached, that He has been raised from the
dead, how do some among you say that there is no resurrection of

---

6. In fact, Paul's imminent expectation of the *Parousia* appears to have played
a prominent part in several of his specific instructions to his converts. Cf. his
counsel in 1 Corinthians, particularly on marriage (cf. 1 Corinthians 7, especially
vv. 26-31).

7. William Barclay makes the keen observation that the Aramaic word is left
untranslated, strongly suggesting that even in the Greek community of Corinth it
was a catchword, slogan, battle cry, or watchword (*Mind of St. Paul,* p. 222).

8. There is some serious question as to when Philippians should be dated. The
Pastoral Epistles are of an entirely different character, as they are addressed to
pastoral assistants rather than to churches.

the dead? But if there is no resurrection of the dead, not even Christ has been raised; and if Christ has not been raised, then our preaching is vain, your faith also is vain. Moreover we are even found *to be* false witnesses of God, because we witnessed against God that He raised Christ, whom He did not raise, if in fact the dead are not raised. For if the dead are not raised, not even Christ has been raised; and if Christ has not been raised, your faith is worthless; you are still in your sins. Then those also who have fallen asleep in Christ have perished. If we have only hoped in Christ in this life, we are of all men most to be pitied. But now Christ has been raised from the dead, the first fruits of those who are asleep (1 Cor. 15:12-20).

This lengthy passage has been quoted to emphasize that the certain hope of the believer's resurrection was *based upon faith in the resurrection of Christ and not on the Parousia.*

However, there is likewise no doubt that in his earlier letters Paul, expecting the *Parousia* imminently, coupled the believer's resurrection with the second coming of Christ. When his converts in Thessalonica were disturbed because some of their number died before Christ returned, Paul gave them assurance that the dead would be raised *when Christ returned* (cf. 1 Thess. 4:15-17). The great resurrection chapter climaxes with these words: "In a moment, in the twinkling of an eye, at the last trumpet; for the trumpet will sound, and the dead will be raised imperishable, and we shall all be changed" (1 Cor. 15:52). This passage does not *explicitly* tie the believer's resurrection to the *Parousia,* but such is strongly implied (cf. 1 Cor. 15:23). What is of most significance is that *all believers are pictured as being resurrected at the same time.* It is a *general* resurrection.

Yet when Paul speaks of the believer's hope of resurrection in 2 Cor. 5:1-9 (previously discussed in part), there is an entirely different note. Admittedly, this is a difficult passage to interpret, but Paul appears to be discounting any *intermediate state* between death and the Second Coming. He clearly contrasts being absent from the body (death) and being at home with the Lord. Some commentators suggest that to be at home with the Lord is something other than the resurrection of the body, but such is difficult to substantiate.

When it is seen that this passage (2 Cor. 5:1-9) is an essential part of the greater context (2 Cor. 3:1—6:10), which is Paul's characterization of his ministry, and is very closely tied to the immediate reference to tribulations and the threat of death (cf. 2 Cor. 4:7-18); then it becomes clear that Paul is *primarily confessing his lack of fear of death,* because it will make possible his being at home with the Lord. This is very similar to a passage in Philippians:

> For to me, to live is Christ, and to die is gain. But if *I am* to live *on* in the flesh, this *will mean* fruitful labor for me; and I do not know which to choose. But I am hard pressed from both *directions,* having the desire to depart and be with Christ, for *that* is very much better; yet to remain on in the flesh is more necessary for your sake. And convinced of this, I know that I shall remain and continue with you all for your progress and joy in the faith (Phil. 1:21-25).

Some New Testament scholars[9] suggest that Paul's experiences in Ephesus, bringing him close to death, resulted in a *deeper understanding* of the significance of death and particularly how it related to the believer's hope of resurrection.[10] Paul's constant brush with death very possibly gave him the deeper understanding that the believer's hope must be *primarily* related to his death. He *must* have hope in the hour of death.

This "must" relates to Paul's basic anthropological concept and its implication relative to new life in Christ. For Paul, immortality could not be contemplated without resurrection—of the body! A new body was indispensable to life after death. Paul could *not* conceive of personal existence in some nebulous, disembodied form without a body. When we speak of an intermediate state—between death and the *Parousia*—by definition it can only be some type of bodiless existence, which Paul vividly describes as nakedness. Neither can Paul envision a subpersonal existence after death in some kind of shadowy Sheol—which probably was his pre-Christian belief—from which at the *Parousia* the believer is

---

9. Cf. F. F. Bruce's Drew Lecture on immortality given on November 6, 1970, and entitled: "Paul on Immortality," *Scottish Journal of Theology* (Vol. 24, No. 4), November, 1971. Professor Bruce strongly defends the theory that Paul in his later thought saw the believer's resurrection as taking place at the time of his death.

10. It is generally agreed that Paul's correspondence with the Corinthian church primarily took place during his approximately three-year stay in Ephesus (cf. Acts 19, especially vv. 8, 10). There are several references to severe trials and an almost daily facing of death (cf. 1 Cor. 15:31).

brought back to life. The new man has *already shared* in the resurrected life of Christ—*in the inner man.* To be brought by death into a state of semiconscious existence was abhorrently unthinkable to Paul. Instead, Paul appears to have—by bitter personal experience—grasped the necessity of the believer receiving his new resurrected body *at the hour of death.*

What does this do to the promise of the *Parousia?* Some would attempt to spiritualize or demythologize the repeated New Testament teaching about the *Parousia.* But such an attempt ignores *another dimension* of eschatological truth that was very close to Paul's heart. Not only did Christ's triumph guarantee personal salvation, but it also promised the *redemption of the world.* Christ is—by virtue of His resurrection—the Lord of history! Paul had a vivid picture of this final day of fulfillment.

> For the creation was subjected to futility, not of its own will, but because of Him who subjected it, in hope that the creation itself also will be set free from its slavery to corruption into the freedom of the glory of the children of God. For we know that the whole creation groans and suffers the pains of childbirth together until now (Rom. 8:20-22; cf. Acts 3:21; 2 Pet. 3:13).

In this study it is impossible to digress to examine the truth of the *historical* significance of the *Parousia.* It must suffice to observe that, even if Paul disassociated the believer's hope of resurrection from the *Parousia,* this did not *in any way* make the *Parousia any less* essential for the consummation of the saving purpose of God. The *Parousia will* usher in that glorious "day" of *cosmic* consummation!

On several occasions Paul identified the future age as "heaven." Christ would be coming *from* heaven.

> The first man is from the earth, earthy; the second man is from heaven (1 Cor. 15:47). And to wait for His Son from heaven, whom He raised from the dead, *that is* Jesus, who delivers us from the wrath to come (1 Thess. 1:10; cf. 2 Thess. 1:7; 2 Cor. 5:2).

The believer's hope was a "hope laid up . . . in heaven" (Col. 1:5), and the man of faith has his "citizenship . . . in heaven" (Phil. 3:20).

The future age is also termed the "kingdom of God" and the "heavenly kingdom." "The Lord will deliver me from every evil deed, and will bring me safely to His heavenly kingdom; to Him *be* the glory forever and ever. Amen" (2 Tim. 4:18). Paul repeatedly says that those who do evil cannot hope to inherit the kingdom of God.[11]

An important part of the believer's hope in the future age is deliverance from the fate of those who do not have faith in Christ. The day of Christ will be a day of wrath and judgment for the unbeliever.

> But because of your stubbornness and unrepentant heart you are storing up wrath for yourself in the day of wrath and revelation of the righteous judgment of God (Rom. 2:5). For we must all appear before the judgment-seat of Christ, that each one may be recompensed for his deeds in the body, according to what he has done, whether good or bad (2 Cor. 5:10). For after all it is *only* just for God to repay with affliction those who afflict you, and *to give* relief to you who are afflicted and to us as well when the Lord Jesus shall be revealed from heaven with His mighty angels in flaming fire, dealing out retribution to those who do not know God and to those who do not obey the gospel of our Lord Jesus. And these will pay the penalty of eternal destruction, away from the presence of the Lord and from the glory of His power (2 Thess. 1:6-9; cf. Rom. 2:8-9, 16; 14:10-12).

Paul can confidently state: "Much more then, having now been justified by His blood, we shall be saved from the wrath *of God* through Him" (Rom. 5:9).

One of the most intriguing questions that has haunted the mind of man concerns the specific nature of the future age. What will heaven be like? Endless conjectures have been made, but Paul is wisely silent about this. It is impossible to adequately depict eternal verities in temporal concepts. But Paul does, however, give a most assuring word to the man of faith. What will heaven be like? You have a foretaste here—in the Spirit.

Paul uses some of the most vivid metaphors in the New Testament to depict this.

> Now He who establishes us with you in Christ and anointed us is God, who also sealed us and gave *us* the Spirit in our hearts as a pledge (2 Cor. 1:21-22). In Him, you also, after listening to the message of truth, the gospel of your salvation—having also believed, you were sealed in Him with the Holy Spirit of promise,

---

11. Cf. 1 Cor. 6:9; Gal. 5:21; Eph. 5:5; 2 Thess. 1:5. Paul makes some reference to the kingdom of God being present (cf. Rom. 14:17; 1 Cor. 4:20; Col. 4:11), but it is significant that it (kingdom of God) is never related to the *Parousia*.

who is given as a pledge of our inheritance, with a view to the redemption of *God's own* possession, to the praise of His glory (Eph. 1:13-14; cf. 2 Cor. 5:5; Eph. 4:30).

In these passages two well-known legal and commercial terms are used: "to seal" *(sphragidzō)* and "pledge" *(arrabōn).* The Spirit is the believer's Seal and Pledge. The seal was placed on something—for instance, a building or a bundle of rods—as a mark of identification, which denotes ownership. It was an authentic guarantee that what was delivered was from the sender and its contents were intact. Thus Paul vividly says that the Spirit authenticates the believer as belonging to God. Yet the significance of the seal suggests more than a mark of identification—the sealing points to the future, which is made abundantly clear by the second metaphor.

The believer is sealed by the Spirit, who is a Pledge of future inheritance. The word *pledge (arrabōn)* means "first installment, deposit, and down payment."[12] Legally a pledge was an advance part-payment that *obligated both parties.* Commercially it was a sample of the promised product that gave assurance of the quality of the purchase to the buyer, and committed the seller to fulfill his obligations.

The spiritual application is plain. The Spirit is not only the *Guarantee* of the future age, but is a *Preview* of what lies ahead. What will heaven be like? It will be like the presence of the Spirit in the believer's life—and much more.

This blessed truth is even more vividly depicted by Paul in these words: "And not only this, but also we ourselves, having the first fruits of the Spirit, even we ourselves groan within ourselves, waiting eagerly for *our* adoption as sons, the redemption of our body" (Rom. 8:23). The key word here is "first fruits" *(aparchē).* It is actually a specimen crop of the coming harvest. So the Spirit is a Foretaste—in kind—of the glory which will one day be fully known.

Here the new man, living under the Spirit, reaches the end of his pilgrimage. He is at home with his Lord, having finished the race.

---

12. Cf. A and G. The modern Greek uses the word *arrabōn* for an engagement ring, signifying the promise of the coming marriage.

Bibliography

Arndt, W. F., and Gingrich, F. W. *A Greek-English Lexicon of the New Testament.* Chicago: University of Chicago Press, 1957.

Barclay, William. *The Daily Study Bible.* Philadelphia: The Westminster Press, 1959.

————. *Flesh and Spirit.* Nashville: Abingdon Press, 1962.

————. *More New Testament Words.* New York: Harper and Row, 1958.

————. *The Mind of St. Paul.* London: Collins, 1958.

Beet, Joseph Agar. *A Commentary on St. Paul's Epistle to the Romans.* New York: Thomas Whittaker, 8th ed., n.d.

Blass, F., and DeBrunner, A. *A Greek Grammar of the New Testament and Other Early Christian Literature.* Tr. and rev. by Robert W. Funk. Chicago: University of Chicago Press, 1961.

Bultmann, Rudolph. *Theology of the New Testament.* Tr. by Kendrik Grobel. New York: Charles Scribner's Sons, 1955.

Burrows, Miller. *What Mean These Stones?* New Haven, Conn.: American School of Oriental Research, 1941.

Curtis, Olin F. *The Christian Faith.* New York: Eaton and Mains, 1905.

Dodd, C. H. *The Epistle to the Romans. The Moffatt New Testament Commentary.* New York: Harper and Brothers Publishers, 1932.

Hall, Calvin S., and Lindsey, Gardner. *Theories of Personality.* New York: John Wiley and Sons, Inc., 1957.

Morris, Leon. *The Apostolic Preaching of the Cross.* Grand Rapids, Mich.: Wm. B. Eerdmans Publishing Co., 1959.

Moule, C. F. D. *Idiom Book of the Greek New Testament.* 2nd ed. Cambridge: Cambridge University Press, 1959.

————. *The Epistles of Paul the Apostle to the Colossians and to Philemon. The Cambridge Greek Testament Commentary.* Cambridge: The University Press, 1957.

Nielson, John B. *In Christ.* Kansas City: Beacon Hill Press, 1960.

Robertson, A. T., and Davis, W. Hersey. *A New Short Grammar of the Greek Testament.* New York: Harper and Brothers Publishers, 1931.

Sanday, William, and Headlam, A. C. *The Epistle to the Romans. International Critical Commentary.* New York: Charles Scribner's Sons, 1899.

Stacey, Walter David. *The Pauline View of Man.* New York: St. Martin's Press, 1956.

Stewart, James. *A Man in Christ.* New York: Harper and Brothers Publishers, 1935.

Taylor, Vincent. *Forgiveness and Reconciliation.* London: Macmillan and Co., 1956.

Vincent, Marvin R. *Word Studies in the New Testament*. Vol. III. New York: Charles Scribner's Sons, 1889.

Wiley, H. Orton. *Christian Theology*. 3 vols. Kansas City: Beacon Hill Press, 1940, 1943, 1952.

Winer, George Benedict. *A Grammar of the Idiom of the New Testament*. Andover, Mass.: Warren F. Draper, 1897.

Subject Index

Footnote references in parentheses ( ).

Debt, 72, 73
Decay, 26, 213
Decentralization, 42
Deeds, 26, 49, 219, 221
Defense mechanism, 214
Deismann, Adolf, (84)
Delivered, 51, 65, 72
Demands (of God), 74
Demons 46, 54, (58), 124
Dependence, 80
Depravity:
—acquired, 47, 53
—original, 46, 53, 54, 139; defined,
41-43; forming inner man, 219;
Genesis account, 43; in Adam, 40,
41; in new man, 140, (140), 141,
154, 156; in Romans 6:6, 102; inner
man (heart), 42, 50, 168; of mind,
46; released (by man), 172, 208; removed (by God), 172, 208, (instrumental value), 174; self-sovereignty, 42, 46, 53, 105, 140, 168, 172
Description: cf. with definition, 41, 42,
79; of faith, 79; of sin, 45, (modern),
53
Desires (outer man), 25, 26, 31, (31), 33,
42, 48, (48), 49, 50, 54, 105, 112, 132,
137, 141, 150, 153, 154, 160, 220, 221
—evil, 48, 224; flesh (cf. "flesh");
fulfilled, (31), 48, (48), 132, 141,
160, 222; cf. inner "wish," 49, 220;
morally neutral, 48, 105, 221; new
(created), 224; old (disciplined),
222; sin, 221; Spirit, 221
Development, 155, 167, 191, 192, 194,
198, 199, 206, 215, 216, 217, 218, 225
Devil, 43
Dimension, 50, 55, 63, 80, 90, 117, 155,
156, 157, 181, 226, 227, 229, 238
Discipline, 142, 144, 154, 158, 160, 206,
210, 221, 223, 224, 232
Disembodied (spirit, soul), 21, 231, 237
Disobedience, 39, 40, 43, 54, 73, 74, 144;
act, 40
Disposition, 219, 222
Dissipation, 37, 224
Diversity (& unity), 33
Divine: assistance, 89, 90; dilemma, 74;
initiative, c. 8; 78, 79, 80, 81, 83, 84,
90, 92, 111, 112; response, 79; Spirit,
24; standard (will), 56, (56), 58, 59,
162, 202; Word, 10

Division, 120, 121, 125, 137
Doctrine, (10), 11, 12, 17, 81, 132
—of man, 6, 18, 19
Dodd, C. H., (86)
Dogma, 10, 11
"Don't you know?" 144, 146
Dooley, Tom, 53
Door, 78, 174
Down payment, 240
Drives (outer man), 26, (48), 49, 54, 110,
219

Early Church, 75, 89, 118, (119)
Earthen vessel, 212, 213
Edify, 151, 193, 194
Education, 54
Elemental things *(stoicheia)*, (58), 60
Ellipsis, 217, (217)
Emblem, 70
Emotions, 23, 87, 115
Enablement, c. 21; 44, 141, 180, 190
End, 56, 58, 63, 156, 174, 226
Enemy, 52, 65, 73
Energy (energize), 87, 180, 181, 182,
183, 185, 186, 187, 188, 190, 191, 194,
198, 201, 202, 203, 218
Enlightenment (spiritual), 179
Enmity, 42, 47, 50, 53, 73, 74, 97, 105,
140
Enslaved (by sin), 45, 47, 50, 51, 53,
(58), 72, 76, 103, 105, 142, 151, 160,
171, 174, 180
Entered: Christ, 102, 103, 107; church,
123, 125
Environment, 54, 152, 196, 219, 223;
stimuli, 220
Erroneous, 51, 53, 94, 195, 201
Eschatology, c. 26; 226, 227, 228, 238
Establishment, 165, 194, 195, 198, 199,
206
Estrangement, 52, 73, 74, 76, 77, 98
Eternal: age, 228, 229; death, 63; glory,
228; God's love, 74; life, 21, 229; mes-
sage, 12, 68; perfection, 215; verities,
239
Eternity, 54, 228, 229, (229)
Ethic (divine), 56, 58
Ethical, 46, (56), 93, 94, 96, 132, 162
Evangelical, 8
Evil: good & evil, 21, 23, 24, (know the
difference), 43; attitude, 42, 47, 49;
compulsion, 52, 104; desires, 48, 224;
ends (of sin), (58); enticement, 195;

67, 80, 94; of law, 55, 95, 151, 158, 162
—of the flesh, 32, 50, 137, 160, 161, 167, 222
Works-righteousness, 165
World, 21, 31, 39, 40, 43, 53, 68, 78, 186, 211
—evil, 158, 165, 183; Gentile, 37, 72; men, 87, 117, 121, 122; view, 228, 239
—under self, 139, 140, 142, 167, 181

—under sin, 139, 142, 165
—under Spirit, P. V; 139, 141, 142, 165
Worry, 114
Worthy, 77, 94, 115, 124, 182, 199, 200, 209, 211
—Communion, 124, (200)
—not intrinsically, 200
Wrath, 19, 63, 64, 74, 76, 83, 91, 239
Wretched, 51, 52, 54, 71, 104
Written, 56
Wrongness, 42

Scripture Index

Greek Word Index

Footnote references in parentheses ( ).

katharisas, (208)
katharismos, (106)
katharos, (106)
koimaō, (61)
koinōnia, 118, 119, 124
koinōnoi, 124
kurieuō, 45, (106)
logidzomai, (95), 146
logikēn, (171)
lutron, (72)
mē genoito, (100)
melē, 25
metamelomai, (82)
metamorphoō, (210)
metanoeō, (82)
metaschēmatidzō, 233
nekroō, (138)
nekros, (61)
nekrōsate, (138)
noēma, (24)
nomos, C. 6, (80), (92), 162
nous, 23, (23), (24), (49), (82)
oikodomē, (193)
oikodomeō, (193)
orexis, 25, (48)
ostrakinos, 212
ouk oidate, (100)
paidagōgos, (58), (83)
parabasis, (40)
paradidōmi, (63)
parakalō, (171)
parakoē, (40)
paraptōma, (38), (40)
parastēsai, (171)
paristēmi, (168)
pathēmata, 25, 31, (48)
pathos, (48)
peiradzō, 195
peirasmos, 195
peripateō, 158
perisseuō, 192
phronēma, (49)

phroneō, (49)
phroureō, (185)
phthora, 230
pimplēmi, (157)
pistis, (78), (79), (81)
pleonadzō, 192
plēroō, 192
plērousthe, (157)
pneuma, 24, 109
pneumati, (157)
praxis, (221)
prosagōgē, 74, 97
psuchē (psychē), 21, (21), (22), (25)
ptōma, (25)
ridzoō, 194
sarkin(k)os, (29), 32
sarx, C. 3, (19), (22), 25, 26, 27, (30), (48), 109, 153, (153)
skeuos, (206)
sōma, (22), 25, (25), 26, (26), 27, 30, 47, (47), 121
sōma tēs hamartias, 47
sōmati, (150)
somatos tēs sarkos, (30)
sōtēria, 126
sphragidzō, 240
stēridzō, 194
stoicheia, (58)
stoicheō, 160
teleion, 215, 216
teleioō, (215)
teleios, 215, (215)
teleiōtēs, (215)
thanatos, (61)
thanatou, (62)
thelēmata, 25, 31, (31), (48)
thelō, (49)
themelioō, 194
thnētos, 230, (230)
ton aiōnion, (239)
tou noos tēs sarkos, (30)
touto, (81)
zōē, 21, 229